Rereading Doris Lessing

Rereading Doris Lessing

Narrative Patterns of

Doubling and Repetition

by Claire Sprague

The University of North Carolina Press

Chapel Hill and London

© 1987 Claire Sprague

All rights reserved

Manufactured in the United States of America

Library of Congress Cataloging-in-Publication Data

Sprague, Claire.

  Rereading Doris Lessing.

  Bibliography: p.

  Includes index.

  1. Lessing, Doris May, 1919– —Criticism and
interpretation. 2. Lessing, Doris May, 1919–
—Technique. 3. Repetition in literature. I. Title.

PR6023.E833Z897 1987   823'.914   86-30879

ISBN 0-8078-1747-3

ISBN 0-8078-4187-0 (pbk.)

An earlier version of chapter 4 appeared in *Papers on
Language and Literature* 17 (1982): 181–97. An earlier
version of chapter 5 appeared in *Modern Fiction Studies*
26 (1980): 99–116.

The paper in this book meets the guidelines for
permanence and durability of the Committee on
Production Guidelines for Book Longevity of the
Council on Library Resources.

91 90 89 88 87   5 4 3 2 1

In Memory of My Sister Annette

Contents

ILLUSTRATIONS

Acknowledgments

Every written work has a vast shadow world of indebtedness that can never be properly acknowledged. I have a unique debt to the community of Lessing scholars, whose generosity and openness have been unexampled. I should like especially to note the stimulation and the support from some of the members of that community—Betsy Draine, Virginia Tiger, Roberta Rubenstein, Paul Schlueter, Ellen Cronan Rose, Katherine Fishburn, Eve Bertelsen, Pat Hoy, Clare Hanson, Nicole Ward Jouve, Dee Seligman, Carey Kaplan, Mona Knapp, Judith Johnston.

To friends like Zola Schneider, Irv Schneider, the late Warren Susman, Bea Susman, Ruth Kaye, Rhoda Wolf, Roz Stein, Sandi Cooper, John Cammett, Ulla Dydo, Jules Brenner, Lee Brenner, Ann Lane, the debt is different and very deep—as it is to my son Jesse who grew up with this work and shared in its growth in very special ways.

For voyages that took me in and out of the ordinary, to the usual critical, historical, psychological, political, and other areas of knowledge that are regularly applied to literary works and to those areas that rarely enter mainstream literary discourse, to numerology, naming, archaeology, architecture, art history, I have Doris Lessing, that prickly, omnivorous intelligence, to thank.

I am also happy to acknowledge the support of Brooklyn College in the preparation of this volume. A Faculty Incentive Award gave me the kind of time seldom available to faculty immersed in teaching. So did grants from the National Endowment for the Humanities and the City University of New York PSC/CUNY Research Award Program.

Rereading Doris Lessing

Introduction: Doubling as Dialectic and Repetition

> I begin to see things double—doubled in history, world history, personal history . . . You must feel plunged as I do into the madness of vision, into a sense of the relation between separated things that you cannot explain.
>
> William Butler Yeats to Dorothy Wellesley

> *Every attitude, emotion, thought has its opposite held in balance out of sight but there all the time.*
>
> Doris Lessing, *The Four-Gated City*

> Who would wish to be a tablet upon which time writes every instant a new inscription?
>
> Søren Kierkegaard, *Repetition*

> After a certain age . . . there are no new people, beasts, dreams, faces, events: It has all happened before, they have appeared before, masked differently, wearing different clothes, another nationality, another colour; but the same, the same, and everything is an echo and a repetition.
>
> Doris Lessing, *Particularly Cats*

Otherness is a constant sting in Doris Lessing's work. Her birth in Kermanshah, Iran (then Persia), and her upbringing in the Loma-gundi region of Zimbabwe (then Southern Rhodesia) would seem to have placed her even further from the centers of Western culture than William Faulkner was in Oxford, Mississippi. Not too long ago both could have been called local color or regional writers. Their work demonstrates that the center is everywhere—if we can be made to see it.

English, white, female, Lessing grew up at least thrice alienated in colonial Africa. The English ruled a country and its overwhelmingly black population by conquest and in the process duplicated the power patterns that placed women in limited, subordinate roles. Lessing was not at home in Africa and even less at home in England, where she has lived for over thirty-five years and where she has written all her published work save her first novel, *The Grass Is Singing* (1950), and a few short stories.

Her politics made her a fourth kind of exile. As a leftist and ultimately a card-carrying Communist, she contended with established power in yet another way. Later she traveled to other outsider stances, to antipsychiatry, for example, and more recently to Sufi mysticism, an interest now at least twenty years old. (Sufi epigraphs appear in *Landlocked* [1965].) Some think of Lessing as an antenna for our times, a remarkable probe for what lies in wait just around the corner. Paradoxically enough, while her ideological journeys have been extravagant, her narrative adventures have been modest. Her recent space fiction novels are not experimental in prose style or narrative form. The same thing could even be said of *The Golden Notebook* (1962), which became an instant classic. Its disruptions of chronology and voice are minimal. Yet Lessing's example is radical. To say why and how is not easy. Her determinedly antimodernist practice is only in part related to her Marxist commitment. As much to the point is that modernism was not exactly in the fifties and rarely in England a viable choice. Though Lessing was an admirer of a writer like T. S. Eliot despite his rightist politics (as many leftists were), the example of his discontinuities or his use of language did not carry over into her writing. Nor did the example of Virginia Woolf affect her fictional forms.

Lessing's "profoundly dialectical consciousness" or her "competing codes" have been central to the interpretations of major Lessing critics.[1] These interpretations imply a view of dialectic that needs to be made more explicit. They have not been specifically Marxist; instead they have assumed that "dialectic" refers to the conflict between opposites, a conflict that can involve interaction as well as polarity. They have not assumed that this conflict must result in the creation of a third force that some systems of dialectic have called the "unity of opposites." Their use of dialectic has been justifiably broad and nondogmatic.

But the place of dialectic in Lessing's thought needs more examination in its specific antecedents. The concept of dialectic has, in our time, been almost exclusively associated with Marxism. It is necessary to reassert its connection to other systems of thought—especially to the mystical and the psychoanalytical.[2] When Martha Quest refers to "*the pairs of opposites*" and "*all those books*" in The Four-Gated City (1969, p. 539), she is probably, in that context, referring more to mystical than to Marxist antecedents. The phrase "the unity of opposites" exists in Christian mystical tradition as *coincidentia oppositorum* (Cousins); its recurrence in Jung's work as "paired opposites" derives from centuries of commentary. Its place in the Marxist canon is well known. The common elements in theories of dialectic, normally ignored, are of some consequence for an understanding of Lessing's thought. It is one thread between the political and the religious Lessing; the vocabulary of dialectic that Marxism and mysticism and some forms of psychoanalysis share may be one source of the attraction Lessing came to feel toward religious mysticism.[3]

Although Jung generously studs his works with "paired opposites," and his influence on Lessing has been assumed by much American criticism, it would be a shock if Lessing's work failed to register an awareness of Freud's precedence. Saul Green's French soldier, for example, yearns to be freed from Grandfathers Marx and Freud, not from Grandfathers Marx and Jung. He wishes that "just once, just once in his life, he felt or thought something that was his own, spontaneous, undirected, not willed upon him by Grandfathers Marx and Freud" (Golden Notebook, 643). For an earlier generation of intellectuals, Marx and Freud were fathers rather than grandfathers. Together these fathers were assumed to have unlocked the most arcane and recalcitrant secrets of human history and behavior. Saul Green's allusion documents a historically accepted indebtedness.

"Freud's whole theory of mental life" is, of course, "a theory of conflict" (Mitchell, 21). Once posit an unconscious, as Freud did, for example, it becomes one term in an eternal and mysterious dialectic with the conscious self. Another psychoanalytic dialectic, that between the manifest and the latent content of dreams, has more profoundly engaged Lessing. In fact, she probably finds the psychoanalytic theory of dreams, both the Freudian and the Jungian, more usable than any other aspect of psychoanalytic thought. (The use of oedipal theory is most marked in The Grass Is Singing [1950].) From The Grass Is Singing on, dreams are critical registers of the past and present for her characters.

Jung's oppositions carry him to mystical, alchemical, religious, and mythical lore, to regions highly recessive in Lessing's thought until The Four-Gated City. His perception of "paired opposites" is most suggestive in its extension to include male and female principles. This kind of elaboration, implicit in Freud, has important suggestions for Lessing's approach to gender roles. The split into two sexes is in some cultures the primeval disaster for humankind, the split from which we have never recovered. Lessing examines and anguishes over that split, or that dialectic, throughout her career.

Lessing came to Freud and to Jung from a prior political education that defined the difference between appearance and reality as social dialectic. Her formal schooling ended when she was fourteen; it continued within the political Left. Like Martha Quest's, Lessing's immersion in left-wing life probably began when she was fifteen and continued until she was about fifty. Her peace activism in the sixties survived her formal departure from the Communist party. The legacy of these years lies in the habit of mind called dialectic, not in the ideological dogmas of Marxism. That habit of mind, particularly in the forms it took in Marxist circles in the thirties, forties, and fifties, seems to me to have had a permanent effect on Lessing's thinking and on the shape her narrative strategies took —and continue to take. The influence of Marxism must be sought for in a way of thinking about experience, not in specific political positions or elegant theoretical formulations.

Lessing's "profoundly dialectical consciousness" sees double and multiple forces in constant interaction. It is a consciousness that displays itself in the way characters and narrative patterns are deployed. It is not limited to political or thematic statement. It has a formal component. It can describe the way characters and narrative forms are juxtaposed just as it can describe the specialized kind of juxtapositions between parts of the self that psychoanalysis calls doubling. The term "doubling" can be used for both kinds of dialectic if its use assumes multiplication beyond twoness, for Lessing multiplies as frequently as she doubles characters, naming and numerological patterns, environments (walls, rooms, houses, cities, planets), and narrative forms (diaries, notebooks, parodies, archives).[4] Lessing's vision of doubleness and multiplicity is embodied in what used to be called a set of objective correlatives. More simply put, we can say that pattern and meaning in Lessing's fiction interpenetrate in complicated and unexpected ways. Lessing's dramatic projections are a way of questioning and enlarging the singleness and stability of personality—especially for women—and of narrative conventions. These multiple forms are the subject of my explorations in this book.

Lessing's naming/doubling pattern is tied to repetition. As Paul Barker notes in his review of *Landlocked*: "In paradoxical contrast to Martha Quest's fear of repetition, it is by repetition that Mrs. Lessing chiefly operates" (27). "Chiefly" exaggerates, but Barker uses the word to assert Lessing's strategic use of repetition. He cites women's names—Myra, Molly, Moira, Mary, Margaret, Martha—as examples of deliberate "sameness" and as an obvious form of self-duplication, for Doris is "also May" (28). The repetition Barker identified more than twenty years ago continues to resurface in Lessing's novels and stories. (Regrettably, the stories will not be discussed in this volume.)

The repetition of M names is not, however, merely self-reflexive. Its full meaning begins to be addressed, I think, when A's are joined to M's and when both are seen as descendants of Alfred and May Quest, the primal parents in the Lessing corpus (as suggested in an article on *The Four-Gated City*, revised and included here as Chapter 5). The repetitive use of J is less clear. It is often used for child or kinship figures (not necessarily in the literal sense). Caroline would have been named Jeffrey had she been born a boy. (Lessing's first two children were named John and Jean.) Jonathan, Janet, Jasper fit this hypothesis. Other J names do not: for example, Johor, George, Johnny, Jack, Jimmy. However, like the repetitive A's and M's, these repetitions suggest human enslavement to recurrence.

The parallels with Lessing's real-life constellation of family names are strong and persuasive, but the fictional pattern is not dependent upon the biographical evidence. The pattern begins with relatively fixed male and female values that sometimes become frighteningly unstable and lead finally to a reversal of gender signals and an acceptance of multiple, complicated, more androgynous selves. Lessing's female and mixed doubles substantially modify the extreme sexual polarization inherited from the nineteenth century (Heilbrun, 54).

Although Lessing's fiction begins with a polarized male/female naming pattern, such a polarity never existed in her own life. The family naming habits subverted gender polarities, for Lessing's father was known to the outer world as Alfred and to his family as

Michael, while his mother preferred her middle name, Maude, to her first name, Emily.[5] Their daughter chose the slight disguise of her own middle name for her fictional May Quest. The circularity of these patterns underlines the sense of fatality in much of Lessing's fiction, which lies so uneasily beside its professed socialism, a socialism ironically called "the happy philosophy" in The Golden Notebook (428). These naming patterns seem to say, with Julia in Retreat to Innocence (1956), "We are all interchangeable" (124). This interchangeability or repetition is one face of Lessing's fatality. It surfaces frequently in her fiction. The message is the same when Doug, married to Martha, has an affair with a Molly; or when Richard, once married to Molly, remarries a Marion (she describes him as in love with a type, not with a particular woman); or when Saul concocts women called Mavis and Marguerite for the diary he knows Anna/Molly will read.

From Mary and Moses of The Grass Is Singing to the multiple selves in The Making of the Representative for Planet 8 (1982) and The Diaries of Jane Somers (1984), Lessing explores fixed, fragmented, double, variable, and multiple identities. Gender and naming patterns become part of that exploration. Mary and Moses, female and male, white and black, disintegrate and destroy one another as Martha and Mark of The Four-Gated City do not, as Al·Ith and Ben Ata of The Marriages between Zones Three, Four, and Five (1980) do not. The equality of shared M names in Mary/Moses represents their equal victimization. Only much later in Lessing's career do such shared names suggest a positive bond of equality.

In imagining female/male doubles like Mary/Moses or Martha/ Mark or Alsi/Marl/Masson and female/female doubles like Anna/ Molly, Martha/Marnie/Maisie/Marjorie/Marie, or Al·Ith/Murti·, Lessing explodes the nineteenth-century male/male doubling pattern. That pattern has its simplest form in the Jekyll/Hyde personality. Jekyll, unable to integrate his violent, amoral self, hides it in another self, although both still inhabit the same body. (We are even told that Hyde means hide.) Once the second self is projected upon another character or characters who have separate objective existences, the second self assumes a more dramatic, complicated character. Furthermore, the primary self of nineteenth- and much twentieth-century literature—Frankenstein, Jekyll, Dorian Gray, Golyadkin, Ivan Karamazov, Spencer Brydon, Marlow, Henry Sutpen, Asa Leventhal, Hazel Motes—is male, and his secret sharer is also male. The one example of a female/male double cited in the standard volumes on the double in literature (Tymms, Rogers, Keppler) is Brontë's Cathy/Heathcliff, and it is significant that their creator is a woman. None of these works cites a woman who has a female secret sharer or double. Only current feminist criticism (e.g., Gilbert and Gubar) has uncovered female secret sharers.

Thus Lessing's extraordinary gallery of doubles and multiples overturns prior models.

In forcing her readers to pay attention to numbers, Lessing takes them to another kind of off-limits territory—to decaying tearooms and flaky old ladies, to an environment without "serious" intellectual credentials. By calling the fifth novel in a series The Four-Gated City, Lessing draws attention to the numbers four and five as she does in The Golden Notebook, in which her major character keeps four notebooks that are, however tenuously, "transcended" by a fifth. Three has another kind of meaning, one inscribed in Lessing's exploration of thirds in The Golden Notebook, A Man and Two Women, and, most obviously, in the title The Marriages between Zones Three, Four, and Five.

Lessing's numbering patterns have their private relevance but seem more heavily ideological than her naming patterns. Three is the traditional number for the family and for the Hegelian-Marxist dialectical triad. In that triad, two forces, thesis and antithesis, clash and are resolved in synthesis. Christianity also provides Western culture with a trinitarian godhead. In number lore, of course, all numbers have their elaborate and overelaborated meanings. In that lore the by now commonplace coexists with the commonsensical and the mystical. The four rivers in Genesis express the almost universally accepted four-squaredness of the earth, its four corners, four winds, four seasons. The four corners of the earth survive in our speech and in our psyche long after the discovery of earth's roundness. Jung builds on the ancient sense of four as wholeness or completeness; it is the circle squared. For him, four adds to the masculine trinity the missing feminine. (Even, as opposed to odd, numbers have historically been considered feminine.) When extended to signify the earthly paradise, the four-gated city, four forever beckons and is forever elusive in Lessing's fiction. On the simplest and, for Lessing, perhaps the most crucial level, four represents the sides of a room, an enclosure that can be a sanctuary or a place of love or the site of a mystical journey as well as a prison.

The city image is the room writ large; the city and the room can oppose or complement each other.

Five appears to be a peculiarly Eastern number. For Mark and Lynda it represents the explosion of the limits of the room, of boundary. For Jung five is an abnormal mandala. In rejecting three and four, can Lessing be suggesting a pattern that overturns two of her major parental thought systems, the Marxist triad and the Jungian mandala? Perhaps. The real point seems to be that five, like the fifth volume in the Martha Quest series, breaks, transcends, yet includes the four walls which trap the Lessing heroine and within which she works out the shape of her freedom. In the Canopus volumes Lessing reverses her use of three, four, and five in the Martha/Anna novels, for in *Marriages* ascent moves in more traditional mystical fashion toward the One: Three is a "higher" zone than Four, Four a "higher" zone than Five, and One the highest zone of all. This pattern reversal indicates in yet another way Lessing's current devotion to mystical journey.

Lessing's extension of the principle of doubling to environments provides a framework for her need to see the individual in constant juxtaposition with the collective. In one of the first reviews of *The Golden Notebook*, Irving Howe notes the replacement in fiction of what he calls "social man" by "psychological man." For him, as for many readers, one of Lessing's strengths is her refusal to accept that replacement and her powerful grasp of "the connection between Anna Wulf's neuroses and the public disorders of the day" (17). The private and the public, the individual and the collective, make a permanent dialectic in Lessing's work. One way she dramatizes that interaction is to make her environments mirrors of the self. Something unprecedented happens to the character-environment interaction in *The Four-Gated City*; the walls, rooms, and houses people inhabit become living extensions of their bodily selves. Two antipodal houses, the Coldridge house and the house that Jack built, are intricately structured and described as coverings for the selves who live in them. When the Coldridge house is bought by the local council and its inhabitants dispersed, the sense of psychic and physical demolition has a preternatural edge.

In *Briefing for a Descent into Hell* (1971), the incipient solipsism of *The Four-Gated City* is full-blown. Charles Watkins's environment becomes evil when he permits the idea of evil to enter his consciousness. In *The Summer before the Dark* (1973), environments have a reality connected with Kate Brown's psychic journey through offices, hotels, the Spanish inn, Maureen's room. In *The Memoirs of a Survivor* (1974), the major characters walk through a wall into another dimension. In the Canopus volumes environments sometimes have unexpected and exceptional presence. The marriage tent or the mountains leading to Zone Two in *Marriages* or the wall of ice in *The Making of the Representative*, for example, have memorable tactile power. The conclusion of *Making* may press its transcendent point too much. Of interest is Lessing's willingness to suspend the tactile joys of living for that transcendent point, for in that novel the surviving inhabitants of Planet 8 explode in stellar fashion into millions of molecules. Their survival as bodily entities is no longer important. In *Making*, therefore, Lessing openly abandons the body and the environment.[6]

Memoirs and *Making* return to Lessing's smallest created environmental unit, the wall, which Lynda and Mark so urgently try to expand or destroy. In these more recent novels the wall is no barrier. In exploding the wall, Lessing in effect explodes the metaphor of the earthly paradise. When the wall comes down, it takes with it not only the four walls of the room but the four gates of the earthly city—and with those gates go progress and history. In other novels actual and dream cities are dramatically counterpointed. Their conception develops with some complexity from the young Martha to Ambien II, who is haunted by the mystery and beauty of the Rohandan geometric cities.

The veld Doris Lessing knew was a vastness without the human figure, her home a tin-roofed long house, a happening, a "timid" (*Martha Quest*, 10) and temporary intrusion on the eternal vastness. The Turner farm that is reclaimed by the land in *The Grass Is Singing* duplicates the fate of the house Doris May Tayler grew up in. When Doris May Tayler Wisdom Lessing returned years later, she could not identify the spot where the house had stood. City and veld, to adopt Mary Singleton's phrasing, are always interacting facts and metaphors in Lessing's fiction. But the veld, although indelibly a part of Lessing's imagination and perhaps more permanent than the city, was not to become Lessing's symbol of human achievement. Unlike so many other writers, Lessing refuses to damn the city and extol nature. She is stubborn in her insistence on the city as the center of human interaction. The city must be confronted, accepted, altered. It is the quintessential locus of human history. Lessing refuses to sentimentalize either the city or the natural world.

Perhaps Lessing's primary variation on straightforward narrative patterns resides in her commitment to mixed forms that often take the shape of antifictions. *The Golden Notebook* is a major breakthrough in both respects. It introduces four and five in new ways, wedding number to narrative pattern as each notebook is given its own mode of speech, insight, and subject matter. The inner Golden Notebook is the fifth, the "freeing" notebook, as the fifth Free Women section is both coda and conclusion. Furthermore, the notebooks are a form of antifiction; they are what doesn't (except they do in this novel) get into the published work. The "real" fiction is Free Women, but the notebooks are "reality." The narrative contraries in *The Golden Notebook* are immensely rich. Within the six major forms, the five notebooks and the one novel, other narrative forms luxuriantly explode: newspaper headlines, diary entries, film script, parody, letter, short story, fragments of a novel in progress, and so on.

These numerous contrapuntal forms question reality and art; they are a dialectic that was immensely satisfying to Lessing, as her various remarks about *The Golden Notebook* in her introduction to it and in several interviews abundantly show. She values complexity and fluidity and found a way to represent both by her mixed forms —which she preferred to discover without the example of modernist works. These mixed forms, most radically elaborated in *The Golden Notebook* and the appendix to *The Four-Gated City*, are reused with variations in all her subsequent novels.

The antifictions can also be called the shadow selves to the public published work, which is essentially what Lessing says when she defines the notebook sections of *The Golden Notebook* as raw material and the Free Women sections as conventional novel (*Small Personal Voice*, 81). We might then think of the notebooks as the rich shadow to the public Free Women, as the complex storehouse of material that is reshaped, even laundered, reduced, travestied, for public consumption. There are shadow fictions within the shadow notebooks: parodies, letters, work in progress, movie scripts. *The Four-Gated City* contains a less obvious set of shadow fictions in Thomas's testament, Dorothy's diaries, Martha's notes, Mark's walls.

These buried texts become an anguished echo to the primary fiction. In these two works, *The Golden Notebook* and *The Four-Gated City*, Lessing insistently records her dissatisfactions with the limits of existing forms, with the limits of writing itself.

In the appendix to *The Four-Gated City*, Lessing strings together ten documents in chronological order without indicating who chose them. Headnotes explain their origins. In these letters, official documents, and one newspaper account, Lessing continues to try out more overt modes of obliterating her authorial presence. These forms, the primary forms of *Shikasta* (1979), and other Canopus novels, transform Lessing herself into a chronicler or a gatherer or a librarian. But Lessing's desire to obliterate her presence in her fiction is long-standing. One could speculate on the relationship of this desire to the internalization of Marxist insistence on "objectivity." Lessing's long-remarked uncertain manipulation of point of view in the Martha Quest novels may be related to a desire for a certain kind of objectivity. Her efforts to present comment dramatically in those novels are sporadic, often unclear, contradictory, and sometimes simply inept. In *Landlocked*, Lessing has a more aware, a more commenting Martha perform functionally as a center of consciousness. Three years earlier, in *The Golden Notebook*, Lessing had retreated totally from her fiction. Anna was finally revealed as the author of Free Women as well as of the notebook sections, an explanation that pretty much eliminated Doris Lessing as an authorial presence.

The contrapuntal "objective" forms of *Briefing*—letters, medical dialogues, interviews—occur within the outer world that is set against the protagonist's inner voyage. *Memoirs* reworks the inner and outer metaphor more successfully. It uses the wall to separate and to describe two opposite worlds, a division that makes for the basic narrative and experiential division of that novel. The Canopus novels are like found objects, manuscripts in a bottle from the future. Lessing has no apparent existence in them. Chroniclers and participants take over the author's role; only primary sources have value. The newspaper clipping that announces Mary Turner's death or Charles Watkins's amnesia, or the newspaper headlines that torment Anna Wulf and Mark Coldridge, become a different kind of history in the Canopus volumes—one that is on the whole acceptable because it is Canopean. Occasionally, when Shammatan representatives speak, as in the epistles from Tafta or the Chinese spies, the documents are meant to be seen as lies because they contradict the Canopean chronicles.

Lessing sits behind all her documents; they are the form her authorial withdrawal takes in Canopus. Her return to first-person narration in The Diaries of Jane Somers is a return to a simpler invisibility, for, of course, most of the Canopean documents are first-person letters and reports. The Canopean chronicle and participant accounts, with their all-too-often uncritical patina of "objectivity" (a socialist realism code word), presumably provided a satisfying way to obliterate direct authorial participation. Lessing's earlier uses of "report" were more critical; her Marxism was always skeptical. She was never a true believer; she is now. The Canopean documents reflect belief in the truth and power of record, of history, of folk memory, and therefore appear to resolve, at least for a while, Lessing's long and prickly encounter with the nature of fictional and historical truth.

The Canopean explosion of temporality into timelessness can now also be seen as one resolution of Lessing's troubled exploration of aging and dying. The transcendence achieved by the inhabitants of Planet 8 seems equal and opposite to the acceptance of decay and dying achieved by Jane Somers in The Diaries. The species and futurist approach of the Canopean novels fragments into the individual and vividly present approach of the later novel's extraordinary portrayal of a middle-aged Janna who sees in the ninety-year-old Maudie the self she may become. The women are older and generationally separated, but the names "Janna" and "Maudie" nonetheless recall Lessing's best-known other female secret sharers, Anna Wulf and Molly Jacobs of The Golden Notebook. Molly, once an older sister, has been transformed into the mother figure. The problems of aging and dying in Lessing's work are situated squarely in the painful, eternally unresolved dialectic between mother and daughter. Lessing returns to that dialectic again in her latest novel, The Good Terrorist (1985), where once more the biologically related mother and daughter are doomed to violently acted-out irreconcilable differences. Her Good Neighbour and her Good Terrorist make another equal and opposite pair. The repetitions in these titles invite Lessing readers to think about equivalences ironic and otherwise between two protagonists and two novels apparently so different.

Each novel Lessing writes confirms the patterns of doubling and repetition I have identified. In her most recent novel Lessing for the first time in her career drops the slight disguise of her naming patterns and gives a fictional character a name transparently close to her own. It is easy to see in Dorothy Mellings, the good terrorist's mother, a stand-in for Lessing herself: their names, their ages, their Old Left backgrounds, and so on are alike. Alison Lurie speculates that Alice Mellings is named for Lewis Carroll's Alice. But the name "Alice Mellings" has a longer and more profound place in Lessing's work. For one thing, Lessing's first Alice was a Martha mirror/double in *A Proper Marriage*. For another and more important thing, Lessing's career-long naming patterns bring "Alice" much closer to home, to the persistent A/M naming constellation.

The Good Terrorist repeats the familiar Lessing doubling of names, numbers, and houses. Replete with A, M, and J names, the novel also has a house and an antihouse whose numbers replay Lessing's uses of three, four, and five (one is number 43, the other 45). It does not explore narrative patterns, which may be one reason for its simplistic effect. Its language is as tired as the Dorothy Mellings version of Doris Lessing who stands behind the foreground action commenting on her disastrous daughter and her housemates. Circularity and fatality are overpoweringly contained in "poor" Alice's name.

Lessing's formal patterns stand on their own. That they sometimes intersect with biographical facts only makes the patterns more available and more meaningful to the critic and the future biographer. They can enlarge our understanding of the genesis of the literary work and of a writer's lifelong artistic compulsions. It seems remarkable today that the literary world accepted the proposition that *The Waste Land* was an impersonal poem. What we now know about Eliot's life at the time he was writing *The Waste Land* enlarges our understanding of the poem without destroying its literary integrity. In opposite fashion, the equivalences between Lessing's life and her fictions have been too casually assumed and used to attack her work as mere transcription from life. The differences between life and art turn out, as always, to be at least as crucial as the similarities, if not more so. Lessing's selectivity has still to be properly and fully appreciated.

Consider, for example, the interesting fact that Lessing bore two sons and a daughter yet has focused on the mother-daughter relationship in her fiction. When Anna imagines her fictive Ella with a son, she does so in order to achieve revenge and power over the Michael who deserted her (she perceives herself as passive and victimized) in "real" life. Lessing's reductions in number and gender of the children she bore into one daughter in her fiction is one example of the kind of artistic selection and transformation that hostile Lessing critics say she does not make.

In pitting her women against multiple mirrors—other women, men, environments, fictions—Lessing is saying that in contraries there are both progression and vision. Her duplications of characters, environments, fictions, names, and numbers have another effect. They modify the straightforward surface of her novels. The resulting resonance is part of her power as a writer. Lessing has also been tasked for general heavy-handedness. For one reader, "She has no wit, and only a very serious kind of humor" (Sale, 22). Her naming and number games are a form of play that may not appeal to all readers. But the games are there and ought to be seen.

Perhaps a study of shaping can try to speak through its own shape. This book could have been patterned according to the strategies I have defined and examined: Lessing's doubling, naming, numerology, environments, narrative forms. It could, less aptly, have gone the more common academic route of chronological comprehensiveness—an ultimately inflexible and especially cumbersome route given its focus and Lessing's prodigious output: nineteen novels, sixty-five short stories, plays, poems, and autobiographical, critical, and journalistic essays. For my meditations about her repetitions and her contraries, a pattern of juxtaposition that looks at Lessing whole, without overall chronological armor, seemed most suitable. Lessing's sly subversions of her realistic surfaces called for something more subtle, flexible, interactive.

My pattern of selection and juxtaposition does, nonetheless, manage to look at almost all of the Lessing novels, some exclusively, in single chapters (The Grass Is Singing, Retreat to Innocence, A Ripple from the Storm [1958], The Golden Notebook, The Four-Gated City), others in group or synoptic chapters (notably the other Martha Quest novels, Briefing for a Descent into Hell, The Memoirs of a Survivor, the five Canopus novels, The Diary of a Good Neighbour, The Good Terrorist). The Golden Notebook is considered alone, yet it is placed with The Four-Gated City, as it should be, for these two novels comment on one another. I call them Martha/Anna novels. I hope I have added something new to the abundant critical discourse that has grown up about these blockbuster works. For one thing, I have shifted the emphasis away from the divided to the multiple self. Novels that have received either little or no attention, like *The Grass Is Singing*, *Retreat to Innocence*, and *A Ripple from the Storm*, seemed worth more discussion. *Grass* and *Retreat*, Mary and Moses, Julia and Jan, are provocative still. I continue to find *Ripple* one of the most exciting political novels in English. Lessing's need to double and repeat persists in the Jane Somers *Diaries*, whose focus on aging and dying makes a gritty counterpoint to *The Making of the Representative for Planet 8* and a similarly gritty expansion of the mother-daughter dialectic Lessing so persistently examines. A planned chapter on colonial and Canopean politics got taken over by/imbedded into my chapter on cities. That chapter discusses *Shikasta* in some detail and other novels—*Briefing for a Descent into Hell*, *The Memoirs of a Survivor*, and *The Sirian Experiments*—less fully. I reluctantly put aside drafts of other chapters on the remaining novels and stories. They will have to wait for other times and other places.

Like feminist criticism, Lessing criticism is changing. (The two criticisms have a parallel/intersecting history.) Lessing critics need to confront those problematic, subversive meanings and patterns that lie beside, within, above, and below the realistic surfaces of the Doris Lessing novels, for Lessing's surface subversions are only the beginning of her story.

Part I

Antiphonal Narratives

1

The Grass Is Singing (1950)

Roberta Rubenstein describes Julia and Jan, the protagonists of *Retreat to Innocence*, as a "distinctly dialectical pair, expressing antithetical issues in both political and psychological contexts" (*Novelistic Vision*, 50). Mary and Moses, of Lessing's first novel about racism and repression, *The Grass Is Singing*, are as dialectical as Julia and Jan in conception and meaning. In their opposition and intersection the two sets of characters prefigure, as hindsight conveniently permits us to say, the themes of an entire career.

Thus, although *Grass* and *Retreat* are separated by the first two novels of the Martha Quest series, they are worth examining together. Both have been considered minor novels; both represent approaches Lessing was to redirect. Comparing them makes *Retreat* less of a sport, it seems to me, and situates it more clearly in the Lessing canon.

The repeated initial letters of each set of names resonate noticeably within their so straightforwardly realistic contexts. The metaphor of difference and sameness inscribed in the names "Mary" and "Moses," "Julia" and "Jan," excites Lessing throughout her career. Both sets are female and male; one is also white and black, mistress and servant; the other is English and European, apolitical and political. The women belong to the power elites of their respective countries. Mary/Moses, Julia/Jan—their initials suggest a sharing undercut by their more profound differences. Their names recall the incestuous Fred and Freda of the short story "Each Other" and Martha and Mark of *The Four-Gated City*. The incestuous element has its relevance even in these novels, especially if incest is defined, as it has been, as an act that overturns established social conceptions of priority. The reversals of priority in the relationships between Mary and Moses, Julia and Jan, contain incestuous elements that relate them to the literally incestuous Fred and Freda. In fact, the major difference between Fred and Freda and the earlier-conceived couples is their seeming peership, as opposed to the obvious inequalities that define Mary/Moses and Julia/Jan.

Writing about first novels later in a novelist's career is dangerous sport for a critic. The critic, knowing what happened, finds it all too easy to discover a whole career in a first work. Yet what has happened cannot be ignored.

Lessing's first novel takes an essentially documentary or case history approach to its divisions of gender, race, nationality, and class. Despite the anticipated limitations of this approach, The Grass Is Singing has an unexpected vitality and complexity that have excited a new generation of critics (e.g., Bardolph, Bertelsen, Draine, Morphet, Taylor, Weinhouse).[1] It stands on its own. It also looks ahead to other novels. (Ironically, years after Anna Wulf refused to allow her first novel to be turned into a film, her creator unbent and gave the permission Anna had denied. As Killing Heat, The Grass Is Singing now exists in film form.)

The plot has familiarity, clarity, and power, for it simultaneously acts out and subverts "the 'black peril' story structured around the transgression of racial and sexual taboos" (Taylor, 8). In the process of fusing the psychological and the political, Grass examines other kinds of divisions—between farm and city, dream and waking life, feeling and reason, sound and silence, name and character—divisions that Lessing will explore throughout her career.

From the opening headline, "MURDER MYSTERY," and its one-paragraph news account, Mary has center stage as victim, a role she shares with the confessed murderer, the houseboy Moses, her husband, Richard Turner, and the outsider Tony Marston. Since the as yet unnamed black houseboy has confessed, the mystery is in the motive. In the reconstruction that is the novel, Mary becomes as much case history as individual, an exemplum of one of the opening epigraphs: "It is by the failures and misfits of a civilization that one can best judge its weaknesses." Thus, even before the novel opens, the reader is enjoined to consider the individual and the collective together. The authorial voice tells us that Mary is a type:[2] "She had the undistinguished dead-level appearance of South African white democracy. Her voice was one of thousands: flattened, a little sing-song, clipped. Anyone could have worn her clothes" (46). Her "anyone" quality contains special exaggerations. Her innocence is, for example, extreme. It represents the arrested development of white southern Africans, of women especially. Lessing intrudes a long paragraph on Mary's ignorance about her condition relative to other conditions in the world, "How could she know?" (44). She knows no history, is unaware of class or race in any genuine sense. On the personal and social level Mary's innocence is pathological; it keeps her a child psychically and sexually. After Mary drops out of school and comes to town to work as a secretary (as Martha Quest and Doris Lessing did), she chooses to live in a girls' club. Office life, little-girl clothes, and sexually innocent dates are her world. Her insulation is threatened when she is past thirty and unmarried. That isn't done: "She was not playing her part; for she did not get married" (48). Given her "profound distaste for sex" (the sounds of parental intercourse still ring painfully in her memory), only social pressure could drive her to marriage.

Mary's childhood was so close to the poverty line that she had almost been relieved when her two older siblings died from dysentery "one very dusty year." Their deaths eased the constrictions of the family's life. For a while the parents stopped their endless quarreling: "The loss was more than compensated by the happiness of living in a house where there were suddenly no quarrels, with a mother who wept, but who had lost that terrible hard indifference" (43). Her alcoholic father, a railway pumpman, is someone she hates. When first the mother and then the father die, Mary is presumably at least partially freed from what Martha Quest is later to call "the tyranny of the family" (*A Proper Marriage*, 82–83). Before her move to town, boarding school away from "her fuddled father, her bitter mother," was her only happy time (44). In town and in the office, "sheer contentment put a bloom on her" (45).

From the placidity of her office life, Mary moves into polarity with Dick Turner, where their total incompatibility shortly surfaces. Each has entered marriage filled with illusions. Mary thinks, for example, how nice it will be to "'get close to nature'" (67). Dick expects a farm wife, a worker, and a mother. "Their inexorably different minds" hasten their mutual disintegration. The obdurateness and hostility of the land and weather conjoin with their differences to ensure their defeat, madness, and death.

To these simplified polarities of male and female, town and farm, human and veld, the factor of racism is the most destructive addition. The entry of Moses into the Turner household comes when Mary is at her last turning point. Mary, Moses, and Dick make a fatal triangle in which Moses' motive must be inferred. Social realities and narrative purpose forbid an insider's view of Moses. Blacks have no identity for whites—as the novel insists. It is no accident that Moses is named only when he has entered a personal relationship with Mary; no accident that only one other black, Samson, who served Dick before his marriage, has a name; no accident that neither Moses nor Samson (nor Mary before her marriage) has a surname. African blacks are as invisible to European whites as Ralph Ellison's American blacks in Invisible Man are to American whites. Ellison's protagonist has no name at all.

Moses enters Mary's life when she is almost totally broken, listless, indifferent, no longer energized by her various projects—chickens, a tobacco crop, a store, having a child, and so on—and still recovering from her failed flight back to town to reclaim her old job and life. At this critical juncture, "when any influence would have directed her into a new path, when her whole being was poised, as it were, waiting for something to propel her one way or the other . . . , her servant, once again, gave notice" (195).

His replacement is Moses, the only black ever to acquire individuality for Mary. Significantly, the special relationship between Mary and Moses begins violently when Mary whips him in the field. Moses reawakens Mary's unresolved incestuous feelings for her father and her identification with what the authorial voice calls her mother's "arid feminism" (44). In breakdown, dreams dramatize for the reader Mary's imprisonment in her childhood, her failure to have resolved the limits of her relationship with her mother and her father. Social clichés expect the virile black male to lust for the white female and the white female secretly to return that desire. What Moses in fact reawakens are the only strong sexual feelings Mary has ever had, and they are connected with her father, not with her husband, to whom orthodox psychoanalysis says they should have been transferred.

Dreams are the key to Mary's inner realities. They serve as a dramatic psychological register that the limits of Lessing's protagonist and the novel's narrative strategies cannot accommodate. Dreams free the limited character from the confines of limited consciousness, for only in dreams can Mary unite her past and her present. The disguised insights of dreams never appear in her waking life.

Moses is an active presence in Mary's many troubled dreams. She is seized with terror that he will touch her in the dreams he inhabits. Three crucial dreams wake her up "sweating with fear" and wanting to end "the new human relationship" that exists between herself and Moses (218). When Dick has another bout of malaria, Moses insists on staying overnight so that Mary may sleep. That night her dreams of childhood explicitly connect Moses with the father figure and recall, for the reader, Moses' voice, "firm and kind, like a father commanding her," on that remarkable day when Mary permitted the barrier between white and black to break down, the day she sobbed in front of Moses and allowed him to put her to bed (212).

In the first dream, Mary's playmates ask her how to play. This possibility of leadership is undercut by her mother, who calls her inside. Mary, feeling afraid as she enters the house, is "sickened" by the sight of her father holding her mother in his arms and runs away. In the second dream, Mary is blindfolded while her mother, brother, and sister watch. Her father catches her head and holds "it in his lap with his small hairy hands, to cover up her eyes" (226). Once again, the odors and feel of her father, her blindness, and her closeness to the father's penis repel, frighten, and attract her: "the sickly odor of beer . . . her head held down in the thick stuff of his trousers—the unwashed masculine smell" (226). She panics while her father and her siblings laugh. She wakes screaming.

In the next dream Dick is dead because of the native's negligence. Mary is relieved, exultant, and guilty. The implied identification of the three men in her life becomes explicit:

> He approached slowly, obscene and powerful, and it was not only he, but her father who was threatening her. They advanced together, one person, and she could smell, not the native smell, but the unwashed smell of her father. It filled the room, musty, like animals . . . He came near and put his hand on her arm. It was the voice of the African she heard. He was comforting her because of Dick's death, consoling her protectively, but at the same time it was her father menacing and horrible, who touched her in desire. [229]

The incestuous conflation of father, husband, and servant could not be more clear. The name "Moses" connotes both paternity and deliverance, and Moses indeed functions as both father and deliverer in the novel. Mary, who feels complicit in her father's death, kills Dick in her dream (or at least represents by that death his psychic unimportance for her), but cannot kill Moses. On the contrary, she almost invites Moses to kill her. Moses, the ultimate victim, paradoxically takes on the ultimate power of dealing death. By submitting to that death, by almost seeking it out in the woods on that last night of her life, Mary performs an ambiguous act of penance.

Her death seems the only resolution to the dialectic that ties her to Moses: "They were like two antagonists, silently sparring. Only he was powerful and sure of himself, and she was undermined by fear, by her terrible dream-filled nights, her obsession" (232). The pathological white fear of black is nowhere better demonstrated than in the fear Moses continues to excite in Slatter and in other whites even after he has voluntarily given himself up to the police.

The conflation of the three men in Mary's life is subtly and effectively accomplished. Thoroughly convincing, it shows Lessing in firm command of psychological and social meanings, able to construct and to tie together several strands of motivational matter—personal, social, racial, psychological, historical. The three men who melt into one man in Mary's dream also recall the central footnote to the *The Waste Land*, which describes all the men and women of the poem as melting into the single figure of Tiresias.[3] Lessing's penchant for duplicating and merging figures becomes a lifelong fictional strategy.

The conflation of mother and daughter is less complex but more contradictory. The dream view of Mary's mother contradicts Mary's conscious view of her. Mary sides with mother against father and repeats in life her mother's victim role. But the dream shows Mary's mother in collusion with her father against Mary, as his partner and sexual mate. Mary cannot consciously accept this construction of her mother's loyalties.

What Mary fears most, the repetition of her mother's life, a repetition that haunts Lessing heroines, she accomplishes by marrying Dick. The authorial voice tells the reader that Mary's nameless mother had a life "so unhappy because of economic pressure that she had literally pined to death" (45). When her mother dies, Mary abandons her pathetic and alcoholic father: "By dropping her father she seemed in some way to be avenging her mother's sufferings" (44). In this case, as in so many others, things are either/or for Mary. Later she will see herself pitted against her husband, against the field workers, and against the stream of servants who come under her household rule and who are finally and fatally at once merged and individualized in Moses.

Marriage returns Mary to the poverty and rage of her childhood, to the cage of repetition she had hoped to escape. As soon as she crosses the threshold into her marital home, she feels "back with her mother, watching her endlessly contrive and patch and mend" (72). The language of doubling perfectly suits Mary's duplication of her mother's life; the memory of her mother recurs "more and more frequently, like an older sardonic double of herself walking beside her" (126). Mary's doomed struggle to resist repetition settles her face into "two masks, one contradicting the other . . . Sometimes she would present the worn visage of an indomitable old woman who learned to expect the worst from life, and sometimes the face of defenseless hysteria" (126). Such physical stigmata of inner division become a regular feature of Lessing's work.

Mary's loyalty to her mother and hatred for her father are muddied by Lessing's strange comment that Mary "has inherited from her mother an arid feminism, which had no meaning in her own life at all, for she was leading the comfortable carefree existence of a single woman in South Africa" (44). "Feminism" is Lessing's word, not Mary's or her mother's. It rings oddly because it is outside the world of the novel—besides being used inaccurately to mean female hatred of males. The phrase "arid feminism" initiates a long-term ambiguousness about feminism in Lessing's work and in her public pronouncements, which the internal nature of her work often contradicts. The important fact about Mary's mother is not her "feminism," but her imprisonment to poverty and the family.

The incestuous elements in Mary's relationship with her father, her husband, her servant, have social as well as sexual meanings. In nineteenth-century fiction sexual meaning tended to be covert; in our time overt sexual events frequently stand for social dislocation. If we see in incest an act that overturns established social conceptions of priority, then the reversals of priority in the relationship between Mary and Moses are revealing. Moses controls Mary rather than the reverse. This is unsettling to Charlie Slatter, the upholder of white racism. If, as he says, " 'blacks keep women in their right place,' " then black males are as patriarchal as white males. For Slatter, the overturn of the proper power relationship between white and black and male and female that takes place when white women boss black men, as Mary does when Dick is sick, is a major factor in Mary's murder: "'Niggers don't understand women giving them orders. They keep their own women in their right place'" (28). Slatter is no misfit in southern Africa; he prospers because he is both racist and patriarchal.[4]

Thus the internal meanings of *Grass* contradict the superficiality of the authorial remark about the "arid feminism" of Mary's mother. Furthermore, the men in Mary's life are neither free nor powerful. They are marginal and defeated. The father who attracted and repelled her and whom she blames for all the problems of her childhood is described as a cipher in his own home. So is Dick, who annoys Mary by calling her "Boss." Moses exhibits a different kind of powerlessness. He may acquire emotional power over Mary, but he has virtually no social, economic, or political power. Both gender and race are related to power in the novel in unexpectedly complicated and contradictory ways.

Mary has never really craved power, although she can relish as well as hate her stint as field overseer. She enjoys the authority; she even enjoys using the whip which is its emblem and with which she strikes Moses. Nevertheless, Mary enjoys order, predictability, and impersonality more than she enjoys power. Office routine provided her with an ideal system: things happened safely "one after another in a pattern, and she liked, particularly, the friendly impersonality of it" (44). Mary cannot get circumscribed order and impersonality in the fields or in her farmhouse. Her speeches to the field hands on the work ethic are ludicrously out of place; she refuses to give rest breaks and is insufferably rigid as an overseer. She tries to have things "happen safely one after the other" in everything she does.

When she can totally control her projects, she is successful. But her success is based on short-lived compulsive hyperactivity. Her cleaning, sewing, painting, and chicken raising are the acts of a woman on the edge of hysteria, as the woman behind the wall in *Memoirs of a Survivor* is over the edge in her frantic sweeping of leaves. Mary's hyperactivity contrasts with Dick's incompetence. She seems related to the Lawrentian conception of womanhood in her placement of logic and dominance over feeling and submission. Whereas Dick can permit petty pilfering, she cannot; whereas Dick can joke with Samson, Mary can never joke. When Mary complains of black smells, Dick laughs and repeats what Samson once told him: "'You say we smell. But to us there is nothing worse than a white man's smell'" (161). In fact, one of the things Mary comes to hate about Dick is his black field-hand look. The closer Dick gets to his land, the less white, or the more black, he becomes.

Mary's compulsive efficiency conjoins with her sexual immaturity to make a very negative picture of her. That is Lessing's overt text. Her less overt text shows Mary functioning well as a single woman: sexually unaware, arrested, frigid—whichever word we choose to apply—but functioning well in a town environment magically independent of cataclysmic seasonal extremes of drought and rain. If people hadn't "'made her get married'" (135), Mary would have pursued her comfortable, independent, stereotypically female secretarial role. Her survival would have been limited, but it would have been survival. People would have been kind to her "because she had 'missed the best things of life'" (49), meaning husband, home, children. But home for Mary translates as "a wooden box shaken by passing trains," husband and marriage as "her father coming home red-eyed and fuddled," children as "her mother's face at her children's funerals—anguished, but dry and as hard as a rock" (49). The early traumatized Mary refuses genuine participation: she "liked other people's children but shuddered at the thought of having any of her own. She felt sentimental at weddings, but she had a profound distaste for sex" (49).

Mary should never have married. That is a strong ironic subtext of the novel. Mary had found her proper place in her single life as an office worker. When she was lifted out of that environment, like other organisms she perished (a lesson often inscribed in nineteenth-century naturalist novels). Lessing imagines other scripts for Mary. In one, "she might have run away again ... and this time done it sensibly, and learned how to live again, as she was made to live, by nature and upbringing, alone and sufficient to herself" (142). Hence the reader confronts the irony that Mary as secretary is freer than Mary as wife.

Her visceral rejection of sexuality, marriage, and motherhood, her hatred of being female, is most fully and intensely projected upon black women: "If she disliked native men, she loathed the women" (132). She cannot bear to see maternal black women "sitting there on the grass, their legs tucked up under them in that traditional timeless pose ... peaceful and uncaring" (132). She is even more repelled by "the way they suckled their babies, with their breasts hanging down for everyone to see; there was something in their calm satisfied maternity that made her blood boil" (132).

The complications of gender and race are further exacerbated by the human relationship to the land. Perhaps only William Faulkner before Lessing has in our time so effectively insisted that people reveal themselves by how they relate to the land. Without her upbringing on the veld, Lessing's exceptional relationship to the natural landscape is unimaginable.

As a title, *The Grass Is Singing* speaks to the victory, even to the eternity, of natural forces, although its meaning in the context of its source, T. S. Eliot's *Waste Land*, is more uncertain. The landscape of the novel begins in the dust and dryness that defined Mary's childhood. Mary, who will never see the sea, is the first of many landlocked characters who struggle against a "vast, harsh" landscape. "It will rain . . . after I am dead," Mary correctly predicts (281), tying weather and land to human fates as they are tied in *The Waste Land*.

Before her death Mary has a number of reconciliations and insights. She realizes that she has never ventured into the bush, never walked beyond the marked-off portions of the farm or listened to "that terrible shrilling, and had never seen the beetles who made it" (274). She has an extraordinary vision of the land reclaiming the timid human intrusion upon it, effacing the house and every other sign that human beings once lived there: "the house, the store, the chicken-runs, the hut—all gone, nothing left, the bush grown over all! Her mind was filled with green wet branches, thick wet grass, and thrusting bushes. It snapped shut; the vision was gone" (273). She runs out seeking death: "The trees hated her, but she could not stay in the house" (274). The claustrophobic room is finally worse than the threatening, hating, vaguely sexual trees.

Mary knows "she had never become used to the bush, never felt at home in it" (223). When she thinks of the "encircling veld where little animals moved, and unfamiliar birds talked," she feels "a stirring of alarm" (223). When, as in the last section of *The Waste Land*, Mary "hears the thunder growl and shake in the trees, the sky lit up" (284), she knows Moses, her deliverer, will appear. Moses comes at her with his appropriately scythelike weapon: "And then the bush avenged itself: that was her last thought" (285).

Thus, at the moment of her death, Moses and the scythe are identified with the personified bush and Mary with its enemy. The natural forces she has denied all her life have taken her. Moses functions as an extension of the bush in this melodramatic climax to the novel, which romantically and stereotypically identifies blacks with natural forces. Such an identification is problematic, to say the least, but it does present the alienation of whites from the land they have expropriated.[5]

Mary's conception of farming the land is essentially rapacious, more akin, in fact, to Charlie Slatter's than to Dick's. She views her relationship to the land and to the people who work it much as she views all of her relationships, as a battle of wills. She likes "the sensation of pitting her will against the farm" (154). After she whips the then-nameless Moses, for example, though frightened at his look, she feels victorious, "a satisfaction that she had won in this battle of wills" (167). Like Lawrentian women, she works against, not with, the farm, the natives, and Dick. When she finally discovers the magnitude of Dick's incompetence during her overseer period, she forces him to agree to a tobacco crop. She looks "at the farm from outside, as a machine for making money" (169–70). Dick gives in despite his view of tobacco as "an inhuman crop; it wasn't farming at all, it was a sort of factory thing, with the barns and the grading sheds and the getting up at nights to watch barn temperatures" (112).

Dick is the only white man in the novel who loves the land, but he is the wrong person in the wrong place at the wrong time. The farm is his life: "He knew the veld he lived from as the natives know it" (173). If he were taken from the farm, "he would wither and die" (173). His favorite acres are those previously ravaged by a mining company that he has replanted with trees. Unlike Mary, Dick has no dream of escape to town with the money the tobacco crop is supposed to bring. So he is immensely relieved when natural catastrophe, a drought, rather than his usual mismanagement, aborts the crop. At the end of the novel, sensing the finality of his separation from the land, Dick descends inevitably into madness. To save his land from Slatter's exploitation, he even considers setting a torch to everything on it.

Their polar relationship to the land is another example of the fatal incompatability between Mary and Dick. But the relationship of whites to the land they stole from blacks has special ironies. The very land seems to fight the whites, as snow and ice fight the inhabitants of Planet 8 in *The Making of the Representative for Planet 8*. If whites succeed financially at farming, as Charlie Slatter does, they succeed at the cost of ruining the land. (Slatter's farm has "hardly any trees left on it. It was a monument to farming malpractice, with great gullies cutting through it . . . But he made the money, that was the thing" [111].) If they care for the land, as Dick does, then it fights them. Whites either rape the land or are ruined by it. No harmonious relationship between whites and veld seems possible under colonialism.

The structures men build on the land are as significant as their relationship to it. Dick sees his house positively as an extension of himself, as an object his hands have created. He does not see its discomfort or its ugliness. The reader first sees the Turner house through the outsider eyes of Tony Marston, who recoils at "the bare crackling tin of the roof that was warped with the sun, at the faded gimcrack furniture, at the dusty brick floors covered with ragged animal skins, and wondered how those two, Mary and Dick Turner, could have borne to live in such a place" (33–34).

When Mary's eyes were, like Tony's, outsider eyes, they were profoundly assaulted by the Turner house. Its rectangular shape, tin roof, and two rooms separated by "a heavy curtain of sacking" speak of poverty to her (71). Painted petrol boxes serve as cupboards. One relatively luxurious object, "bought for the occasion . . . a proper old-fashioned bed, high and massive," dominates the bedroom. With that bed, Dick feels that he is "capturing happiness itself" (72). What to Dick represent "victories over discomfort" are to Mary a sickening throwback to the poverty of her childhood.

Mary's relation to her house and her land is very different from the African relationship. Once hired, each new laborer is given a day to build his hut. The new huts coexist with inhabited older ones and disintegrating empty ones to maintain a natural and eternal rhythm of becoming, being, and dying. They are natural growths, "dropped . . . magically on the earth in the form of huts" (152).

Lessing's career-long concern with human dwellings and their relation to the land is thus strikingly initiated. Natural rhythms are embraced and remain a contrast to the more commonly compulsive characters and environments Lessing depicts. None of her environments approaches the correspondence between land and people of the African huts in *Grass* until Frederick Larson in *Briefing for a Descent into Hell* has his insight about the river people who correlate their habitats with the rhythms of the river's rising and falling. The river people do not build for permanence, for to do so would be to ignore the river's rhythms. Only once more, in the legendary geometric cities of Shikasta, does some ideal correspondence between people and land seem to exist. (Compare Bachelard's description of this correspondence.)

The store is another constructed environment, one that Lessing raises to major private and social significance. Her description of it is as overtly and self-consciously sociological and historical as Dreiser's description of the department store in Sister Carrie or Faulkner's use of the commissary ledger in "The Bear": "If one was looking for a symbol to express South Africa, the South Africa that was created by financiers and mine magnates, the South Africa which the old missionaries and explorers who charted the Dark Continent would be horrified to see, one would find it in the store. The store is everywhere" (39).

The store's geography is carefully described; it is low, single-storied, "divided into segments like a strip of chocolate" (39). Its colors, odors, and Greek, Jewish, or Indian owners, perceived as alien profiteers, are strong stuff for English settlers. As the local social and economic center, dispensing food, drink, mail, reading matter, and gossip, the store provides for Mary and others "the real center" of life. For her as a child, it was "even more important . . . than to most children," since the family quarters were almost always within sight of it and she was always asked to run errands there (41). When she was older, it was "the place where her father bought his drink" (41) and where the family ran up never fully paid bills. (Compare Martha Quest's pleasurable trips to her local store, where the storekeeper's sons, Joss and Solly Cohen, introduce her to a radical reconstruction of her claustrophobic culture.)

Lessing carefully calculates her introduction of Dick's desire to run a kaffir store on the Turner farm. It cannot occur too early, as it represents a violation of the farm. In the catalogue of disasters that mark the Turner farm—pigs, bees, turkeys, rabbits, tobacco—it is the last. Mary resists and rages, but at last capitulates to running the store. Her return to the hated store of her childhood is even worse because it is a kaffir store only African women will frequent.

Thus Lessing endows the store with two faces: it is a social institution and the private nightmare of a specific woman. It focuses Mary's psychological crisis and her racism. That "the ugly menacing store of her childhood" should follow her into her own home seems a dreadful "omen and a warning" (130). Explaining her feelings to Dick would be futile because he has become associated with her childhood "grayness and misery . . . and it would have been like arguing with destiny itself" (132). Flatly and finally, the authorial voice announces: "It was the store that finished Mary" (134).

The positive spaces Mary has known belong to her single life: boarding school, the girls' club, the office. They provide what the bush and the conflated homes of childhood and marriage cannot provide. Negatively, presumably in keeping with the term "arid feminism," they provide impersonality and circumscribed order—clear, limited boundaries that exclude feeling and sexuality.

Mary cannot accommodate to farm, bush, or marital home. Her deterioration into catatonia, into a world with almost no speech, is an extreme example of how language reflects character in the novel. The commentary on language imbedded in Grass joins the naming patterns to heighten meaning and atmosphere. Silence becomes a metaphor for disguise, repression, ignorance, and isolation. The community receives Mary's murder with "silent unconscious agreement" (10). In Briefing for a Descent into Hell Lessing has her protagonist use the "You gotta have words" of Eliot's Sweeney. But in her first novel, only the grass sings and the people refuse words.

Like the incestuous elements in the Mary/Moses relationship, the inability or refusal to use words is a symptom of severe social pathology. The nearly catatonic household Tony enters mirrors the almost subhuman quality of life Mary and Dick have come to live. Dick, normally solitary and taciturn, easily accepts the almost total silence during their meals. Mary cannot finish sentences. To Tony she seems to have "forgotten how to speak" (254). Making a sentence becomes "an overwhelming effort. For weeks on end she spoke to no one but Dick and the servant; and even Dick she saw for five minutes in the morning and for half an hour before she dropped exhausted into bed" (194). Moses' efforts at conversation never take. Mary can only order or criticize. When Mary talks to herself, "the sound of that soft, disjointed crazy voice was as terrifying as the sight of herself in the mirror" (209).

The atmosphere of silence and "wordless criticism" coexists with three named languages, the kraal language of the Africans, kitchen kaffir, and English. Kitchen kaffir, the language white and black use with one another, is a fake language both white and black must learn. Men fresh from the kraal do not know it; women fresh from the town do not know it. The reader learns these language realities casually as an aside, as readers often discover crucial information in Lessing's fiction (that Martha Quest has left her daughter, for example, or that May Quest has died). Blacks speak their own language when they are together or when they are responding to a new outrage of Mary's. The nameless black Mary whips across the face speaks his own tongue first in response to her question. When she does not understand, he switches to English. Of his native tongue, Mary says, "'Don't talk that gibberish to me'" (164). (Mary's final undecipherable speech could also be called gibberish.) When he switches to English, Mary is equally offended, for "most white people think it is 'cheek' if a native speaks English" (165). This native has already marked himself out. In refusing the synthetic kitchen kaffir, he refuses the language of servitude. Lessing has built into her first novel another durable concern, the meaning and uses of human speech and silence.

The silence of the human actors contrasts with the shrilling of the cicadas and the beetles. Their incessant undecipherable noise, another kind of gibberish, reminds Mary just before her death that she has never walked beyond the demarcated portions of the farm. The beetles and the cicadas are the only voluble creatures in the novel.

Names in the novel are another form of silence that speaks very loudly. Mary and Moses are linked by their fates. Their common initial M's announce and reinforce their linkage. Both are victims, as the reader comes to know and as the white settler community will never permit itself to know. For that community, Mary and Moses reenact ritual scenarios: black buck rapes white woman or blacks thieve from whites. Neither has a surname. Dick never discovers Mary's last name when he looks for her in town; neither does the reader. Mary acquires a surname only when she marries, for only with marriage does she acquire full social identity. That she has no surname before marriage may be the clearest feminist statement in the novel. (Compare the name she acquires, Turner, with Lessing's original surname, Tayler.) Moses never acquires a last name. Only white males are connected with surnames, with, as we may say, full social identity from the white point of view. Mary and Moses, unequal as white and black, are relatively equal in social powerlessness, Mary by her gender and class, Moses by his color.

There are three biblical Marys, the mother of Jesus, the sister of Martha, and Mary Magdalen. If Mary has any relationship at all to the biblical Marys, it is to the Mary whose sister is Martha, for in the context of Lessing's work, Mary is indeed a sister to Martha. The biblical Mary has become associated with the contemplative life, her sister with the active life. The biblical meanings of Mary and Martha seem tangential, whereas the collocation of Mary and Martha as sisters does not (compare Rubenstein, Novelistic Vision, 33; Stimpson, 186). It is oddly prefiguring, for Martha Quest and all the other women named with an M who stream through Lessing's work are Mary's fictional sisters. May, the name Lessing gives to Martha's mother, is a diminutive of Mary, and it is Lessing's own middle name. This striking fictional and biographical intertwining of M names seems self-evidently significant; religious correspondences are less so.

The name Moses faces two ways. It does indeed evoke the patriarch and the deliverer, but by its M sound it suggests equivalence with Mary, equivalence with the woman and in this novel equivalence with the victim. Not until The Four-Gated City does Lessing create, in Martha and Mark, another female/male couple who share initial M's in their names. But Martha and Mark no longer share a victim status. The positive equality of this much later fictional duad is not based on distorted power relationships.

Between the two black males who acquire first names, Samson and Moses, there is a long succession of nameless houseboys, very few of whom are, needless to say, in fact boys. Both blacks are given the names of Old Testament heroic deliverers, probably to signify at one and the same time captive status and the possibility of deliverance. The bound Samson accomplishes his deliverance though he dies for it. Moses, slated for death as an infant, leads his people out of bondage. Lessing ironically gives the young black a patriarch's name and the old black the name of a young, sexually attractive deliverer. A novel whose title comes from The Waste Land and whose landscape needs rain invites us to think about deliverers and deliverance. The potential deliverer of this southern African wasteland is black. Although his role is distorted by white outsiders, his name promises the eventual reunion of the land and its people. It also promises deliverance to the white woman already disoriented, mechanically moving through time and longing for death.

Dick, called Jonah, caught by the discrepancy between his vision and his capacity, yet having a truer relation to the land than other whites, descends into madness after Mary's death, and Slatter finally gets the land he has so long coveted. Dick is the Jonah who has and brings bad luck, not the Jonah who finally escapes from the belly of the whale. He undergoes death without resurrection. The three major victims in the novel have biblical names, a use of biblical associations quiescent in Lessing's work until the Canopus novels, which are heavily indebted to "the sacred literatures of the world" (*Shikasta*, x).

Tony Marston is an outsider to the bush whose surname links him to Mary. His defeat by the white power structure and his own weakness relate him to Mary and to Dick. Like the Turners, he is accounted a failure by the Slatters. Like Mary, he is also fated to repeat his past. Instead of escaping paper work and an office, Tony, defeated by the land and by what Slatter calls his gutlessness, will return to white-collar life. This additional victim of repetition is the only outsider who has been deeply affected by Mary's death and by the glimpse he has had of the Mary/Moses relationship (he sees Moses dressing her). As the only outsider who wants to know why, Tony starts the investigation that the reader, with the help of the omniscient author, must complete. He knows that the truth must be arrived at circuitously, not in a straight line. Through him, Lessing prepares the reader for the long flashback to follow. Tony is a nascent chronicler, the outsider/insider commentator who, if we think of Tony as short for Anthony, may have the first echoic A/M name in Lessing's fiction. He embodies in an early form Lessing's interest in developing outsider perspectives within her narratives, just as the opening newspaper headline is the first archival document in her fiction.

Lessing's naming patterns in her first novel are already strong indicators of meaning, indicators that acquire additional resonance when set against the naming patterns of her subsequent works. They suggest an early need for strategies beyond those provided by the realism Lessing defined and admired in her essays.

The achievement of the novel is Lessing's success in bringing Mary to the point where she can respond humanly to Moses. The terrible irony is that white "personal" response to black can only occur when the white is profoundly disintegrated. This reality is the disastrous reality of colonial Africa.

Mary, introduced simultaneously to the institutions of marriage and apartheid from a sheltered sexual and racial past, cannot survive this double initiation into the realities of power. Caught between Dick and Moses, between marriage and apartheid and all that these institutions represent, caught also in her own pathological denial of Eros, she is doomed to destruction. The vulnerable, more feeling (more female?) white male members of these institutions are also doomed. They are all what the survivor class, represented by Charlie Slatter, calls "misfits, outlaws, and the self-exiled" (10). These empathic failures embody Lessing's attack on white southern African society.

Nor can marriage as actuality and metaphor succeed. Perhaps, Dick hopes early on, the marriage is not so bad after all. For "there are innumerable marriages where two people, both twisted and wrong in their depths, are well matched, making each other miserable in the ways they need" (73). The Mary/Dick marriage is not one of these. After Mary's flight back to town, Dick is grateful for her return to him: "For, although their marriage was all wrong, and there was no real understanding between them, he had become accustomed to the double solitude that any marriage, even a bad one, becomes" (147).

Their "double solitude" deepens, and the real tension in the household is displaced into the Mary/Moses relationship. No *coincidentia oppositorum* can occur within either duad. The separation between these opposites seems unalterable. The "proper old-fashioned bed," meant to "capture happiness itself," will never be the center of the Turner marriage, for the man of Mary's imagination is "endowed with hands and lips but left bodiless" (73). The Turner marriage is the first of a long series of unworkable marriages. Only once, in *The Marriages between Zones Three, Four, and Five*, published thirty years later, can Lessing imagine a unity of opposites—and it must be temporary—a true conjoining of female and male, of sameness and difference.

The critic all too easily pinpoints the themes and patterns of a lifetime in a writer's first novel. In *Grass* the major obsessions of a career-long exploration do seem to exist. *Grass* examines division and imagines harmony. The particulars of that division—between man and woman, white and black, land and person, dream and waking life, feeling and reason, sound and silence, name and character—are the concerns of a lifetime. Some aspects of the novel are foreshadowing, like Mary's extremity in her early forties, the age

Lessing would later fix as the crisis age for women in her major heroines: Martha Quest, Anna Wulf, Susan Rawlings, Kate Brown. In *Grass*, Lessing anatomized this crisis age when she was herself just thirty. Or consider the use of dream as dramatic inner register before Lessing began her own immersion in psychoanalysis. Furthermore, here as later dream enlarges the narrative reach of Lessing's fiction in its ability to transcend the boundaries of simple chronological time and limited character. In the Turner marriage, the first of many failed marriages in Lessing's work, breakdown and madness afflict the man as well as the woman. Madness, rarely gender-specific in Lessing's work, is always rooted, as it is in *Grass*, in a social context. Finally, in that complicated interrelationship between art and life, *Grass* has a unique role: it reappears as in a distorted mirror in *The Golden Notebook* as Anna Wulf's first novel, *The Frontiers of War*.[6] Through Anna Wulf, Lessing distances and distorts her own reflections about her first novel.

2
Retreat to Innocence (1956)

Retreat to Innocence is, like *The Grass Is Singing*, an exploration of di-
chotomy that cannot issue in marriage. In Julia Barr and Jan Brod,
Lessing probes a whole series of obvious oppositions.

It is Lessing's only novel of the 1950s in which the female protagonist has no clear relationship to Lessing's own life. This may be
the source of its weakness, for the flaw of the novel is less in its
supposed party-line conception than in its simplistic conception of
Julia. *Retreat* is also the only Lessing novel out of print because Lessing will not permit its reissue. She has described it as "good material wasted" (to Schlueter, 137), and "a wonderful theme but I did
not do it justice" (to Knapp, *Doris Lessing*, 48).

The London setting is similarly unrealized. In this first novelistic
use of her new London home as the setting for a novel, Lessing
barely notes the natural and the human-made environment. One
or two of the park scenes acquire some life. The interior landscapes, however, never quite come alive. The contrast between
Julia's room and Jan's is perfunctorily made. Not until *The Four-Gated
City*, published twenty years after Lessing's arrival in London and
projected through the eyes of a protagonist newly arrived from
Africa, would Lessing successfully realize the London setting in fiction. (The London setting is fully realized in the nonfictional *In
Pursuit of the English*, 1960.) Perhaps the error in *Retreat* was to locate
her female protagonist in the young, narcissistic daughter of an upper-class liberal English family, a social level that seems entirely
"literary" or "got up" in the novel.

The disharmony that is the subject of the novel surfaces in the
description of the Old Danube coffeehouse whose interior is internally at war with itself: "The commercial modernity of the tip of the
room and the old-fashioned plushiness of the rest did not harmo-
nize at all" (5). But Lessing's description of this divided Old World/
New World setting lacks the power of the description of the store

or the veld in *Grass*. Julia's room is done "in a parody of a bedroom 'suitable for a young girl' " (19), a description that makes Julia sound like other Lessing heroines who parody in order to antagonize their mothers, and indeed, the authorial voice tells us, "This was to tease her mother, whose taste was severe" (19). But Julia backtracks before the paragraph is over to admit: " 'No, this room is me; it is me; it wasn't a joke at all when I made it like this, even though I pretended it was a joke so that my mother wouldn't laugh at me' " (19). She is in fact the kind of young girl who rebels against her mother's example, as Janet rebels against Anna Wulf in *The Golden Notebook* in wanting boarding school, a uniform, the middle-class works. Jan's room is probably the kind of room Lessing liked, one linked with the colors of the sun and foliage like Martha and Thomas's tree room in *Landlocked*. It is "very light, open-faced, candid" (82), jammed with bed, desk, fireplace, papers, and books, drenched in yellows and reds. However, once these opposing environments are defined, rooms and parks take second place, perfunctorily recording but not extending Lessing's anatomy of the human and the natural environment.

Retreat can be described as a novel of limited female initiation, an initiation accomplished through an older male mentor, a Holocaust survivor and skeptical Marxist. Julia's sexual and political innocence is a feature of her age, class, sex, nationality—and her time, the 1950s. She has no experience of World War II and no interest in history or politics. Her innocence relates her to Martha Quest as much as it does to Mary Turner. If she is innocence, Jan is experience, not an inapt set of terms for them, since William Blake is Jan's favorite author. Experience is connected with historical consciousness, political suffering, and multiple "irregular" heterosexual relationships.

Jan is a type who haunts Lessing's fiction; he is related to other male Jewish Left survivors—to Anton Hesse and Thomas Stern of the Martha Quest novels, to Willi/Anton and Michael/Paul of *The Golden Notebook*, and to George Sherban of *Shikasta*. Class seems less crucial in *Retreat* than sex, age, or political allegiance, for Julia's father, Sir Andrew Barr, generationally equal to Jan, empathizes more with him than with his own daughter. Jan's description of Julia's generation as " 'nature resting' " (73) defines a generational rhythm that recurs in Lessing's fiction. The next generation, the generation of the 1960s, was to claim Lessing's sympathetic and extended attention in *The Four-Gated City*. Another generation "resting" surfaces in Emily and Gerald of *The Memoirs of a Survivor*, to be succeeded by the "committed" generation of the Sherbans, George, Benjamin, and Rachel, in *Shikasta*. These generational rhythms represent one strand of Lessing's acute and permanent historical consciousness.

Thus, from one point of view, Jan is a stand-in for an older generation that, like Lessing's, has grown up with "history." When Julia first visits Jan's room, she reads the emblematic set of quotations on the top sheet of a manuscript. The first, "After such knowledge, what forgiveness," is appropriately from Eliot's "Gerontion," a poem about the failures of historical consciousness. Julia becomes angry. "'What right has he to Eliot?'" she thinks possessively, forgetting that Eliot is English by adoption only, as Jan would like to be. Is the second quotation more Jan's because it is Stalin's? It is not particularly political: "'There are no things in the world which are unknowable, only things which are still not known'" (84). The energy and optimism of the quotation contrast wonderfully with the fatigue, depression, and religious longings of "Gerontion." These grotesque opposites are not totally parodic. They show the coexistence for left intellectuals of seemingly incompatible heroes. Eliot and Stalin, that unlikely duo, were equally usable repositories of wisdom for many left intellectuals. The irony goes further, for Stalin's line could as easily issue from a Sufi guru of today.

Although the title of the novel refers to Julia Barr and would seem to point to her as the protagonist, the novel is, in fact, saturated with Jan's consciousness. That consciousness, like Lessing's, is an outsider/insider's, at once not English and English, for Jan is more aware of England's tradition of political liberty than Julia is and also more critical of England's flaws—its imperialist past, for example. After fifteen years in England, Jan speaks Czech too poorly to converse in it with his brother when Franz arrives from Prague for a visit. The brothers have to give up on Czech; Jan has also forgotten his Hungarian and his Russian and refuses to speak German, the language of the Nazis and, ironically, his native tongue. The brothers continue in English. (Jan's big novel is in English.) Lessing's exploration of language in this novel does not take this notation of the multilingual Central European exile versus the monolingual English very far. She is more interested in satirizing ideological and bureaucratic jargon.

Jan's ambivalent relationship to England and to the languages of his past parallels his skeptical communism. Though *Retreat* was published before Khrushchev's de-Stalinization speech at the Twentieth Party Congress in 1956, Jan dares to suggest that Stalin wasn't perfect. Franz wants to know if he has become an anti-Stalinist, a crucial question for orthodox party members. Published before the Hungarian revolt of 1956, which precipitated Lessing's departure from the Communist party of Great Britain, the novel records through Jan's doubts Lessing's own doubts about her formal party commitment. When Julia calls Jan a Communist, he answers, "'Oh, I'm not a communist. I'm an enemy of the people'" (41). Later, Jan accuses the Czech regime of hanging his best friend, Pavel, and identifies his brother Franz with that regime.

Jan's fifteen-year effort to acquire British citizenship is filled with bureaucratic stupidities that will not result in hanging but will, with Julia's "help," force Jan's return to Czechoslovakia. Lessing will not forgive British bureaucracy just because Communist bureaucracy is more repressive. Jan's attack on these two types of postwar bureaucracy surfaces early in the novel, though it is disguised and distanced in his ironic stories. In one, Fritz, a wonderful tailor and loyal Communist, is asked to run an electrical factory in East Germany. Fritz's story becomes a parable about bureaucratic idiocy: "'We can do without suits at the moment, but we can't do without electricity'" (44). So loyal, hardworking Fritz successfully shifts jobs and, discovering he has a talent for mathematics, asks to study it at the university. He is then told that the country needs hospital administrators. At this point, Jan leans back laughing.

The serious Toni story, told without irony, is about Jan's adoration at age thirteen of the twenty-three-year-old Toni, who invited sex without the young Jan's realizing it. Julia's "'And what happened to Toni?'" (49) brings the information that she was gassed by the Nazis. (Jan's mother died at Auschwitz.) Jan tells Julia these stories before they have exchanged names. Stories are his staple mode of discourse.

The first story is the longest and the most redolent of Lessing fiction to come. The story of Willi is really the story of Anna and Willi, names *Golden Notebook* readers will instantly recognize. Willi converts Anna to communism and wants to return to East Germany with her, but Anna, whose party loyalty is suspect, is not cleared for return. Willi refuses to leave without her. Indoctrinated by Willi to place party above personal loyalty, Anna rejects him and finds a more consistent Communist partner. Willi goes to East Germany, but returns to England. This is the down-and-out Willi who gets a handout from Jan at the Old Danube, to Julia's puzzlement and disgust. Jan tells Julia about Willi's genius and bravery as a World War II partisan. Willi, out of place in the postwar world, "'belongs to the age of conspiracy. He can't stand order, and organization and construction'" (39). Some people "'can't bear normality'" (41). Willi's story, told with great irony and empathy, is the kind of interpolated story Anna tells in The Golden Notebook. Willi also seems a prototypical figure much like the individual terrorists thumbnailed in Shikasta.

These stories or antifictions function narratively much as dreams function in Grass. They contrast with and enlarge the flat, nonresonating main narrative. They have the irony, the suggestion of density, that the straight narrative lacks. They imply the aridity of Julia's life, even of Jan's life, which is immersed in a make-ends-meet job while he completes his historical novel and waits for British citizenship, perhaps in part like Martha, who waits for the end of the war so that she can go to England, then later waits for commitment and later still for time to undertake her visionary journeys. Jan's unslakable need to discourse in story form resembles Anna Wulf's similar need in The Golden Notebook.

The story of Anna and Willi and its allusion to partisan life will recall to Lessing readers the Yugoslav partisan story Charles Watkins makes up in Briefing for a Descent into Hell. Jan's partisan story is not dubious or falsely heroic. It has the ring of truth Charles's "heroic" story quite lacks. Like all of Jan's stories, it issues from an imagination fixed within and around World War II. For Lessing this period is paradigmatic. She returns to it again and again, even in the Canopus series. It is an indicator of the painful discrepancy between what was supposed to happen and what actually did happen after the war.

Jan's stories are teaching stories. Through his stories, he teaches Julia about discrepancy in personal and species history. His richly ironic teaching mode is a way to distance his private pain about the failure of his socialist dream. His stories could be called Sufi stories were they not so suffused with pain. Sufi ironies are presented neutrally; their bite is soft and noncorrosive. Whether Jan is telling the story of Max or Helga, who keep being denied British citizenship, or of Ivan the horse, or of "the mustache" (the stereotypic English bureaucrat who examines Jan's fitness to be English), Jan paradoxically removes himself as an actor and infuses his personal pain into his stories.

Jan is a professional writer with a significant prewar publication career (Sir Andrew knows his work) who is beginning to be republished in Czechoslovakia because he is no longer considered, as Jan says to his brother, "'a writer hostile in spirit to the needs of the people'" (310). He begins to get some attention in England; a reporter comes to inverview him. Julia's indirect pressure brings his former English publisher to indicate an interest in his novel in progress, which Julia describes as "'one of those awful novels with a thousand characters all talking at once, ... an incident in every paragraph, and the action taking place in a dozen countries simultaneously. It's all so old-fashioned'" (231). Her summary sounds like a parody of a nineteenth-century Russian novel—the kind Lessing praised so highly in the 1950s.

But when Jan describes the novel to Franz, he describes it as an allegory of the new man whose survival in a hostile world is a miracle and yet not, "'because you can't kill the future'" (317). Jan's new man sounds sometimes like Stalin, sometimes like a secular Christ, sometimes like George Sherban of *Shikasta*. His new man turns bitter when he realizes people want to kill him; in order to stay alive, he is forced to become a killer himself. Then, after leading his people through a war and establishing his new nation, he suffers because his hands are bloody. Naturally, his children's hands, like Julia's, are clean.

Jan decides his novel is realistic, yet he knows it is a parable of our time or of all times, a localized myth of the male deliverer that remains ambiguous. Jan's storytelling powers go back to his boyhood, as he and his brother laughingly recall. His gifts seem divided between the allegorical and the realistic. Perhaps that division displaces his creator's own incipient dissatisfaction with her conception of realistic narrative.

Julia's view of politics has a double face. The weight of the novel is critical of her naiveté and insulation in gender, class, and nationality, but Lessing also makes the reader aware that the younger generation in England and Europe cannot respond to a past it has not lived through. That is a major point in Jan's realistic allegory or allegorical realism. Even Franz, the Communist bureaucrat and apologist, sees that the young people in England and those at home are alike in not having known suffering: "'They are happy: they have no idea what it cost, what it all cost. And why should they have?'" (322). Bobbie, the English working-class waiter at the Old Danube, has no interest in politics though his parents brought him up on William Morris and Keir Hardie and he knows the socialist canon by heart. His stance is cruder than Julia's: "'What's in it for me?'" (111).

Julia's response is saturated with anger and guilt: "'I loathe politics. I hate them. All my generation do. All that filth and dirt and heroics—'" (41). When Julia digs into her past for a political experience, she can dredge up only a conventional touristic homily based on a childhood stopover in a small town in Spain to fix a flat: "'We all laughed a lot. We all liked each other. We had nothing in common, but we liked each other'" (222).

Julia's storytelling powers are almost nonexistent. Her Spanish story is her only story. Its moral is that two people face to face will break down all barriers: "'Don't you see? It's impossible to put two people into the same room together for half an hour without their liking and respecting each other'" (223). Jan sighs and laughs, but Julia persists, making her point that human terms restructure the problem and require other modes of response. She is a simplistic, unconvincing predecessor of Maryrose in The Golden Notebook, who unexpectedly isolates truth and who always attacks political jargon. Unlike Julia, however, Maryrose has a radical personal past; she and her dead brother were lovers. Julia's possibly incestuous feelings for her father are distanced in her affair with Jan. She will never act out or confront these feelings.

Julia's dialogue with her father duplicates the dialectic she has with Jan. He becomes "sharp and impatient" over her desire to escape misery and unhappiness. His attack on her generation as an "I" generation may be the first formulation in Lessing's fiction of the kind of ego insulation Lessing will later oppose to "we-ness": "'I want to be happy. I want this and that. A more self-centred, selfish, materialistic generation has never been born into this unfortunate old country. All you want is to cultivate your own gardens. You really don't give a damn for anyone but yourselves, do you?'" (195). So Sir Andrew registers his judgment of his own committed and his daughter's uncommitted generation, the generation of the 1950s.

When Julia acquires somewhat more insight, she can perceive that however much like Jan her father is, he is also very different. She realizes that "'when it comes to the point, you'd do all the things you blame them for, and laugh'" (266). In short, British cool and British manners can become as violent and unsporting as Communist behavior. British officials did in fact spy on Jan, and Sir Andrew does accept such spying as pragmatic necessity. Julia insists that Jan's commitment has an honesty her father's lacks.

Julia's initiation into sexuality occurs simultaneously with her initiation into politics and recalls Mary's double initiation into marriage and racism. The sexual act is reported after the fact and is never explicitly described here or elsewhere in Lessing's fiction. Julia naively expects marriage to follow sexual intercourse, although Jan, the father figure turned lover, tells her he has no interest in marriage. Jan and her father share more than generational equality and commitment. They have been twice married and have had affairs between and during marriages. Sir Andrew is currently having an affair with a Marie and is continuing his friendship with his first wife, Olga. Jan married his first wife for essentially the same reason Martha Quest marries Anton Hesse in *A Ripple from the Storm*: "'I married her to give her a nationality and save her from the Nazis'" (119). Jan's second wife, still a friend, visits his flat in Friedl Aitken's house. Friedl, another war casualty, lost her husband and one child in the war. One day Julia realizes that Friedl's child, Micky, was fathered by Jan, who was honored to comply with Friedl's request that he do so.

Julia, though furious at what she calls the "group marriage" of the older generation, simultaneously wonders where the idea of "one man" comes from. Even her limited experience undercuts it. Nonetheless, she persists in longing for "'the man I'd be with for ever . . . the one man'" (122). She has explained to Jan her generation's belief in "'getting married young and being faithful to one person all one's life,'" in contrast to the "'divorces and—messiness'" of their parents' lives (66). When Jan explains that his second wife, Maggi, was a friend of Friedl's, Julia interrupts, "'Oh, don't tell me . . . You married her, it might just as well have been Friedl'" (118). Her words are like those Charles Watkins will use in *Briefing for a Descent into Hell* when he says that he might just as easily have married Nancy as Felicity: "It would have been the same" (206). Julia's momentary sense that "'we are all interchangeable'" (124) threatens her construction of the way things are.

Julia needs to reassure herself that she is the Julia she would like to preserve. Her steps to create that reassurance are stereotypically female. She spends a lot of time looking into a mirror. She thinks about clothes; she looks at clothes; she buys clothes. Like so many Lessing fictional women, she realizes that clothes can seem to change personality (143). Old women in the street become frightening mirrors of what she will become. The darker side of her one-dimensionality is her passion for order, which is contrasted with the more casual style of her roommate, Betty. That order suggests Mary Turner's erratically efficient side. Her need to confirm her identity converts into the need to confirm and enlarge Jan's identity, for she still wants to marry him.

Her normal indolence turns into energy once she decides to set Jan's life in order. That means getting his manuscript typed and ready for the publisher. This upper-class young lady knows how to type—a surprise—and she does the job for her man. She also undertakes research for Jan, much as Martha undertakes research for Mrs. Van and Mark Coldridge. She prevails upon her father to offer Jan a job (which Jan, of course, refuses) and wangles an interview with a high official in the British Home Office, which, like her efforts to get Jan's novel published, backfires. Julia also borrows money from her father to repay Jan's loan from Mathias (called Matti) Smith (born Fischl) and his English wife, Elsie.

Julia is roused by her need to shape Jan's life, not by her need to shape her own. This is a subtext of *Retreat*. Sir Andrew knows that his daughter is smart and talented. He also knows that she has decided "not to have talent" (190). Surprisingly, therefore, Julia joins Lessing's extensive gallery of women who shape their lives in response to what they think their men want or need. From this perspective, Julia escapes her shallow Galatea role to raise unconventional questions about how women subvert themselves in their relationships with men.

Virtually ignored in *Retreat* is the relationship between mother and daughter. Julia's mother, named Jane, is a feminist and political curmudgeon. She is in the background, surfacing only once through a letter she writes to Julia. She never appears in person. Her letter is precipitated by Julia's suggestion to her father that she have an illegitimate child, an idea Julia gets after she learns about Micky's parentage.

Julia's fantasy mothering, like Mary Turner's, never begins in infancy: "She did not imagine the child after it was born, or herself living with it in this flat, or with Jan" (199). Jane Barr writes to Julia without alluding to her fantasy of single motherhood, but the letter is an indirect expression of support (202–3). Julia ignores the inner meaning of the letter; her mother gets lumped with her father as a member of the older generation: "'When a man comes to our house, I look at him and think, I suppose you've slept with my mother some time'" (66). Of her father's mistress, Julia says, "'Oh yes, she's very nice, and she's a friend of my mother's too'" (66). Andrew suggests that Julia might like her mother if she took the trouble to talk with her. But Julia's hostility toward her mother is too old and too deep. When Sir Andrew tells her that he and Jane have agreed that of the two, Jane should stand for Parliament because she'll be good at it, Julia is so irritated that she chooses this moment to discuss having "'an illegitimate child'" (197). She must pit herself against her feminist mother who has also always been left-wing Labour and "'as good as a Communist in the thirties,'" while Sir Andrew has always been a Liberal (66).

Her parents make light of Julia's desire for the traditional white wedding, which Julia will of course have when the Jan affair is over and she has turned to her generational peer, Roger Metland. Thus the strong generational disjunction in the novel becomes almost virulent in its mother-daughter aspect. Julia's political and sexual mother outrages her as Martha Quest in reverse outrages May Quest with her sexuality and her radical politics.

On only two brief occasions does Julia think of her physically absent mother positively. Once she imagines her grown child "living beside her in her mother's house in the country, swamped by the generosity of her mother's acceptance" (200). Later, in her confrontation with Elsie, she lifts an appropriately acid and accurate phrase for her "out of an armoury inherited from . . . her mother" (301). Julia will not see that in refusing her mother she is refusing her own identity. Although Lessing must cast some doubt on Andrew and Jane as representatives of the upper class, the weight of the novel comes down positively for all members of the older generation and for Jane Barr's feminism and radicalism.

The part of Julia that is manipulative comes under criticism; it is a related obverse to Elsie Smith's testimony to the Home Office that Jan is immoral and a Communist, testimony that probably loses Jan his current bid for citizenship. Elsie and Julia are interfering and manipulative, one ill motivated, the other well motivated. Manipulation is in this novel defined as a female trait. Friedl seems the contrasting ideal woman, at once political, sexual, maternal, domestic, and loyal to her one man.

Julia's relationship to Jan and to her father and mother has psychological as well as political reverberations. For in having her first affair with Jan, a father figure, Julia seems involved in incestuous feelings that are for her satisfied through a stand-in, as Mary Turner's similarly incestuous feelings are not. Her relationship with her mother is competitive. Whether these tensions were consciously devised by Lessing is, of course, not to the point. Her projections of oedipal/incestuous tensions are there, and are worth comparing with those in *Grass* and other works.[1] Jan and Julia cannot make a marriage literally or metaphorically any more than Mary and Moses can. Jan, in effect—by his age, his politics, and his nationality—becomes a taboo figure, as Moses always is.

The incestuous longings Julia plays out in her first sexual experience make it possible for her to move on to a generational peer. She will sexually initiate and then marry Roger, who is defined by her roommate as "'the masculine equivalent of a cock-teaser'" (281).

The Julia who unhappily cries, "'We are all interchangeable,'" seems at some level as anguished by repetition as Mary is, and as Martha is. Lessing's repetitive naming patterns reinforce and enlarge for the reader Julia's nascent awareness of repetition. Julia Barr and Jan Brod are interconnecting opposites, as both their first and their last names suggest. Julia is also tied to her mother, Jane, by her J name. Names beginning with a J are an interesting addition to the M names so plentiful in *Retreat*. Julia, Jane, and Jan are the first of a fair number of J's in Lessing's fiction that are runners-up to the more profuse A and M names. From Joss, Jasmine, Jackie, several Jacks, Johnny, Jonathan, another Julia, Janet, two Georges, Johor, and so on to Jane/Janna in the recent *Diaries of Jane Somers*, J names make their presence felt. My speculation that they too must be echoes of family names received some confirmation when I learned that the two children Lessing left in Africa with her first husband are named John and Jean. Although J names are sometimes given to fictional children, to Janet Wulf, for example, or to members of the Quest family—Jonathan is Martha Quest's brother —J names cannot be described as located only in children or sibling figures. They can be described as more distanced kinship or doubles figures much like the A/M figures.

Three of the five A names in Retreat are male. Andrew, Aitken, and Andreas are coupled with M names: Andrew/Marie, Micky Aitken, Andreas/Maria. The fourth is Friedl Aitken, the mother of Micky. The only female with an A first name, Anna, appears in an interpolated story with a Willi (in The Golden Notebook a duplicate of Max). The M names are profuse and cut across gender lines: Andrew's mistress, Marie; Micky (he calls himself Jack the Giant Killer); Mathias, nicknamed Matti (his wife's name, Elsie, suggests Ella, Emily, and Stella); Maria, the mother of Andreas (both, like Jan, are natives of Mathey); Maggi, Jan's second wife; Metland, Roger's last name; Max, a friend of Jan's, who never appears. Finally there is the invented Miriam Hauptmann (Miriam is the Hebrew form of Mary).

This profusion of A and M names cannot be described as accidental. These names, like Jan's teaching stories, function narratively to create a resonance that realistic narrative—at least as Lessing perceives such narrative—does not contain. The repetitions are striking, but they do not have the shape they already exhibit in the two Martha Quest novels published before Retreat, where A's are male and M's are female. Perhaps the M's in Retreat are more "female" than "male," figures without the strengths stereotypically associated with masculinity. Certainly the rush of M names—even their sometimes casual repetition, as when the Andrew/Marie pair is perfunctorily duplicated in Andreas/Maria—suggests the melting of characters into one another in a larger human kinship saturated with the special fatalities of family ties.

The repetition of names has its underground atmospheric effect. The undercutting of bureaucratic and ideological jargon in almost every sentence that Jan utters or story that he tells is a major and self-evident objective of the novel. Irony, humor, and teaching stories keep Jan a survivor even when he believes his novel is a failure, even when he returns to Czechoslovakia without the passport he so covets, the kind that will give him identity and mobility. Without it, he shall remain stateless and probably never be able to leave Czechoslovakia. Jan fabricates an identity for the unknown Miriam

Hauptmann who was used to reject Helga's application for citizenship. (Helga, a brilliant Hungarian physicist, is another casualty; she returns to her homeland when her current application for British citizenship is denied.) Jan writes a satiric poem about Miriam that he sends to his brother. A friend sees it pinned to a wall, laughs hard, and later decides to write a satire using Miriam as the central character. Jan breaks out, "'You hear, Friedl? Our Miriam, she's going to be a real person at last. Julia, did you hear? Franz, you tell Nicolas from me, he can't have our Miriam unless he puts in that bit where she sells atomic secrets back to the same country she got them from'" (311). Jan's ability to tell stories and to satirize jargon go hand in hand. His built-in use of what Paul Blackenhurst in *The Golden Notebook* calls "the principle of destruction" is a positive satiric weapon.

Jan's stories and Jan's language, Jan's writer persona, give the novel whatever depth it has. They are to *Retreat* what Anna's notebooks are to the Free Women sections of *The Golden Notebook*. His stories are very much like the ones Anna interpolates in her various notebooks. It is interesting that Lessing never imagined an English writer (Anna Wulf, supposed to be English, comes across as African) until Janna/Jane Somers. Her imagined writers, even when they are male and British like Mark Coldridge, are outsiders, implicitly making the point that writing requires an outsider perspective and the kind of dense and critical immersion into the private and historical past that contemporary English novelists seem to lack. Just six years after *Retreat*, Lessing's most remarkable writer figure, Anna Wulf, who is also a woman, will make her explosive appearance. As a writer with an intense historical consciousness, Anna is a genuine descendant of Jan Brod—indeed, the only one he has so far had in Lessing's fiction.

The "marriage" of Jan and Julia dissolved, Julia can retreat back into her class and its system of protection. She exaggerates the change in herself that her exposure to sexuality and radical politics has brought about: "'I'll never be simple and ordinary again as long as I live. I'll never be able to do anything with an undivided mind— I'll always be seeing myself as Jan Brod would'" (332). How would Jan Brod view the marriage to Roger into which she slips so easily? She appears to want both its legality and its superficiality. Nonetheless, her remarks are significant for their definition of the positive value of the divided mind—especially since criticism about Lessing has so often centered on the evils of division. In Julia the divided mind represents a development in depth and maturity. The positive role of division is as valuable as its negative role.

There are few shadows in *Retreat*. Without the evocative naming patterns and Jan's stories and ironies there might be none. Jan is obviously to be admired, Julia to be found wanting, her transformation modest, her fate conventional. Only one other Lessing novel ends with marriage, *Martha Quest* (1951), but the ending of that novel makes the instability of the marriage clear and its dissolution inevitable. The novel that follows, *A Proper Marriage*, documents its disintegration. Furthermore, Martha Quest, like Jan, like Andrew, like Jane, like Anna Wulf, will have two marriages. Marriages after divorce as a regular event were inconceivable in the nineteenth-century marriage plot. Their presence, with such regularity and matter-of-factness, is one more symptom of the erosion of that plot in Lessing's work.

The societally acceptable marriage Julia makes to a paper cutout figure will not tax her body or her mind. It is not an achievement but a convenience Julia accomplishes by her seduction of Roger. Roger, who scarcely has an existence in the novel, is more interesting for his role in one or two of a number of embryonic triads. These triads announce an interest in triadic relationships that Lessing will return to in her short stories and in her Anna/Martha novels. The man-and-two-women triads in *Retreat* include Julia/Roger/Betty, Julia/Jan/Friedl, Julia/Andrew/Jane, Jane/Andrew/Marie. Jan's two ex-wives are also in the background and in Julia's consciousness as rivals. The two-men-and-one-woman triad occurs less often: Jan/Julia/Roger, Roger/Betty/Richard, Julia/Andrew/Jan. *A Man and Two Women*, the title Lessing gave to one of her short story collections, is another indicator of Lessing's interest in the two-women–one-man triad. In *Retreat* the other woman functions for the primary woman as a rival or wife or mother figure. Friedl, the most developed other woman in *Retreat*, is an idealized helpmeet who in fact functions as Jan's third wife. Friedl and Jan share a house, have a child together. Friedl is the housekeeper personality Martha Quest becomes, Mary Turner fails to be, Julia Barr will never try to be. Although the novel explodes Julia's one-man ideal, it also seems to accept with admiration Jan's later description of Friedl as a one-man woman. Friedl is a woman fulfilled in her maternal and housewifely functions. Like the nameless African women Mary Turner hates, Friedl seems fixed forever in some maternal pose, inwardly at peace, cooking, cleaning, child rearing, lacking in the restlessness that afflicts the typical Lessing heroine—a restlessness even Julia Barr shares. The image of Friedl, like the image of the African women, is an image of longing, a suggestion of female sufficiency no fully realized Lessing protagonist achieves even temporarily until the creation of Al·Ith in The Marriages between Zones Three, Four, and Five.

The novel closes over a Julia safe in her class after a summer of risk. People who have been away on vacation have returned—Friedl, Roger, Betty. Summer frames the novel. Julia meets Jan at the Old Danube because he cannot go anywhere for his holiday. It is the summer of 1955; Julia was born in 1934. Like the dates Julia checks for Jan, these dates are important. Julia needs to be generationally situated. The novel represents a kind of summer before the dark, to appropriate a later Lessing title, for both Julia and Jan. Certainly Julia's summer of experiment coincides with the month or months in the summer during which other Lessing protagonists descend into risk. The pattern of descent and return during the summer is repeated by Anna during her affair with Saul, by Charles Watkins in Briefing, and of course by Kate Brown in The Summer before the Dark. Is it that Lessing's own life was, like Anna's, punctuated by the needs of child rearing? Was her son away for a month or two during the summer as Janet is away from Anna? As Kate Brown's family is away? This defined period of difference can also be correlated with Martha's month-long "descent" in a room in Paul's house in The Four-Gated City. Retreat seems to be the first novel to frame a time of risk for its protagonist that ends with return, though presumably return with a difference, for Julia does not end quite where she began.

The circularity of the summer experience does, therefore, contain some progression for these figures. Julia's new unity, however slight, is internal and independent of others, not defined in terms of a continuing relationship with Jan or a new relationship with Roger. The novel suggests that Julia will go on separately though she lives with a husband. Her marriage to Roger is not a union of opposites, as her union with Jan was, as Al·Ith's and Ben Ata's will be.

The novel isn't great or good, but it is extremely interesting for Lessing students. In it Lessing once again examines a failed "mar-

riage" whose dynamics are private, social, political. Lessing's anatomy of the fifties here has a shallowness quite lacking in her two
masterpieces, The Golden Notebook and The Four-Gated City, which so
brilliantly fuse the political here and now of England in the fifties with individual lives and which have a life that has survived
that decade. Julia's refusal of further risk is characteristic of the English and the fifties as Lessing portrays them in Retreat, whereas
Jan's acceptance of it by his return to Czechoslovakia suits his very
European "historical consciousness." As always, Lessing comes
down for commitment over noncommitment and for risk over safe
repetition.

Lessing doesn't reuse the Julia figure but does reuse elements of
her character: her incestuous feelings, for example; her rejection of
her mother; and so on. The exploration of Julia's incestuous elements is too veiled and too underdeveloped to be fictionally interesting, but it does recall Grass. The attack on the immature female
fantasy of fulfillment through a child and the simultaneous celebration of the "natural" woman in Friedl, as of the silent black women
in Grass and other works, is an example of an unresolved contradiction in both novels.

The newspaper headline that helps to undermine Jan's application for British citizenship, "WE DON'T WANT SUCH PEOPLE"
(108), is all too like the headline that announces Mary Turner's
murder. Both represent outer lies that the novels expose. These
headlines, like the multiple narrative forms, the naming repetitions,
and the use of triads, will acquire greater depth and meaning in
later novels. No work of a major writer should be ignored. The
vehemence of Lessing's repudiation of Retreat must act as an incentive to the curious. The curious will not be disappointed: Retreat is
an interesting novel. The story of its genesis, when and if we ever
know it, will add to our understanding of Lessing's attitude toward
it.

Part II
Remembering Mirrors

What of course I would like to be writing is the story of the Red and White Dwarves and their Remembering Mirror.

Doris Lessing, Preface to *The Sirian Experiments*

3
The Martha/Anna Novels

The decade of the fifties is the critical one of Lessing's career. It fed the first four and a half volumes of the five-volume *Children of Violence* series as well as *The Golden Notebook*, whose present time is 1957 and whose retrospective time is largely the fifties (World War II and the fifties recur compulsively in Canopus volumes). During these years, Lessing joined and left the British Communist party, underwent psychoanalysis, lived through explosive private relationships —and wrote prodigiously. In *The Four-Gated City*, 1956 is explicitly defined as a watershed year in national and international politics (standard mainstream histories may not agree): "1956, as everyone knows, was a climactic year, a watershed, a turning point, a crossroads . . . a four star year, classed with 1942; Stalingrad; or 1949; the birth of Communist China" (291). Hungary and Suez were critical reference points for the Left, Suez for many more Britons; Suez reverberates in plays and novels by the "Angry Young Men." (*The Golden Notebook* emphasizes another memorable event of 1956, the Khrushchev de-Stalinization speech at the Twentieth Party Congress.) The "as everyone knows" has wonderfully ironic overtones in the 1980s, when hardly anyone "knows" about 1956—a development that doesn't at all reduce the effectiveness of Lessing's use of that date.

Without a unique set of personal and political crises, Lessing's interruption of the Martha Quest novels to write *The Golden Notebook* is impossible to imagine, especially since Lessing's work and her pronouncements indicate that like Mary Turner in *Grass*, she likes to have one thing happening after the other, that like the survivor/ narrator in *Memoirs*, she is a sweeper of eternally congesting leaves. That she could resist her compulsion to finish the series in order as planned, to stick it through, to respect linear development, is a mark of the radical power of those years. Only an extreme crisis situation could have made Lessing put aside Martha Quest sometime after 1958 for the Anna Wulf who was possessing her more urgently. Suspending the series to write *The Golden Notebook* (1962) must be the major artistic decision of Lessing's career.

In fact, Lessing was probably writing about Martha and Anna simultaneously for a while. Their interconnections, their duplication and repetition of themes and characters, have long been remarked —indeed, complained about. Such complaints ignore the significance of repetition. Like the repetitions in other writers, Lessing's invite critical examination, not concern that Martha and Anna are too much alike or that Anton, Willi, and Max are the same man or that Lessing has an obsession with names beginning with M.

It would be more to the point to examine the Martha/Anna novels as they comment on one another, to look analytically at their differences and similarities. The years that were lived and written about in these novels are likely to be considered the great years of Lessing's career. They recall William Faulkner's obsessive reworking of repetitive characters and themes in his great years, 1929 to 1936, in the novels *The Sound and the Fury*, *Absalom, Absalom!*, and *Light in August*. Critics (e.g., Irwin) relish and explore Faulkner's repetitions. Lessing critics must begin to do the same with her repetitions.

Art, like life, is inconceivable without repetition. It is enslaving for Martha Quest, who fears that she will repeat "the tyranny of the family" she grew up in (*A Proper Marriage*, 82–83). Yet she is, much later in life, willing to repeat again and again the steps that will lead to her version of transcendental experience. Her creator knows what Martha does not know: that repetition can be used and controlled, certainly in art and occasionally in life.

For repetition, although it suggests an eternity of sameness, is in fact extraordinarily various. It can be boring or exhilarating, pleasurable or painful, an example of discipline or sloth. In psychoanalytic theory repetition can be healing as well as neurotic or psychotic. In literature it can be made up of small elements or large and can refer to meaning or to sound. Although literary criticism has always considered repetition an element of literary pattern, especially in poetry—in epithets, refrain lines, rhyme—or in larger structural relations (as in, for example, *To the Lighthouse*, whose third section duplicates the time frame of the first), only recently has the phenomenon received extended special attention (from, for example, Kierkegaard, Deleuze, Kawin, J. Hillis Miller, Norman).

Repetition seems the opposite of dialectic, for it suggests stasis and sameness, whereas dialectic suggests motion. Yet though we may experience or think we experience repetition exactly, repetition is never exactly the same. Even if we could show that an event recurs in the same place, that event must take place in a different time. All repetition is therefore doomed to be inexact. Contemporary physical theory parallels literary theory in maintaining the impossibility of exactly repeating the location and time of any given event. Thus the phenomenon of repetition, which appears to be unchanging, is itself subject to change.

It might be objected that we can experience duplication as sameness even if measurements tell us otherwise, or that even if the object or event undergoes change in time and location the change is minimal compared with the kind of change dialectic describes. Nonetheless, repetition does not exactly duplicate, just as the dialectical end product cannot be wholly original.

We may, therefore, speak of the coexistence of repetition and dialectic. These two seeming opposites overlap and interact. They certainly do in Doris Lessing's work. Her repetition of names or of names with the same initial letters within a novel and from novel to novel are, for example, clues to realities beneath the appearance of her wholly freestanding characters. Lessing's extraordinary repetitive naming patterns are part of a network of double and multiple female/female and female/male characters that repeat, rework, and explode prior uses of doubling in literature. Her passion for certain numbers is as integral as her passion for exploring environments. And for her the four walls of a room are as significant an environment as are the more traditionally labeled environments of house, city, galaxy. Her repetitive exploration of fictional modes within each novel and from novel to novel is another constant in her work. Lessing's repetitions as a formal phenomenon must be insisted upon because her work has so often been considered merely programmatic in meaning and realist in method.

The paradox of arithmetic division is crucial to an understanding of Lessing's network of double and multiple characters. A cell that splits in two has both divided and multiplied. This paradox governs Lessing's exploration of the problem of fragmentation in our time. When Anna Wulf divides her experience into four notebooks, she is saving herself. Her reunited self does not discard the four notebook selves. Hence division leads to or can lead to multiplication or growth. Unity is achieved by at once incorporating and discarding negative or incomplete selves. This was the lesson of the classic doubles novel of the nineteenth century; but that novel was for men only and did not imagine positive or peaceably coexisting selves and other selves.

There are times in the Martha/Anna novels when all the women appear to melt into one woman and all the men appear to melt into one man in recollection of T. S. Eliot's famous note to The Waste Land: "Just as the one-eyed merchant, seller of currants, melts into the Phoenician Sailor, and the latter is not wholly distinct from Ferdinand Price of Naples, so all the women are one woman, and the two sexes meet in Tiresias" (III. 218). There is no equivalent of Tiresias in the Martha novels, but by the end of Anna's novel male and female meet in Anna as they do in Tiresias.

The intertwining of primal A's and M's never wholly leaves Lessing's work, although it is never again as rich and complex as it is in the Martha/Anna novels. The pattern recurs even in the Canopus and later novels. For example, in Marriages Al·Ith has a sister named Murti·. An Alsi, Marl, and Masson appear in The Making of the Representative for Planet 8. Ambien II of The Sirian Experiments (1981) has a name that combines the letters A and M and suggests an androgynous nature. (Does her male partner have precedence as Ambien I?) Jane Somers, known as Janna (Anna in slight disguise), has a new kind of relationship with the aged Maudie. Although the relationship is simultaneously filial and maternal, Janna holds all the visible power. Alice Mellings is the "good terrorist" in Lessing's most recent novel.

From 1950, when Mary and Moses appear in The Grass Is Singing, and 1952, when A's and M's appear profusely in Martha Quest, to 1985, in The Good Terrorist, Lessing's compulsive use of A and M figures has persisted. These names acquire archetypal status in Lessing's fiction. Their changes in meaning, density, and complexity are an important index to her thought and formal patternings.

The primal parental figures, Alfred and May Quest, may be less stereotypically male and female than they at first appear to be. Alfred was a soldier and May the nurse who tended him during World War I. Alfred's amputated leg suggests the castration that in fact defines his life. Alfred was also the quester who brought the family to Zambesia, where the quest eroded in daily battle with a resistant land, climate, and social structure. A man both hypochondriacal and truly ill, her father has given to Martha his "morbid strain" (*Martha Quest*, 40–41). Whereas Alfred Quest represents the "fatal lethargy of a dream-locked figure" (*Martha Quest*, 24), May Quest is the doer, the organizer, and the nurse who will tend Alfred all his life. In fact, their marriage seems eternally fixed in its original nurse-patient pattern. The woman nurtures; the male accepts her nurture. On another level, the Alfred/May relationship is less stereotypical, for the energy in the house is maternal, and its apathy and depression are paternal. The soldier/father is finally as much a victim figure as the nurse/mother.

The twoness associated with the nineteenth-century double co-exists with multiples in Lessing's work. The two women who open three of the five Martha Quest novels, as well as the two who open and close *The Golden Notebook*, make a provocative distorted mirroring pattern. The sets of women are both united and at odds with one another to make, as Marxist terminology might have it, a true dialectical equation. Or, to put it another way, Lessing's two women are never equal and opposite. The two mothers, Mrs. Quest and Mrs. Van Rensberg, who open the first Martha Quest novel are, for example, united against their children but divided against each other by nationality and religion and further divided when their daughters are compared (May Quest is certain her Martha is better than Marnie Van Rensberg). *A Proper Marriage* opens with Martha and Stella, who are described as more "guardian and ward" than friends. *Ripple* opens with Martha and Jasmine in reversed roles, for Jasmine, once Martha's mentor, is now her equal. The last two novels open with Martha alone, signaling the diminution of her need to use other, stronger women as mirrors to resist or emulate (or signaling a change in Lessing's original plan for her opening scenes?).

When the reader reaches Saul's injunction to Anna in *The Golden Notebook* to write about "the two women you are," Molly is revealed as a part of Anna that has been temporarily given a separate, objective existence. Anna can leave Molly at the end of the novel: "The two women kissed and separated." Their separation does indeed duplicate the classic conclusion to the doubles novel, but the kiss is unique. It is a signature to the remarkably pacific nature of the Anna/Molly relationship. For Molly's separate existence has never threatened Anna with the violence or dissolution so regularly connected with the male other self.

Yet something of the nineteenth-century doubles pattern does exist in Lessing's work. Marnie, Maisie, and Molly are presented as emotionally freer women than Martha or Anna. Furthermore, they are not connected with intellect, as Martha and Anna are. Stella and Jasmine are sterner, more exigent, controlling figures. Nevertheless, none of Martha's or Anna's female others can be called violent, criminal, or asocial. Martha's most extreme other female self is Lynda, who is in a unique category and who does not appear until the fifth and last novel in the series.

"Double novels" today, whether female or male, are less likely to be "Devil novels," in part because they have developed "in a social context" that no longer "places a negative value upon what is free and uninhibited" (Rosenfield, 334). But female doubles seem to be special. They may function less to ensure ego protection than to define a self (Abel, "Reflections"). Through her female doubles Martha does learn to define herself. As she develops, she begins to function as a teaching mirror for other female selves. Marjorie learns from her and takes over her group role when Martha leaves for England, as Martha took over Jasmine's group role when Jasmine left for South Africa.

Negative doubles are less likely to be female peers (Stella is an exception). They are more likely to be parental or male figures. Parental doubles, the Quests, the Maynards, are negative except when they are grown-up daughters—Martha, Anna, Kate Brown. (Mrs. Van is another exception.) The mother-daughter battle is never resolved in the Martha Quest novels. Lessing displaced it in The Golden Notebook by eliminating the biological mother's presence. (It is resolved incompletely and provocatively in two later novels, The Memoirs of a Survivor and The Summer before the Dark.) Female doubles are collaborative, whereas female/male doubles are combative until Martha/Mark come onstage. Through these doubles Lessing explores—altering, questioning—gender roles. Her doubles and multiples are not merely a way to note either the fracturing of identity or the establishment of identity. They are one of several strategies used to project complex private, societal, and formal concerns.

Lessing's Martha Quest novels are closer to the German than to the French version of the series novel. Contemporary feminist critics (Rose, Tree, Stimpson, and others) have defined the series as a female Bildungsroman whose locus is Martha's developing consciousness. Still, the French example is also worth looking at in relation to Lessing. In Balzac and Zola there are reappearing characters but no central protagonist. In their novels, the portrait of a society dominates over the portrait of an individual. Their protagonists are multiple.

The brilliant exemplar of the French mode in our time is William Faulkner. Faulkner's example both emulates and undermines the mode. By its irregularities, the Yoknapatawpha series ironically comments on the simpler patternings of earlier sequence novels, as Lessing's Canopus series comments on the simpler patterns of the Martha Quest series. Faulkner's series grew without a master plan.

Lessing claims to have had a master plan. In 1963 she said she had planned the quintet "twelve years ago" (Newquist, 57). Some critics (Jouve, Enright, Knapp) have been skeptical of her claim. Lessing has not, however, publicly enlarged on it. Some changes have been simple; the three chapters per four parts of *Martha Quest* become the four chapters per four parts of the remaining four volumes, for example (Sprague, "Dialectic and Counter-Dialectic," Knapp, *Doris Lessing*). The expansion may have come merely out of a need for symmetry or for greater amplitude or out of a desire to create a special patterning based on four. Although it can be claimed that all of Martha exists in the fifteen-year-old adolescent who opens the series, these "seeds" may not have been slated for full development. Was the nascent "seer" and "hearer" of these early pages meant to become the mystic Martha of *The Four-Gated City*, or was she meant to become the portrait of the artist as a woman? How ironic was Martha's conception of the "noble city, set foursquare" (*Martha Quest*, 11) originally meant to be? Martha's city is nonracist, but it excludes everyone she hates and can be described as a teenage fantasy of revenge. The appendix to *The Four-Gated City* seems to represent material unassimilable in the original plan. The mere size of the fifth novel suggests that it has burst the boundaries of its predecessors, although it technically adheres to the format of four chapters per four parts. It can be and has been claimed that the Martha of *Landlocked* and *The Four-Gated City* is a different person from the Martha of the first three volumes (see especially Jouve). Questions relating to the artistic genesis and development of the Martha novels have only begun to be addressed. Their exploration is bound to confront biographical as well as internal evidence.

The discrepancies between Lessing's fictional characters and her own life are, as suggested in the introduction, extremely interesting. One example is Lessing's reduction of the three children she bore (John, Jean, Peter) into the single Caroline (named for Lessing's grandmother Caroline May, from whom Lessing also gets her own middle name). In the context of the Martha Quest novels, this reduction makes a great deal of sense. It economizes and highlights. Of course, it also wish-fulfills. Martha refuses to have the second child demanded by her culture, the one "to save the marriage," but Lessing herself did not refuse to have the second child and even a third child by her second husband. Furthermore, by altering the sex of her first child from male to female, Lessing highlights and intensifies the mother-daughter antagonism that runs throughout the quintet. Thus, whatever private satisfaction this change occasioned, it had major artistic consequences.

Another example of her manipulation of biographical elements may be the incorporation of her three children into The Golden Notebook in a disguised way that suits the more formally deliberate doubling and multiplying of personality that goes on in that novel. Tommy, Janet, and Michael are Anna's three children, and they duplicate in number and gender Lessing's actual three children. Anna is their functional mother and Molly finally an Anna self temporarily endowed with separate fictional status. These manipulations of biographical detail have provocative implications for the critic of today and the biographer of tomorrow.

The following chapters, on The Golden Notebook and The Four-Gated City, explore Lessing's separated and merging selves as well as other repetitive and dialectical strategies in these novels. They are not exclusively focused on the repetitions and collisions between the Martha/Anna novels, but they do make a beginning. They are an effort to see the provocative patterns beneath Lessing's deceptively flat surfaces.

4
Doubletalk and Doubles Talk:
The Golden Notebook (1962)

Who am I, then? Tell me that first, and then, if I like being that person, I'll come up; If not, I'll stay down here till I'm somebody else.

Lewis Carroll, *The Annotated Alice*

He used to wonder at the shallow psychology of those who conceive the ego in a man as a thing simple, permanent, reliable, and of one essence.

Oscar Wilde, *The Portrait of Dorian Gray*

Lying there I remember the Anna who can dream at will, control time, move easily and is at home in the underworld of sleep. But I was not that Anna.

Doris Lessing, *The Golden Notebook*

Critical response to *The Golden Notebook*'s intricate structure became substantial only some ten years after its publication. Its "shifting narrator, unstable or merging characters and . . . non-chronological arrangement of events" were deliberately disorientating strategies (Lifson, 97). It took a while to recognize Anna Wulf's role as Anna-editor or Anna-writer or Anna-scriptwriter, or to accept Free Women as fiction, or to question the "truth" of the notebooks. The novel, tied together by juxtaposition and contradiction, achieves its at best momentary stasis only with the very last line, when one of the many fictive Annas walks away from a fictive Molly in belated acknowledgment of Anna's in fact earlier separation from Molly.

In a 1971 essay now regularly used as a preface to *The Golden Notebook*, Lessing has insisted that her "major aim was to shape a book which would make its own comment, a wordless statement: to talk through the way it is shaped."[1] These often-quoted words refuse to think of pattern without meaning. Within a short time after this essay/preface appeared, a number of articles addressed themselves to the patterns of the novel.[2] Most critics have accepted Lessing's claim that the novel is about fragmentation and unity; others prefer to shift the ground of discourse, for Lessing herself seems to be sending out a paradoxical message about these polar terms. She says that her two themes are fragmentation and unity; then, after describing the inner Golden Notebook as the end of division, she interpolates this startling statement: "There is formlessness with the end of fragmentation" (vii). This paradox should make the reader beware of overdoing any judgment that the inner Golden Note-book—or even the outer, for that matter—represents unity or syn-thesis. The existence of alternate or discrepant endings (Blue Note-book 4 and Free Woman 5) should be enough to suggest continu-ing process, contradiction, irony, uncertainty—anything but clear, unambiguous unity.

An example: The opening line of The Golden Notebook has no magic until one returns to it after having read the entire novel, or at least until it reappears as Saul's line in the inner Golden Notebook. It then acquires an extraordinary resonance. No one could expect the pointedly ordinary, almost wholly monosyllabic line, "The two women were alone in the London flat," to acquire such resonance. When it is placed against the closing line of the novel, "The two women kissed and separated," the reader begins to learn how artful and how provocative the opening and closing lines are. Their sim-plicity and their intricacy seem to me an emblem of Lessing's craft in The Golden Notebook.

Lessing also suggests that Anna and Saul " 'break down' into each other" and "into other people" (vii). "They hear each other's thoughts, recognize each other in themselves," and in the inner Golden Notebook they write collaboratively so that we "can no longer distinguish between what is Saul and what is Anna, and be-tween them and the other people in the book" (viii).

I should like to suggest an additional way of defining the merging and separation of characters in The Golden Notebook, one that pro-poses these permeable selves as another structural pattern that works effectively and together with the narrative pattern. In other words, structure inheres in the disposition of protagonists as much as in the collision and interweaving of the five notebooks and the Free Women sections.

If Anna's other selves are called doubles, then another rich layer of meaning emerges. If these doubles are divided and examined by gender, the results are significant, for the central character conflicts are not between Anna and her female doubles but between Anna and her male doubles. Anna sees herself in her other female selves while she sees men as "others" for almost the entire novel. The male doubles are connected with destructive powers whose existence in herself Anna evades or denies.[3] Lessing's naming strategies are a witty and important indicator of her larger explorations of gender.

Although Lessing directs the reader's attention to the presence of split and merging selves, she does not direct it to the complex interaction between Anna's female and male selves. Her rather testy use of the cliché "the sex war" in her preface trivializes her own meticulous attention to the relations between men and women in the novel. It is an ironic echo of Paul Tanner's pronouncement that "the real revolution is women against men" (213).

In a novel filled with colliding forms and chronologies, the symmetry and clarity of the opening and closing lines of the Free Women sections are at once particularly pleasing and particularly deceptive. The novel is not primarily about the two women, Anna and Molly, for Anna and Molly are effectively separated at the beginning of the novel. The opening line is not Doris Lessing's line. It is written by Saul Green, who gives it to Anna, who gives it to the reader. Anna writes Free Women with Saul's help. Saul says: "I'm going to give you the first sentence then. There are the two women you are, Anna. Write down: 'The two women were alone in the London flat'" (639). Doris Lessing's presence is nearly obliterated.

How are we to take Anna's obedience to Saul's command? How are we to take Saul's description of Anna as two women? Saul tells the reader what she already knows, that Molly is an aspect of Anna. When the two women kiss and separate, is Anna saying good-bye to all the Anna/Molly figures in the novel, to Ella/Julia, Maryrose, Marion, Muriel? Are we witnessing the conclusion of a symbiotic doubles relationship akin to Conrad's Captain and Leggatt in "The Secret Sharer" or to James's Spencer Brydon and his alter ego in "The Jolly Corner"? Only in part, for in a novel filled with deceptions and false clues, the Anna/Molly relationship is not the central relationship. Furthermore, Free Women is a highly laundered version of the notebooks.

While the reciprocity between Anna and Saul is self-evident and even brutally forced upon the reader's attention, Saul's relationship to his earlier selves, to Tommy, Paul Blackenhurst, Paul Tanner/ Michael, is less obvious. Anna/Molly and Anna/Saul are, so to speak, the archetypal, explicitly defined doubles in the novel. Free Women tells us that Anna is two women, making it easy to accept the female/female double as a structural layer in the novel. Lessing's seemingly simple and actually devious strategies should make us wonder at Saul's arrival onstage as a full-blown secret sharer. The explicitness of the Anna/Saul relationship is an invitation to notice earlier versions of Saul. Tommy, the two Pauls, and Michael are predecessors; Willi/Max, Nelson, De Silva are lesser ones. Names are as usual a clue to connections. Lessing's Pauls become a Saul, in witty reversal of the biblical Saul's conversion to Paul. The major male characters, Tommy, the two Pauls, Michael, and Saul, are insistent, cynical inquisitors and consciences, as Anna's female selves are not. We might even say that the nineteenth-century madwoman in the attic has in The Golden Notebook become the madman in the attic.[4] The male doubles create motion in the novel. Only one woman, Anna, the mother of them all, is an active principle. She is present everywhere, from the beginning to the end and back again, as her palindromic name suggests.[5]

There is, in short, a complex layer of doubling in The Golden Notebook. That layer includes mixed as well as same-sex doubles. Like the more obvious Free Women/notebooks overall patterning of the novel, this pattern has its disguises and ambiguities; its meaning is also slippery. But the pattern is there. When the novel opens, the two women who appear to be reuniting after a year apart are already psychically separated. The female/male doubling, disguised at first, ascends in clarity and significance as the novel proceeds. The final collision of Anna and Saul is climactic. Their separation ends the inner novel as the deceptive separation of Anna and Molly ends the outer Free Women novel. We might say that Anna/Saul represents the esoteric content of the novel and Anna/Molly its exoteric content, the content that satisfies the uninitiated. The separation of the two women represents a form of the double talk and doubles talk that pervades the novel.

An extended theoretical definition of the double in its various psychoanalytic and literary forms seems less germane than a contextual one.[6] We can agree that the second self normally exhibits displaced asocial characteristics that the public or the more compliant self cannot acknowledge. (The reverse is sometimes true, as in Poe's "William Wilson.") This basic distinction is a useful starting point. The self that divides in two, as it does in Jekyll and Hyde or in Dorian Gray and his portrait, has been less interesting to novelists of our time than the more complex figure whose other self has an objective existence. In the phrase "secret sharer," Joseph Conrad fixed for us the fascination and the complexity of that freestanding other self. Virginia Woolf's Clarissa Dalloway and Septimus Smith and Saul Bellow's Asa Leventhal and Kirby Allbee are more recent examples of secret sharers. Lessing's contributions to the genre are remarkable and heretofore unacknowledged. Her doubles are, for example, regularly female/female and female/male, unlike the classic male/male double. She develops her conception of the "free" self and its relation to the primary self with wit and originality, in part accepting, in part contradicting, and in the process extending our conceptions of the double figure.

Like other doubles, Molly Jacobs has elements Anna would like to have, her Jewishness and spontaneity, for example. Anna could never say, with Molly's "loud jolly laugh: I've got the curse" (340). Molly may seem and even be "freer," but neither she nor her other versions can be linked with the criminal or the mad self, as several of the male doubles can be.

At the opening of Free Women, Anna and Molly, separated for a year while Molly was abroad, have not been living together for a while. Once so close as to be mistaken for sisters or lovers, they are both over thirty-five, divorced, "free" women currently living without men. Both are mothers; one has a son, the other a daughter. They have shared an apartment, the services of Mrs. Marks/Mother Sugar, and sometimes men—De Silva sexually, Richard (Molly's former husband) almost sexually. Molly sends men—Nelson, Saul, Milt—to Anna. Both women became Communist party members despite themselves. They call themselves "free" women in a very limited, ironic sense: they are not attached to particular men at present and are open to affairs. Both want to remarry. Even their differences seem more complementary than antagonistic. Like other literary doubles, they are almost twins.

To their friends, who simply cannot see their physical differences, they are interchangeable. Molly is tall, boyish, light-haired; Anna, "small, thin, dark, brittle, black-eyed" and "always the same" (9). The "always the same" identifies a crucial difference between the two women. Anna envies Molly's pleasure in role changing, her "capacity to project her own changes of mood" (9). Molly admires Anna's single talent for writing. Molly's many talents and many selves seem suitably embodied in her profession as actress. Her acting, like Saul's, defines her ability to risk, to change, while Anna seems fixed in her role as writer-observer rather than writer-actor. Anna develops the capacity to change roles only privately, only in the long dark night of the soul she acts out with Saul.

Anna is, however, much stronger than she seems. Although her earlier move to her own flat seemed undertaken in order to accommodate her lover Michael, it accomplishes more. Anna and Molly will never again live together. Furthermore, Anna has begun to find her conversations with Molly too ritualized. She has tired of talking about how men fail women. When Anna and Molly talk, it is usually about Tommy. Only Tommy and Saul see Anna's notebooks. Molly is not even permitted to know they exist. Molly is Tommy's more passive mother, Anna his more active one.

Indeed, Anna functions within Free Women as an informal social worker, mediating between Tommy and Richard, between Molly and Richard, between Marion and Richard, trying to save Tommy. Hence the ironic Free Women 5 assignment of Anna to welfare work is neither inappropriate nor entirely unprepared for. It recognizes one of Anna's very female gifts. The increasing strength of her mediating function is an additional sign of Anna's growing independence from Molly, who had once "frankly domineered Anna" (9–10). (Isn't that independence an unremarked result of Anna's analysis?) It is a paradox that Anna's mediating role expands as she herself comes closer to breakdown. The most crucial sign of Anna's independence from Molly is what she withholds from Molly—her writing self and her relationship with Saul. Anna has in effect written Molly off. Molly barely appears in the Blue Notebook, the notebook of "truth." (Mrs. Marks/Mother Sugar seems to take her place in the Blue Notebook.) The concluding line of Free Women 5 belatedly confirms the Anna/Molly separation that has occurred before Free Women opens. Anna's "integration" may be ironic and uncertain; her independence from her older sister is not.

Of Anna's other female selves—Ella, Julia, Marion, Maryrose,

Mrs. Marks—Ella is the strongest and most developed "other" besides Molly. Although Anna, like Lessing, warns readers and critics against finding autobiographical analogues in her writing, she is quite open in using her own life in her fiction. In naming Ella, she says: "I, Anna, see Ella. Who is, of course, Anna" (459). Anna also transforms her daughter, Janet, into Ella's son and names him Michael after her departed lover. Ella and her former lover, Paul Tanner, therefore function as shadow doubles of Anna and Michael just as the Ella/Julia pair functions as a shadow double of Anna/Molly. Presumably Lessing sits above her creations paring her fingernails as she contemplates their movements.

Ella and Paul are primary characters in what may become Anna's second novel, "The Shadow of the Third." Within that novel, Ella is writing and does finish a novel about a young man who commits suicide (Tommy? herself?), apparently on the spur of the moment. In fact, without his knowing it, the young man has been planning suicide for a long time. The apolitical Ella, an editor for a women's magazine, is a kind of Miss Lonelyhearts. (Is she another version of Anna's mediating role?) Her double, Julia, "plump, stocky, vital, energetic, Jewish" (170), is a Communist and a minor actress with minimal function in this novel within a novel within a novel. Ella seems an altogether more conventional Anna, although Anna has "to fight to write about sex" (482) and Ella can talk about orgasm. Unlike her creator, Anna, Ella does not suffer from writer's block, and as a professional journalist, she is, to use Molly's ironic phrasing, " 'integrated with British life at its roots' " (666). Ella's sexual discussion is less "free" than it seems, for it mirrors conventional fifties thinking about vaginal versus clitoral orgasm. Her "integrity is the orgasm" seems more parodic than genuine. Yet Anna can tell us more about Michael through Ella's Paul than she can in her own voice.

The title of Anna's projected novel, "The Shadow of the Third," seems to refer to the idealized wife figure, to Paul's wife, Muriel, to Marion, perhaps even to Maryrose, who is the idealized partner for African Paul. Anna notes "the motif of Paul's wife—the third" (206). Frightened of her dependence on Paul, Ella also paradoxically clings to the third as a sort of protection. In one of her dreams, she becomes Paul's abandoned wife. Another time, Ella's third becomes her younger alter ego, "formed from fantasies about Paul's wife" (448–49).

There seem to be two constants in Anna's conception of "thirds," an "Ella herself" and wives who are linked to what Anna/Ella call "normality," really "conventionality," connected with the "'respectable' life which in fact Ella refuses to have anything to do with" (449). Ella plays out and is victimized by attitudes she disclaims: dependency, bourgeois faithfulness, domesticity. Anna displaces and exaggerates in Ella her dependence on men, her own inability to "get over" Michael, her own ambivalence toward marriage.

Turning Michael-her-lover into Michael-her-son gives Anna rather transparent power over and revenge against the lover who left her.[7] She had no such power over Michael-as-lover when they were together. Anna was in fact imprisoned, tied to illusions about their relationship, tied to waiting for Michael to show up, tied to serving him food and love without complaint and on his terms. The metamorphosis of Michael into a son is a metamorphosis into powerlessness; Anna can dominate Michael the son as she was unable to dominate Michael the lover. Perhaps Michael's transformation is predicted by his name, the M he shares with Molly.

Anna, on the other hand, begins her fictional life with a name that suggests greater independence, greater power, than Michael or Molly can ever have. For in the name "Anna," Lessing reverses the explosion of male A's and female M's that characterize the Martha Quest novels. Anna is stronger than Molly, as Alfred, Adolph, Anderson, Athen, and Andrew are, on the whole, stronger than the Marthas, Mays, Marnies, Maisies, and Marjories who pervade the Martha novels. Anna takes on the male A and gives the female M to Molly, for as we have seen, Anna creates Molly, who may be as fictive as Ella. From this point of view Anna and Molly can even be considered a male/female double. From this point of view Anna is by her very conception more male than female.[8] The naming pattern suggests another postulate: Anna, we may say, begins life as an androgynous figure. If so, she does not become androgynous because of her interaction with Saul. She was born androgyne.

What happens to male names in The Golden Notebook? As suggested earlier, the many male A names and female M names in the Martha Quest novels are reduced and often reversed in The Golden Notebook. Molly, Ella, Marjorie, Maryrose, Muriel, and Mrs. Marks continue the female pattern of names. Male names tend to follow the female pattern—Michael, Max, Milt—or to fall outside the A/M pattern entirely—Paul, Saul, Tommy. However, Tommy as a name is close to

Molly; both have internal double consonants, middle and final vowels. It may be significant that Thomas means twin. If so, Tommy, like Molly, is by his name as well as his role identified as a second self. Like the Pauls, Michael, and Saul, Tommy prods, questions, annoys. Like them, he is malicious and cynical, as the doppelgänger figure so often is. Tommy wants to know what Anna really believes in. He wants her to give him a reason for living. Anna's own submerged violence, cynicism, and nihilism are mirrored in Tommy as they are in Michael, the Pauls, and Saul. Anna probably displaces her own contemplation of suicide into Tommy and into Ella's young, unnamed, male protagonist. Tommy can be aptly called the destructive principle of the Free Women sections, as the Pauls and Saul are the destructive principles in their respective notebooks. Because he appears in the novel first, Tommy is paradoxically a harbinger of the African Paul Blackenhurst, who belongs to Anna's past. Tommy is also a preparation for Saul, who has yet to appear in Anna's life. Destructive principle and inner conscience are openly joined in Tommy, African Paul, and Saul, less openly in Michael; Paul Tanner has little of the inner conscience role.

Tommy accuses Anna of dishonesty, of masking her divided existential state by calling it a phase, by calling Tommy's own perilous condition a "bad phase." He insists: "If things are a chaos, then that's what they are. I don't think there's a pattern anywhere—you are just making patterns, out of cowardice. I think people aren't good at all, they are cannibals, and when you get down to it no one cares about anyone else. All the best people can be good to one other person or their families. But that's egotism, it isn't being good. We aren't any better than animals, we just pretend to be" (275). In this passage Tommy effectively "names" his own version of doubling. What he describes is the victim/cannibal concept developed more fully by African Paul Blackenhurst, by Ella's father, and by Anna and Saul. The victim/cannibal principle "names" the human/nonhuman material later dramatized in the Mashopi pigeon shoot episode. Tommy's naming provides the reader with a crucial link between the Free Women and the Black Notebook sections, sections that will not be pieced together until much later, when Anna, becoming her own projectionist at last, reruns her divided experience in montage.

Paul Blackenhurst, the central actor of the Mashopi episode, is kin to Tommy. His brilliant cynicism dominates a section filled with unstated human/pigeon/insect analogues. Anna's recall of that African episode is precipitated by "a fat domestic London pigeon" who is kicked and killed in a comic-grotesque street drama. The brief episode, reported without comment, triggers Anna's memory. In her recall, five members of the African group, Anna, Willi, Maryrose, Paul, and Jimmy, undertake to collect pigeons so that Mr. Boothby may have a pigeon pie.

The remarkable afternoon that follows is a tale of coupling and death. The analogues with the general human condition and the five who see and act are disturbing. Thousands of "apparently identical" grasshoppers couple while Paul, the "projectionist" of the afternoon, toys like a god with the insects, shifting sexual partners, killing some, announcing the death by evening of the thousands "by fighting, biting, deliberate homicide, suicide, or by clumsy copulation. Or they will have been eaten by birds" (418). In the meantime, Maryrose thinks of her brother's death, and Jimmy fights with his fear of death. Paul, the handsome, the fearless, will actually die first—in perfect absurdist fashion. The pigeon shoot is interrupted by another concurrently played drama of death between an ant and an anteater that proceeds while Willi reads *Stalin on the Colonial Question*[9] and while Paul tries to get Willi to acknowledge the existence of a "principle of destruction" he can never acknowledge, for Willi's communism cannot accept the cannibal within. Paul parodies present and future myths of progress and purpose as he continues his pigeon shooting. A beetle intervenes between anteater and ant. Paul shoots his ninth pigeon. The final image: "Now we saw the jaws of the ant-eater were embedded in the body of the beetle. The corpse of the ant-eater was headless" (432). The image, reminiscent of Virginia Woolf's similarly mutually destroyed snake and toad in *Between the Acts*, produces its special ironies among the group.[10] Finally, the five, "slightly sick with the smell of blood," return to the hotel and separate "with hardly a word" (433).

This extraordinary section is Lessing's most successful dramatization of what Anna, Tommy, Paul, and Saul accept as "the principle of destruction." The actors are now victims, now cannibals; the action is copulation, combat, and death. Paul is the most memorable projectionist in *The Golden Notebook*. Anna's "self-punishing, cynical tone" is writ large in him (90). History fascinates him because it so

perfectly satisfies "his intellectual pleasure in paradox" (77). Anna
calls Paul's ruling passion "the enjoyment of incongruity" (105). Although Anna shares Paul's passionate perception of incongruity,
she cannot so easily or so powerfully display her mockery. Paul's
cynical predictions about what will happen after the war hit postwar actualities more closely than the Left's official predictions
about a better postwar world. His "spirit of angry parody" foresees
the ironic mediocre sameness of workers' housing and workers'
lives under both socialism and capitalism (93). His predictions fail
only for himself: he dies by walking into a plane propeller, perhaps
in parallel with Maryrose's brother, who is crushed by an Allied
tank. By his life and death Paul exemplifies the principle of destruction and incongruity.

Paul and Maryrose make "'a perfectly matched couple'" (433),
really a magazine cover couple, but like the grasshoppers that the
human actors rearrange to couple by matching size, who then return to their outsize partners, the matched human pair will not
couple. Maryrose prefers the memory of her incestuous affair with
her brother. Her attitudes toward incest, jargon, and ideology have
the ring of truth. Immune to ideas and feeling imposed from outside, "she had a capacity for silencing us all. Yet the men patronized
her" (90). This "unattainable beauty" of the group may be its only
genuine radical—an incongruity that Paul and Anna must relish.
She can say to the intense ideologues who surround her, "'I have
no view of life'" (428). Maryrose seems a transparent wish-fulfill-
ment projection of Anna, as Paul is a projection of her "negative
self."

The second Paul, Paul Tanner, appears in the Yellow Notebook.
His wife is a Muriel, but his sexual life is with Ella, as the earlier
Paul's actual sexual experience was with Anna, not with Maryrose.
This Paul is a psychiatrist like the Michael who is his original. He is
negatively critical like Tommy, African Paul, Michael, and Saul. All
five men are connected with death and great energy like the male/
female dwarf in Anna's recurrent joy-in-spite dream, like so many
other second selves (e.g., Conrad's Leggatt, Stevenson's Hyde, and
the alter ego in "The Jolly Corner"). Paul destroys in Ella "the knowing, doubting, sophisticated Ella," putting "her intelligence to sleep,
and with her willing connivance" (211). He rejects Ella as writer:
"his voice is always full of distrust when he mentions her writing"
(208). The other Paul, Tommy, and Saul want to strengthen the

knowing, doubting Anna. Paul Tanner, who ties with De Silva for title of most destructive double, encourages Ella's artistic impotence. In effect, he encourages her suicide.

Paul Tanner can be described as a purer or less clouded form of Michael, a fictional figure Anna uses to distance uncomfortable truths about Michael—his criticism of her as "authoress" and mother, for example. Anna manages to play down Michael's erosion of these two crucial Anna selves as she manages to submerge the fact that Michael will never divorce his wife and marry her. On the night this realization sinks in, she fails to achieve orgasm. Naturally, Michael most dislikes "the critical and thinking Anna" (331). Anna cannot unite "Janet's mother, Michael's mistress," and does not try to, for they "are happier separated" (336). Although Michael's ironic discourse lacks the malice of Tommy, the Pauls, and Saul, it nevertheless seems to undercut every comment Anna makes. A displaced Prague Jew, a survivor who is, like Thomas Stern, "the history of Europe in the last twenty years," Michael simultaneously responds to and mocks Anna's remaining shreds of optimism about the human condition (332). Michael is experience to Anna's innocence in a replay of the Julia/Jan interchange in *Retreat from Innocence*.

Lessing's naming game continues when her Saul who was Paul comes onstage. He complements, combats, and completes Anna. Once Anna acts out her long dark night of the soul with her destructive double and all her multiple selves, she can contain and separate from Saul. In a novel with many characters who either act on stage or change roles consciously and frequently—Molly, Tommy, African Paul, Julia, De Silva—Saul is the consummate chameleon: "In any conversation he can be five or six different people" (573); "Shock. Literally, I saw him come out of the personality he had been" (582); "I don't know who will come down the stairs" (590). During their lowest point of mutual madness, Anna has a long night of dreams in which she and Saul play roles against each other: "We played against each other every man-woman role imaginable. As each cycle of the dream came to an end, I said: 'Well, I've experienced that, have I, well it was time that I did.' It was like living a hundred lives. I was astonished at how many of the female roles I have not played in life, have refused to play, or were not offered to me. Even in my sleep I know I was being condemned to play them now because I had refused them in life" (604).[11] This dream follows a series of metamorphic dreams in which Anna is both the "malicious old man, and the spiteful old woman, or both together" (563), or mad Charlie Themba, an Algerian soldier, and a pregnant Chinese peasant. These changes of sex, age, shape, and color, this melting into one figure and all figures, recall again Eliot's footnote about Tiresias in *The Waste Land* and underlines the terrible potential of multiplicity as both disintegration and possibility.

Anna's night of dreams marks a genuine turning point. Anna and Saul have indeed doubled, divided, and interchanged selves. Their relationship climaxes and pinpoints the novel's complex use of doubling. The next morning Saul pushes Anna to begin her new novel; she is able to admit her writer's block and able to walk out of her room at last to buy her golden notebook.

The insights Anna and Saul derive from one another are prepared for through Anna's slow deciphering of her repetitive joy-in-spite dream. Its disguising elements are slowly worked away. At last the dream becomes identified with an actual person in Anna's life, with De Silva, the latest and most nihilistic exemplar of the principle of destruction: "incarnate, the principle of joy-in-giving-pain." He appears in the dream "without disguise, just as he is in life, smiling, malicious, detached, interested" (503). The description is perfect. The disguise has yet to drop altogether. Only in her final bout of madness with Saul does it drop totally, revealing to Anna that both she and Saul are De Silva, the malicious male/female dwarf: "I slept and dreamed the dream. This time there was no disguise anywhere, I was the malicious male-female dwarf figure, the principle of joy in destruction; and Saul was my counterpart, male-female, my brother and my sister" (594). Anna and Saul are each other, like Anna and Molly, Anna and Michael, Maryrose and her brother, Anna and Paul, Ella and Paul. Their climactic interchange illuminates the function of the other couples in the novel. Anna's breakthrough is, of course, liberating. It means that she may be able to free herself from repetitive behavior patterns. The dream with "no disguise anywhere" permits Anna to wake up "filled with joy and peace" (595). She realizes that she has at last dreamed her destruction dream positively, as Mother Sugar had admonished her to do. She has at last internalized the destructive principle.

At one point in the Anna/Saul combat Anna accepts the victim/cannibal view of human interaction proposed by Tommy and by

Ella's father and accepted by Paul Blackenhurst. To Ella's father, "'People are just cannibals unless they leave each other alone.'" For him, the human animal is isolated, solitary: "'People don't help each other, they are better apart'" (464). Anna, committed to social action yet antagonized and repelled by its evils and its limits, purifies her negative self through this father figure.

Anna can only accept the cannibal figure in her own voice in the inner Golden Notebook. "'You simply don't get to be wise, mature, etc., unless you've been a raving cannibal for thirty years or so,'" she tells Saul, identifying serenity and wisdom with "'a history of emotional crime'" (626). In the continuing didactic discussion that follows, Anna defines the interdependence of victim and cannibal and the conditions under which role reversal will occur. She also borrows a didactic nugget from the Yellow Notebook. This time she appropriates Paul's rather self-congratulatory and intellectualized view of himself and Ella as two of the boulder-pushers of this world.[12] The victim/cannibal construction, developed through Tommy's attack on Anna, the events of the Mashopi afternoon, and the Anna/Saul interaction, is more convincing. It is dramatic; it is objectified; it allows for violence. It represents in fact another form of the doubling mechanism.

Saul is, of course, a cannibal. For Anna to see herself, however provisionally, as a cannibal is a considerable achievement. She has always preferred to see herself as victim, particularly in her relations with men. Despite her anger at her emotional imprisonment to Michael/Paul, she is always the dependent partner, waiting and anxious. Anna is not "free" with men unless she lacks special feeling for them. (Her encounters with the American doctor, Nelson, and others are examples.) Through Saul, she achieves some measure of freedom from repetition. So she achieves some release from the stereotype of women as victim.

Anna's surname, like her first name, underscores the fact and the ironic limits of her "freer" condition. She is significantly not Anna Freewoman, but Anna Freeman Wulf. Lessing has given her a triply masculine name.[13] Does Lessing believe that male power is writer power?

Max/Willi, Michael, and Milt are shadowy doubles of Tommy, Paul, and Saul. Perhaps the male M names in The Golden Notebook represent acts of mastery and revenge; perhaps they represent more "feminine" males? Certainly, as we have seen, Anna makes the naming of Michael an explicit act of mastery and revenge. By comparison with the Paul/Saul figures, Max and Milt are recessive and hence perhaps more suitably males with M's. In Free Women 5, for example, Anna and Milt (Saul's "fictional" equivalent) do not undergo a journey into the self together. They do not help each other to write. Milt has no diary; he does not read Anna's notebooks. Anna does not buy a golden notebook. However, Milt does close the four notebooks and remove all the newspaper clippings from Anna's walls. After five days, he and Anna separate.

The Paul and Saul names, so totally outside the A/M pattern, may represent a maturing movement away from the self and from father analogues. As names they probably also twist and/or duplicate an autobiographical source, much as Anna and her creator do.[14]

An awareness of the naming patterns of The Golden Notebook enlarges the meaning of "thirds" in the novel as it enlarges Lessing's conceptions of male/female and female/female relationships. Thirds are almost always the idealized shadow wives of Anna's lovers and regularly "the woman altogether better than I was" (637). Anna generally empathizes with these hidden selves; she is jealous only of Saul's largely fictive other women, perhaps because they are "other" to her wifely role, for Anna is usually the "other woman" in the triangle, forever displaced by a mother or a wife and forever guilty of betraying mother or wife.[15] As noted before, Lessing triangles, although occasionally a woman and two men (Anna/Paul/Willi), are more regularly "A Man and Two Women," the title of one of her short stories: Ella/Paul/Muriel; Anna/Michael/Michael's wife; Anna-Molly-Jean/Richard/Marion; Anna/Saul/the women in Saul's diary.

Considered from another perspective, Lessing's primal family triad, Alfred/May/Martha, a man and two women, is repeated with a difference in The Golden Notebook. It becomes Anna, Anna's lover, and her lover's wife. Lessing's compulsion to create thirds suggests her need to repeat her original family constellation. (This primal triad recurs in Al·Ith, Ben Ata, and Vahshi of Marriages.) It seems also to suggest the daughter's guilt, which in The Golden Notebook is more adulterous than incestuous.[16]

Lessing's doubling habit works in other ways. It extends, for example, to Janet and Tommy. Janet is Anna's child; Tommy is Molly's. In fact, Anna is the functional mother of both. Late in the novel, Anna's dream about Janet and Tommy confirms her double mothering role.[17] It also reflects Anna's anxieties about the relationship between being a woman and being a writer. She dreams that Janet is "plump and glossy with health," Tommy "a small baby" she is starving (651). Janet has emptied her breasts; there is no milk for Tommy, who vanishes "altogether." Anna wakes "in a fever of anxiety, self-division and guilt" (652). Her waking self does not understand the dream. Has she failed herself? The dream occurs after Anna wonders if Tommy's reading of her four notebooks has triggered his suicide attempt. The Tommy of the dream may represent someone else, as Anna, familiar with the disguises of dream, herself suggests. True. Given the prior expression of guilt about Tommy, however, the dream figure is at least Tommy. He may, more significantly, also be the writer self that Anna obliterates in Free Women 5.[18]

These suggestions about Lessing's naming patterns, their relation to her biography and the meaning of her thirds, represent other modes of perceiving the doubletalk and doubles talk in The Golden Notebook. "Doubling" is also useful as a description of the major structural antithesis in the novel between and within the notebook and Free Women sections. For as Lessing has herself said, the notebooks are to the Free Women sections what antinovel is to novel or what raw experience is to the finished work.[19] The notebooks are richer than Free Women, as our interior self is richer than our external self, as experience is richer than art. The notebook/Free Women juxtaposition is the most evident juxtaposition in the novel. It can be called a form of doubling, one that forces us to consider structure and character together. We might, then, think of the notebooks as the rich shadow to the public Free Women, as the storehouse of esoteric knowledge that is reshaped for public consumption. That reshaping presents Free Women as the only segment of the novel that does not internally qualify its structure or its meaning. This seemingly integral section turns out, of course, to be the most deceptive part of the novel, its only complete "fiction."

Lessing's use of pattern to reflect personality and vice versa recalls Poe's "Fall of the House of Usher," in which house is reflected in tarn, refrain lines are reflected by echoes, and Roderick is reflected by his twin, Madeline. So in The Golden Notebook the various Anna/Molly and Anna/Saul juxtapositions parallel and intensify the overall juxtaposition of notebook to notebook and notebook to Free Women. Like all the various "fictions" within the larger or outer Golden Notebook, such as "The Shadow of the Third," "Blood on the Banana Leaves," or Saul's Algerian novel, these doubles and multiples force us to see at least double, force us to question any single view of personality or reality.[20]

The varied narrative forms—diary, letter, book review, parody, short story, film script, headline, news item, synopsis—are mirrors for Anna as much as people are. We would know this without Anna's saying so. Part of her "welfare work" for the party is to read and mark stories and articles published abroad that are suitable for British consumption. Anna describes these "great piles of magazines" as a "mirror into which I have been looking for over a year" (351). Her use of the term "mirror" for writing (it occurs often for people) occurs in the Blue Notebook, supposedly the notebook of truth.[21] The long entry for 15 September 1954, judged a failure at presenting truth, is totally crossed out. The reader is privy to this crossed-out material. Anna/Lessing, by her cross-outs and her inclusion of other handwritings, black lines, pinned-in newsprint, typescript, musical symbols, the £ sign, interlocking circles, asterisks, doodling, brackets, and clipped and banded material, speaks to the excisions that falsify published writing. Lessing describes the cross-outs, handwritings, black lines, asterisks, doodling, pinned- and pasted-in materials. She does not show them. The reader sees only the brackets that head each notebook section. Anna, certain that "the real experience can't be described," thinks "bitterly, that a row of asterisks, like an old-fashioned novel, might be better. Or a symbol of some kind, a circle perhaps, or a square. Anything at all, but not words" (633). But Lessing, Anna's creator, chose not to pursue in her subsequent fiction direct visual presentation of raw worked-over, interpolated, or discarded materials.[22]

The narrative forms and mixed-media materials project the multiplicity of personality and truth. They also suggest that the much-proclaimed theme of fragmentation has been oversimplified. The doubling, multiplication, and interchanging of the self are not accurately defined as evils. Anna says that the notebooks represent a way of splitting the self to save it from chaos. She is right. The splitting works. Seeing the self in or as others is a necessity. We are multiple. The inner Golden Notebook is not golden in any fairy-tale sense; it does not represent great or glorious synthesis. It does not contain a single Anna. All the selves of all the notebooks are in it, occasionally merged (Paul and Michael), still interchanging

(Anna imagines Ella in an affair with Saul), still identifiable. The inner Golden Notebook does not homogenize personality. (Anna's madness also continues in it.) Its other selves will continue to function for Anna much as Rinehart functions for the nameless narrator of Ralph Ellison's *Invisible Man*. Like Rinehart and the Martha of *The Four-Gated City*, Anna can try out different selves in her quest for possibility over fatality. She may contemplate herself as various Mollys, various Sauls in various roles. She may, for example, see herself as mother in Anna, Molly, Ella, and Marion, and through these acted and unacted selves exorcise guilt or explore unacceptable acts and attitudes.

In projecting so many female/female and female/male doubles Lessing explodes the classic novel of doubling, which is wholly male. Her rich exploration of female doubles has few precedents: Charlotte Brontë's Jane Eyre and Bertha Rochester, Woolf's Mrs. Ramsay and Lily Briscoe. Lessing's exploration of female/male selves is equally bold. The Anna/Saul predecessors are also few: Poe's Roderick and Madeline Usher, Emily Brontë's Cathy and Heathcliff, Woolf's Clarissa Dalloway and Septimus Smith. Other examples will be hard to find, for opposite-sex doubles are even more rare in clinical literature than they are in fictional literature.[23]

But no other writer has both retained and burst the boundaries of twoness. The nineteenth-century doubles novel did not go beyond twoness to the complexity of multiple mirrors. Twoness and multiplicity coexist in *The Golden Notebook* to signify that being more than one is a fact of life and not necessarily a threat to identity. Lessing manages to convince us of this abstraction although we also believe in the reality of characters openly described as "fictive": Ella, Julia, the Anna of Free Women, and others. Anna is a cosmos: "the Anna of that time" (153); "that other Anna's eye is on me" (351); "the Anna who goes to the office, argues interminably with Jack" (362); "two other Annas" (562); "I was not that Anna" (614); "sick Anna" (623 and passim); and so on. *The Golden Notebook* overturns and redefines the nineteenth-century version of split and merging selves.

The doubling, multiplication, and interchanging of the self also mottles the realistic surface of the novel. People, events, and settings connect, merge, and separate in ways not always easy to define. Anna's "others" are at once real and not real. They are almost freestanding figures, "almost" in the sense that so many are fictions created by Anna. Despite their presentation as fictions, they are real enough to invite belief in their existence. Thus they are both free-standing figures and creations with visible puppet strings.

As a principle, therefore, doubling both speaks and shapes. It contains, sorts, accepts, links, and questions contraries—joy and spite, male and female, anarchy and order, victim and cannibal, art and life. Some of Anna's selves are, like the traditional other self, freer, more uninhibited, closer to the criminal than to the socialized self. Jekyll's "My devil had been long caged, he came out roaring" ("Henry Jekyll's Full Statement of the Case"), can describe Anna's "devils" (Tommy, the Pauls, Saul), her hidden, violently energetic cannibal selves. Other Anna selves are not so clearly evil or overwhelmingly frightening. Some may be frightening enough (Ella/Tommy's suicide impulse) or socially unacceptable enough (African Paul's harsh irreverences) to displace into a double. Some may represent unrealized parts of the self (Molly's role changing). As a whole, the doubles show that the self is multiple and must shed its single skin. Lessing goes further. In *The Golden Notebook* acceptance of the destructive male self seems necessary to survival, to the reunification of the self, and to the process of writing.

It takes Anna almost the entire novel to realize that the destructive principle is inside as well as outside her. In a way, the novel is "about" her search for its location and meaning. Mother Sugar's instruction to Anna that she dream her destruction dream "positively" means that Anna must recognize its presence within herself. She has preferred to see the destructive principle outside her and in men only, in Tommy, Michael, the Pauls, Saul. On one level, then, men make war and women do not. But as Anna's repetitive dream shows, she, and by extension all women, contain the destructive principle their upbringing as women so strongly denies. The "male" principle of destruction is therefore both male and not male. Fundamentally without gender or containing both genders, Anna perceives it as male and must unlearn that perception. Her triply masculine name suggests complicity in sexual stereotypes, while other aspects of the novel question these stereotypes.

The act of writing also wears a double face. It frees Anna and Saul to separate and simultaneously suggests the androgynous nature of the writer and the eternal antagonism of Anna/Saul principles. Anna cannot live with Saul: he would destroy her; they would destroy each other. But Anna must, through Saul, accept her own cannibalism. The woman as victim/angel must recognize herself as cannibal/monster and ultimately reshape these categories.

On another level, Anna/Lessing accept and play out to a parodic end the societal perception of the male as power, violence, aggression. On one level male power is indeed writer power. At its most reductive, this playing out makes Anna a writer in Blue Notebook 4 and the inner Golden Notebook and a marriage counselor in Free Women 5. Why does Anna obliterate her writing self in Free Women? The answer is not easy. It must lie in Lessing's desire to juxtapose to the very end. Blue Notebook 4 contradicts Free Women 5. Anna chooses to finish her conventional novel conventionally. Free Women is not a portrait of the artist as a young man. In it Anna is neither artist, nor young, nor a man. So at every turn Lessing seems to resist and to mock her own composition of a portrait-of-the-artist-as-a-woman-near-forty-with-writer's-block.

On yet another level, Anna triumphs, for she is the maker of Saul and his avatars, of Molly and of her companions. Anna makes the decision to turn Saul into Milt in Free Women 5. Anna's palindromic name suggests her great hidden circular or unending power, her possession of a kind of eternal fecundity that is a writer's power and a woman's power. Anna will come back; she is indomitable, forever returning, like her name, to and from herself. She is the maker and the mocker of the male and female myth.

5

Multiple Mirrors:
The Four-Gated City (1969)

> On whatever theoretical horizon we examine it, the house image
> would appear to have become the topography of our intimate
> being.
>
> Gaston Bachelard, *The Poetics of Space*

> I've been turned inside out like a glove or a dress. I've been like
> the negative of a photograph. Or a mirror image. I've seen the
> underneath of myself.
>
> Doris Lessing, *The Four-Gated City*

> The thing is that in *The Four-Gated City* . . . various aspects of myself
> were parcelled out between the different characters. They were a
> fairly interesting map of myself.
>
> Doris Lessing, in Bertelsen, "Interview"

There is a golden notebook in *The Golden Notebook*, but there is no
four-gated city in *The Four-Gated City*. From its opening lines, the
dominant style and material of *The Four-Gated City* are at odds with
the evocative magic of the title. The word "four-gated," surely more
romantic than literal, suggests towers and flying banners rather than
the realities of the medieval walled city. But the "grimed muslin,"
the "no particular color," the several "-ish" colors, and the "gritty
smear" of the opening lines totally undercut any legendary associations the word "four-gated" may have for the reader. The evocation
of the shabbiness, the dreariness, the deprivations, of post–World
War II Britain matches the classic portrait of 1948 in the opening
lines of Orwell's *1984*. Both openings are fit texts for the popular
saying that Britain won the war but lost the peace.

The first equivalent of the four-gated city is London. London is the dream city of *Landlocked*, the city positioned at the end of a spirit-healing voyage across water that will take Martha Quest out of her landlocked inner and outer state. The actual London, like the actual Communist party, ends the dream. The death of London as the four-gated city has already happened in the opening lines of the novel. Or, to put it differently, the opening lines show London beyond death and in decay, hurtling toward the degenerated city of *Memoirs of a Survivor*.

In the Martha Quest novels the ideal city exists only in the future. In the Canopus novels ideal cities exist only in the past. The Golden Age of Rohanda/Shikasta has innumerable analogues in human history, analogues that Anna Wulf would call "lying nostalgia." The functional truth, however, the important truth, is that only the past and the future contain four-gated cities. This is a truth in all of Lessing's work. The four-gated city will never fully exist in the present. It will always be in the title—in another place, in another time —never in the text.

The overarching dialectic of *The Four-Gated City* is the painful discrepancy between the connotations of the title and the content of the novel. The dream of a better environment shapes the novel in very special ways. If *The Golden Notebook* is original in its disjunctive presentation of personality, chronology, and narrative frame, *The Four-Gated City* is original in its presentation of personality in relation to environment.[1] We have become accustomed to describing the title of *The Golden Notebook* as the outer Golden Notebook and the one in the novel as the inner Golden Notebook. So the various walls, rooms, houses, Londons, and imagined cities of *The Four-Gated City* can be described as inner cities in counterpoint with the outer city of the title. Mark's *City in the Desert* is one example of a city inside the novel that echoes, however partially, the outer city in the novel's title.

This inner/outer discrepancy is one of the many ways Doris Lessing's passionate vision of contradiction presents itself in *The Four-Gated City*. That vision is as much a shaping principle in the *Children of Violence* series as it is in *The Golden Notebook*, where notebooks collide internally with one another as well as with the framing novel. The series, all too regularly seen as a linear female Bildungsroman,[2] has, in short, another kind of progression, one that can be described as lying beside or within the simpler chronological progression. As the fifth and last novel in a series that contains a four in its title, The Four-Gated City establishes its connection with its four predecessors and invites us to examine how it shares and how it shatters connections with those predecessors.

It continues to double and multiply female and male characters, but it does so in a radically new way that simultaneously questions the binary mode of assessing personality, experience, and history. Martha comes, for example, to accept layering as much as juxtaposition as a definition of growth. In a recent interview, Lessing confirms that "in The Four-Gated City what happened was that various aspects of myself were parcelled out between the different characters. They were a fairly interesting map of myself" (Bertelsen, "Interview," 109). "Various aspects" of Lessing are "parcelled out" in the entire series as well as in The Golden Notebook. The A and M names that stream through the earlier novels and signal Martha's "aspects" are in this novel both narrowed and extended in meaning. The M names continue—Martha, Matty, Margaret, Miriam, Mary Coldridge, Mary (Nanny) Butts, Mellendip, Mavis Wood, Miriam (Aaron's mother), Maynard, Mark. Rita can be described as a positive repetition of her mother, Maisie; Phoebe as a negative repetition of her sister, Marjorie. The M's have it in this novel, for the A names barely exist (there is an Arthur married to Mary and an Aaron, a fictionalized Thomas Stern). The secondary J's also make their appearance: Jack, Jimmy Wood, Jill, Joanna, Jane.[3]

Lessing develops a narrower concept of self and antiself in the Martha/Jack antithesis, extends the concept of collaborating doubles in Martha/Mark and Martha/Lynda, and creates a new concept of a collaborating triad in Martha/Mark/Lynda. Martha's relationship with Mark is the most durable and complex of all Martha's relationships with men. It is in fact the most durable heterosexual relationship in all of Lessing's fiction. Mark is as much a displaced part of Martha's self as Lynda is. The unique threesome they make represents a new conception of male and female selves and an interesting resolution of the problem of "thirds" that obsesses Anna Wulf, especially in her novel in progress, "The Shadow of the Third." Published seven years after The Golden Notebook, The Four-Gated City resolves and extends a number of stances from that earlier novel. In Martha and Mark, Lessing creates a very different alternative to Anna and Saul.

Mark is Lessing's first major male protagonist with the female M.

His M-ness makes him equal to Martha and she to him and gives both greater strength than either could have had alone.

The term "doubling" has often described special sets of fictional characters. I am enlarging it to apply to Lessing's double and multiple/parallel environments and antifictions. "Doubling" is a good word to describe Lessing's extension of the concept from characters to environments—to walls, rooms, houses, and cities—and to internal fictions within the larger fiction that is the novel. Environments and fictions can mirror other environments and fictions just as functionally and powerfully as characters mirror other characters.

As an analogy to Lessing's strategy, Poe's "Fall of the House of Usher" may be clarifying. In that story the physical house is as alive as its male and female owners, reflecting, even enlarging, its empathic relationship with them. The house is a kind of environmental mirror of the inner and outer decay of Roderick and Madeline Usher. The walls, rooms, houses, and cities in The Four-Gated City also function as physical mirrors of psychological realities. Lessing's extension of her doubling pattern to structures seems to me highly original and worth considerable attention.[4]

The walls, rooms, and houses show us developing sets of positions. "The house that Jack built" is set against the Coldridge house. Paul's house becomes a "descendant" of Jack's house, as Francis's house becomes a descendant of his parental house.[5] The walls and rooms Mark and Lynda occupy become the primary options open to Martha and to the Coldridge children, though neither Mark nor Lynda is a negative principle, as are Jack and Jack's house. Martha learns from both sets of walls and rooms, yet inhabits her own room. Her room can represent wholeness as well as limit; its four sides are an analogue of the city's four gates. Martha's room in the farmhouse, the one she shares with Thomas, the one in Mark's house, and the one she uses to induce trance are positive places. Yet, like Lynda and Mark, she wishes to break free of four dimensions into a fifth. The geography of the archetypal Mark and Jack houses is explicitly described in the same chapter. Indeed, the novel's explicit and frequent use of doubling imagery and vocabulary—for example, shadows, mirrors, opposite, underside, inside out, reverse—is a distinctive feature.

Lessing's strategy of contraries works in other ways as well. "Buried" equivalents of antifictions function in this novel much as the notebooks in The Golden Notebook do. In Thomas's ant-eaten, multi-textual memoirs, Dorothy's letters, Mark's and Martha's notebook entries—even in Francis's childhood scrapbook, which bizarrely juxtaposes family snapshots and newspaper headlines—Lessing creates several sets of antifictions within the larger framework of the novel proper. The contrast between *The Four-Gated City* and the published novels by Mark Coldridge and Jimmy Wood makes another kind of comment about the writer's mind, fictional truth, and the sociology of fictional reputations.

Operating simultaneously with contraries is an equally explicit imagery of layering, which is in turn sometimes contrasted with an imagery of stripping or peeling. Layering comes to represent Martha's ability to accept her past, present, and potential selves and to see these selves as coexisting with present events in time. In *The Four-Gated City* Martha can posit "the permanent person in Paul, or Francis, or anybody else" as well as "the details, fragments reflected off the faceted mirror that was one's personality, that responded all the time every second to ... past selves, past voices, temporary visitors" (356). Martha can now accept an essential or "permanent" self and a layered self as well as a divided self. This is a new concept in Lessing's fiction.

Martha, who once hated herself when she was Matty, comes to England after the war as a very different woman. Instead of fearing the multiple self, she courts it. She deliberately experiments with different roles that she takes on with a change of clothes or speech. These roles never threaten to destroy her identity. Martha is closer to understanding and accepting the layers of the self than she has ever been. The earliest image of layering in the novel is analogic evidence of her new acceptance of layering. In London, the ruined postwar city, Martha picks at the thirteen layers of papering in a bombed-out house, imagining the lives that chose, touched, and lived with each layer. She tears off a sample and puts it into Mrs. Van's coat pocket. This sample is as talismanic as Mrs. Van's coat (which both layers and disguises) and Thomas's testament, which has also come to England with her. Martha continues to be sheltered by Mrs. Van, the best of her mothers, and disturbed by Thomas, whose testament Mark will inherit.

Earlier in the series Martha uses the word "repetition" to stand for fatality, and in *Landlocked* she names "the hound, Repetition, her old enemy" (133). She fears "the tyranny of the family" (*A Proper Marriage*, 82–83) throughout the series, even as a middle-aged woman awaiting a visit from her mother. Though never explained clearly enough or fully enough, the act of leaving her daughter, Caroline, with Douglas is meant to free Caroline from the tyranny of the mother, from a repetition of the Martha/May relationship.

In the first four novels, female figures like Marnie and Maisie are examples of the separation and displacement of unacted parts of the self. On the veld, Martha is contrasted with Marnie in personality, ethnicity, and physical type; in the office the same kind of contrast is made between Martha and Maisie. Maisie recurs throughout the series and repeats herself through her daughter, Rita Gale Maynard, who eventually marries Mark. Both Marnie and Maisie are unskilled, uncomplicated, unambitious, fun-loving girls. They may fitly be described as extremer types of the Molly figure in *The Golden Notebook*.

Stella of the Stella/Andrew couple in *Martha Quest* and *A Proper Marriage* seems less a part of the pattern until her name is set beside those of Anna and Ella in *The Golden Notebook*. The similarities—internal double consonants, final vowels, two syllables—of these names stand out. Couples as well as single figures function comparatively in *A Proper Marriage*: Stella/Andrew, Martha/Douglas, Alice/Willie (compare Willi/Max in *The Golden Notebook*). "The three young wives" experience marriage and childbirth at approximately the same time (*A Proper Marriage*, 82). Martha, Alice, Stella, and their three children are a suggestive earlier version of Anna/Molly/Ella and their three children in *The Golden Notebook*. In *A Ripple from the Storm*, Martha/Marjorie/Maisie and their men are constantly juxtaposed. These limited examples suggest the simpler gender uses of the A and M figures in the earlier four novels.

They exist in a fictional world poorly served by terms like "fictional contrast" and "comparison." "Doubling" and "multiplication" are more richly exact terms for Lessing's remarkable gallery of A and M names, which invite us to look beneath the conventional linear progression of the novels. The repetition distorts their ordinary realistic surface to present us with the kind of dislocation or accident that gives to these fictions a slight sense of mystery. In this sense what Freud calls the *unheimlich* (17:619–39), too strongly rendered in English as the "uncanny," turns the ordinary surface of the novel into something else. Like Leggatt in Conrad's "The Secret Sharer," Lessing's characters have the usual freestanding reality of characters in a realistic novel. Perhaps less surely than Leggatt, but nonetheless like Leggatt, Lessing's characters also acquire another level of reality as displaced or possible parts of the self. Lessing explicitly identifies Mark and Lynda as positive parts of Martha, for example, and other characters, like Maynard, Jack, Phoebe, and Margaret, as negative selves or negative educators.

Lessing's solemn self has received a great deal of attention. Her special kind of gaming self needs more attention. Her naming game transparently reworks her own network of family names. Emily Maude is echoed in names like Ella and Stella. Alfred remains Alfred; his unofficial Michael name surfaces in Anna's lover and son and makes him both an *A* and an *M* figure. The name Anton for Martha's second husband duplicates Gottfried Anton Lessing's middle name. (In Douglas Knowell, called "know-all," Lessing rather obviously puns on the surname of her first husband, Frank Wisdom.)

Alice in *A Proper Marriage* has the first given name to fall clearly outside the pattern of *A* for men, *M* for women. As the only woman character with an *A* name in the Martha Quest novels, Alice tempts us to speculate whether Lessing was already considering a shift of the male *A* to a female protagonist rather different from Martha. The Anna/Molly names in *The Golden Notebook* represent Lessing's only extended use of *A* and *M* for a female couple rather than for a female/male couple. As noted, the *A/M* names reappear in the Canopus novels, in Al·Ith and Murti· of *The Marriages between Zones Three, Four, and Five* and in Alsi and Marl of *The Making of the Representative for Planet 8.*

Maynard, the most important male M before Mark, has a name that privileges May but contains elements of Alfred. Perhaps his male power echoes May Quest's matriarchical power? He is, in any event, the most authoritarian male M in the series, secretly manipulating the lives of Martha's friends—he gets Andrew posted, tries to separate Maisie from her daughter, sets spies at interracial meetings. His surrogate parental role, complicated by his sexual attraction for Martha, has a larger function that is defined late in the final volume of the quintet when Martha judges the Maynards, "her old enemies," as "the most valuable of all her educators" (558). Maynard "had shown her disbelief, in the shape of an accomplished and withering ridicule. She, Mrs. Maynard, had shown her power at its ugliest, when it is indirect, subtle, hidden" (558). Like Jack, the principle of evil and destruction in *The Four-Gated City*, these useful negative educators belong to the underside, to the mirror image, to the other face of joy. In *The Golden Notebook* they would be "named" as the principle of destruction.

The established *A* and *M* naming pattern of the first four Martha Quest novels, as noted in the introduction, takes a significant departure in *The Four-Gated City*. The many male *A*'s almost entirely disappear. Mark's unique M-ness enlarges and strengthens rather than weakens him. Furthermore, the names "Martha" and "Mark" are so alike as to suggest brother and sister rather than sexual partners. Martha once herself describes the two of them as "an old married couple, or a brother and sister" (192). Their names suggest a narcissism, a twinning of the self that is at the heart of the doubling phenomenon. Patty Samuels even calls Martha "Mark's female equivalent" (422). (Martha in turn describes Patty as "also her younger self" [202].) Martha watches in Mark the repetition of her own political development. When Mark turns to communism early in the novel, Martha recognizes in him her old self of ten years before: "They had changed roles" (185), as she and Lynda will later also do. She watches Mark "as if she were watching her own young self" (186–87).

Mark is more than Martha's mirror. Like Anna and Saul, the two are defined as fused or interchanging selves (187). But Anna feared merger with Saul; it threatened dissolution. No such threat exists for Martha and Mark. That classic threat of the doubling phenomenon is overturned in their conception. Martha and Mark are equals. Neither needs to take over the other. Their conception represents a decisive change in Lessing's exploration of male and female qualities. Lessing's conception overrides Martha's apparently continuing complicity in the view that intelligence is masculine (241). When Dr. Lamb suggests that this is her belief, she does not refute him.[6] To some degree, then, her professional mothering and her shadow writing role, compared to Mark's public writing role, are symptoms of her subjection to the almost inescapable cultural norms women are still born into.

If Phoebe/Marjorie, Patty (Patty/Jasmine?), and Rita/Maisie are potential, partial, or temporary "aspects" or doubles of Martha, then Mark and Lynda are more permanent pieces of her. Mark could be called the "public" side of Martha as Lynda is her innermost self, the self that can be apprehended only after many years of living and knowing. Mark is the best kind of public conscience. His "taking

onto himself a burden of guilt about the fate of the Jews in the last
war" is an example of that conscience at work (215). He faults himself for not having sensed Sally/Sarah's approaching suicide. He
fuses Sally/Sarah and Patty together with his knowledge of Thomas
to create the fictional brother and sister, Aaron and Rachel, who
become figures in a successful play. Mark never forgets these figures and their meaning. When he writes another work based on
them, times have changed. The reigning taste, denying Mark's right
and ability to know about Jewishness, rejects the work.

Mark is humane, open, caring. His Rescue schemes go as far as
the human mind can go without breaking the barrier into telepathy.
He remains the best person rationalism can produce. But rationalism is not enough. Neither is Rosa Mellendip's world of "packs of
cards and tea-leaves." Martha defines the Mellendip world as "cozy,
self-satisfied, stagnant, the mirror or shadow-side of the orthodox
scientific world which was also cozy, self-satisfied, stagnant" (511).
What Martha wants cannot be found either "in the backwaters of
'rationalism,' which was the official culture," or "in the mirror of the
official culture" (511).

When Martha begins to hear what people in faraway places are
saying and to see events before they happen, she has traveled beyond rationalism. Her voyage into Lynda's "country" justifies her
years of waiting. Her very female waiting has enormous rewards in
this novel, for the deeply private world of "inner immigration"
(605) turns out to be political on a global scale. It becomes "activist"
in ways profounder than Phoebe's way or Patty's way—the way of
parliamentary or Communist political action—profounder even
than Mark's way. The inner immigrants foresee Catastrophe and
mobilize as many people as possible to survive and so keep the
human race alive.

Martha is fully independent only after she has absorbed first
Mark and then Lynda and has seen the younger generation into
adulthood. Recalling "her old antagonist, the competent middle-
aged woman" (219), Martha comes to find middle age the freest
time of her life. (She is, it should be noted, only thirty-five when
she says this.) Later, while she consciously uses a "particular personality" to manage Paul, she thinks how "extraordinary it was, this
being middle-aged, being the person who ran and managed and
kept going" (354), being "that person who once she hated and
feared more than any other" (360). This awareness triggers a

memory of Mrs. Van, whose approval of her work in the Coldridge household she knows she would have, for Martha stays on the job. She does not leave this third "marriage" and her new brood of nonblood children. Martha's sense of responsibility is too strong, Lessing's evaluation of woman's child-bearing and child-rearing roles too high.

Martha now also judges that she abandoned rather than freed Caroline. She must have been mad, she thinks, quite disagreeing with Jack, who approves her behavior. The birth scars he touches vividly evoke the perfect child's body she gave away. For the first time, Martha unconvincingly rationalizes her decision by rooting it in the Communist ethos of her earlier self. She places the responsibility for her belief that no-family-equals-no-neurosis on Marxism. In that earlier life, "we were all corrupted and ruined, we knew that, but the children would be saved" (70). Caroline's name is later given to a child at the Aldermaston March, who holds a placard that reads: "Caroline Says No." Martha may have relinquished her Marxism, but she has not given up and never does give up her conviction that children provide a chance for renewal. The black child Joseph who concludes the appendix section of the novel is a version of Caroline. He is also a group child and as such a descendant of the group child in A Ripple from the Storm who grows up as Rita. (Kassim Sherban of Shikasta, another group child, can also be described as a descendant of Rita.)

Most readers have accepted Anna as an artist and Martha as a caretaker figure. But this construction of Martha simplifies her. She may have once been meant to become an artist.[7] She certainly bears significant traces of that vocation within her, enough for her to be described as a shadow artist.

Martha and Mark have a collaborative writing relationship that is different from, yet related to, the collaborative relationship between Anna and Saul. Martha is not merely a secretary to her writing men and to Mrs. Van; she is an active collaborator. Her earlier collaborations are indeed purely secretarial. In earlier novels, she types Johnny Lindsay's memoirs, researches and types for Mrs. Van, and becomes the custodian of Thomas's testament.

In her most important collaboration with Mark, she talks through with him the material that is to become A City in the Desert. Mark spends "hours talking to Martha in order to find out what it was he thought" (293). Until their paths separate very late in the novel, Mark talks through all his subsequent books with her (139, 192, 215, 293). These are functional dialogues. Martha even polishes up some of Mark's old sketches for publication. When Mark begins to paper his walls, Martha is again his collaborator, choosing extracts from reports, papers, blueprints, as once she did for Mrs. Van (296–97). Martha and Mark go in and out of a sexual relationship together, never out of an intellectual and emotional relationship. As Martha muses, "The fact was, she supposed, that in a way she was married to Mark. No joke that. It was a kind of truth"—as much a truth as Mark's enduring love for Lynda, his legal, no longer sexual, wife (299). Only much later, when Martha becomes closer to Lynda than to Mark, does Mark write without discussing his work with Martha. By then his plan for saving a remnant of the human race diverges from Martha's and Lynda's.

Martha writes totally for herself only when she is able, after her initiation with Lynda, to make a descent into the self on her own. The writing closest to the self has been prefigured in Thomas's testament, whose chaotic forms filled with insights have analogues in Anna's notebooks and in Dorothy's memos, accounts, and letters. Martha makes an explicit connection between these private suicidal journeys and Mark's journey. She lays Thomas's testament beside Mark's manuscript, which has also been crossed out and written over in different inks and styles. It has become a "debased" copy, overrunning and destroying the original much as, in Martha's myth, the shadow city overruns the inner city.[8] Looking at it "was like watching a battle between two personalities, one trying to take over another" (184). Somewhere in their respective descents, "two very extraordinarily different people made contact" (164). "Thomas had gone down into madness and death"; Mark goes to another "kind of descent, of an entering in," whose conclusion is still, at this point, unknown. This point does, however, end Mark's political naiveté; here he begins his study of the "shadow, or reverse side of what was taught" (185). Martha "rescues" the manuscript by removing Mark's annotations and sending *A City* to the publishers.

During her solitary period of fasting and trance, Martha begins a notebook that comes to resemble Thomas's testament and Dorothy's diary: "But soon sheets and sheets of paper were scrawled and scribbled over as the notes and remarks accumulated, were put down so fast she did not have time to make things legible" (537). While Martha has gone off on her own journey, Mark has gone off on his. His numbered notes and instructions for a new world are a counterpoint to Martha's list of discoveries. His title, "Memorandum to Myself," is in caps; Martha's is in lowercase as befits her shadow writer's role. Mark's final journey incorporates the antimemoirs of Thomas and of Dorothy as well as the material on his five walls. Mark becomes "preoccupied, if you like, obsessed, with the immediate future of humanity and was spending his time in his study with his charts, his figures, his maps, the pages torn from Dorothy's diary, and Thomas's manuscript" (516).

The dead Thomas is a brooding presence over the entire novel. He walks in and talks to Martha. She dreams about him. Mark studies his testament and connects him to Sally/Sarah. He is only a slightly less obvious suicide than Sally/Sarah and Dorothy. Mark's fictional Thomas becomes "the mirror image of his parents and his ancestors; and his future, like theirs, was planned as death in a holocaust" (461). Thomas is also in part a precursor of Lynda: Martha notes Lynda's "great eyes that, like Thomas's once, were full of depths of light into which one could lean, like pools, or clouds or trees; and was invaded by great washes of understanding, insight, knowledge" (520). The narcissistic image is striking. Thomas, Lynda, and Dorothy become heroic figures who have entered the underside, stepped through the mirror and been both illuminated and destroyed. They have also been educators or gurus.

The antimemoirs of Thomas, Dorothy, and Martha are the underside of what is finally put into print. In that sense, they are to the finished work what the notebooks are to Free Women in The Golden Notebook.[9] They are the chaos, the rawness behind the public work, a reminder of the questionable truth of the shaped work. In this novel, Lessing accepts the Laingian premise that madness is vision. For some—for Thomas, for Sally/Sarah, for Dorothy—madness and vision are also death. Though Lynda seems to suffer a kind of defeat, she comes back in the appendix section and in Shikasta. Martha survives without relapses. And Mark, an aboveground visionary, also survives. In this context, calling Martha a secretary/den mother seems inadequate. She is a collaborating alter ego, a secret sharer of Mark's and the head of a family collective. In terms of the novel's appendix, her journey is more radical and more successful than Mark's. Martha, not Mark, comes to represent the remnant that becomes the new world.

Mark's importance needs to be insisted upon. His role has

tended to be ignored and Lynda's highlighted. Both are "aspects" of Martha. When Martha has fully "used" Mark, she can turn to Lynda. Her true maturity develops after she survives her mother's visit and the breakdown that leads to her acceptance of Lynda as a mentor. Maturity in this novel is defined as a visionary coming of age, not as a sexual, political, or intellectual coming of age.

Lynda, for so long a background presence in the Coldridge household, finally becomes a foreground, a "real" presence for Martha—and her last doppelgänger. The "shadow world of the basement" (or "the irrationality of the cellar" as opposed to "the rationality of the roof," to use Bachelard's phrasing [18]) becomes the heart of Martha's universe, as a role reversal of place and person takes place. Martha's crucial voyage to the "shadow world," undertaken at Mark's request to help Lynda through one of her "bad" periods, ends with Lynda running upstairs to get Mark to help Martha. Their role reversal is complete. During their common journey, Martha wonders, "And how could Martha go out, since she was part of Lynda?" (491). She almost joins Lynda on the floor to lick milk from a broken saucer. Martha leaves the basement world only to shower or to gather some food. "The observer and Martha," this novel's equivalent of Anna and her critical intelligence, return from one such journey upstairs with an awareness of just how far "inside of Lynda's country" these selves have gone (493).

After a month's journey into the interior of the self, the two women emerge and rejoin the "normal" world. (Their journey together recalls the month-long journey of Anna and Saul.) Martha's subsequent trips into her interior are solitary. She will not undergo Lynda's long history of institutionalization and treatment, shock therapy, drugs, and so on. That history has taught Martha how to survive in the outer world of doctors, families, friends. She will be able to hide her visionary powers and live in both worlds, the one in which madness has become more subversive than Marxism and the one in which seers and hearers commune.

In her next journey into the self, in Paul's house, Martha struggles with her negative double, with the principle of hate and destruction, the one more familiarly and traditionally called evil. That shadow self, "switched into Hating, which is the underside of all this lovely liberalism," includes the antisemite, the racist, the Nazi. "'The Germans are the mirror and catalyst of Europe'" (539); they are everyone's inner Devil. Lessing's secularism is so eroded in this novel that she finds terms like "Devil" and "evil" eminently usable. Martha later comments on her wrestling with her capitalized Devil: "I've been turned inside out like a glove or a dress. I've been like the negative of a photograph. Or a mirror image. I've seen the underneath of myself" (553). The graphic imagery describes the violent, amoral other self, the Hyde self of nineteenth-century doubles novels, not the one represented by Lynda or Mark. In Lessing's more complicated conception, the double can belong to the unrealized or unconfronted positive self, as Mark and Lynda do, as well as to the destructive or pathological self. Like Anna, Martha must learn from and incorporate both her good and her evil selves. Martha's encounter with the destructive principle seems more clinically or more didactically imagined than Anna's. Furthermore, Martha's experience suggests that the destructive principle cannot be entirely integrated. Some parts of it must be exorcised. This point of view accords with Lessing's embrace of the religious view of evil as ineradicable.

The Four-Gated City, as the final volume of a quintet meant to be "a study of the individual conscience in its relation with the collective," turns fully to the problem of creating a new collective (Small Personal Voice, 12). Whatever the limits of Martha's earlier political group, it did provide an alternative to "the tyranny of the family," the collective forced together by the accident of birth (A Proper Marriage, 82–83). In The Four-Gated City Lessing explores, through a series of "houses," new kinds of family structures. Perhaps these houses can be called mini-cities. Certainly the city is firmly and surely fixed in Lessing's imagination as the quintessential location of human collective life. The city in the desert and its shadow city are explorations of new collectives on a larger societal and worldwide level. In The Golden Notebook, Anna's house seems only nominally a double of Molly's house. In that novel, where the central character is a writer and the title alludes to writing, writing forms are more fittingly central extensions of the self. In The Four-Gated City environments are more suitable mirrors for a protagonist who shares the leadership of a household or a commune.

The Coldridge household is a loose agglomerate based on kinship, friendship, accident, and choice. Its symbolic function is not clear for a long time, perhaps not until Jack's house and Mark's house are set side by side: "For all those years, while Martha had been in Mark's house, Jack had been here, creating a house which was like a perverted millionaire's brothel, and sitting like a spider while women came and went" (405). Surely this is "the house that Jack built," the evil shadow house to Mark's good house. Jack began differently. Martha had once linked him with Thomas Stern: "With Jack, she found herself thinking of Thomas. She did not think of her two husbands, Knowell and Hesse, she thought of Thomas" (51). She is "always at home" with Jack, feeling in him the paradoxical "time and death" that also moved in Thomas (52). Martha knows and accepts Jack's professional lovemaking to many women. It seems good, as good as Jack's creation of a house out of a bombed-out London tenement. Then Jack, undergoing a reversal, becomes a destroyer. But his equivalent of a long dark night of the soul during an illness leaves him possessed by another personality: "Some time while he had been ill the old Jack had simply died, or gone away, and this new person had walked in and taken possession" (406).[10] The "real" Jack never returns (403).

Jack last appears in the Breughelesque Aldermaston March chapter. Everyone is at this peace march, even Jack, marvelously, comically "in search of fresh prey" for his brothel among marchers and watchers (432). He even checks out Lynda as a possible candidate. Jack breaks in his girls by an elaborate process of degradation that depends on his recognition of and response to the destructive double in his victims. His essential weapons are the weapons of torture and "of some brands of psychoanalysis. The common factor . . . is that a part or area of the person manipulated has to be made an accomplice of the person who manipulates" (432). In short, Jack turns his knowledge of the double self to destructive ends.

The body, the outer covering of the self, and the house, the extended environment of the self, correspond with Jack's new self. "The geography of the house," mapped "in terms of sexual fantasy," suits what Jack is and does. Lovemaking has become sadomasochistic to a Jack now "all domination and hurt" (403). When Martha "works" alone in a room in Paul's house, she has to meet the point where Lynda was defeated, pass it, then move on and pass the point where Jack was defeated.

Jack is the principle of evil in the novel and his house the anti-house to the Coldridge house: "Everything was stood on its head and became its opposite in Jack's house" (431–42). The phrasing is one example of Lessing's need to "name" the principles of self and antiself in this novel. Francis and Jill's house and Paul and Zena's house duplicate, with variations, the primary oppositions displayed in Jack's and Mark's houses.

Martha foresees Jack's transformation very early in the novel: "The jiggling wave length was telling her: Jack fell down and broke his crown, Jack fell down and broke his . . ." (40). She knows then that she cannot stay with Jack, "even for as short a time as he would be able to live as he did before he fell down and broke his crown" (41). Lessing never uses the nursery rhyme line, "This is the house that Jack built." She does not need to. The line comes easily and aptly to the reader's mind to join her use of the lines from Jack and Jill.

Lessing maps the Coldridge house and Jack's house fully and specifically in a single chapter (3 of part 3). The Coldridge house comes first; it is a personality, at times uncertainly both layered and divided: "The house continued, if not divided against itself, at least layered in atmospheres or climates: A slight shuffle: Francis had moved upwards when he had left school; so now, from top to bottom it was Francis, Paul, Martha, Mark, Lynda" (375).[11] Here the layering image is less positive than its earlier application to the thirteen layers of wallpaper. In other sections, as we shall see, the house is an organic entity, and the layering image belongs to wholeness rather than to division.

At this time, the children are grown. Francis lives in the attic with his friend Nicky; his cousins, Gwen and Jill, are there so often that they "might as well have moved in" (378).

Paul, "the cuckoo in the nest," occupies "the floor below Francis" (382). He is an earlier school dropout than Francis; his "knife-like need to have, to outwit, to do down," makes him always a counter-figure, one the reader is expected to understand against his traumatic childhood. Both parents abandoned him: his father, Colin Coldridge, by defecting to the Soviets; his Jewish mother, Sally/Sarah, by committing suicide. Paul finds a partner in Zena, "his female image, lithe, black-haired, black-eyed. They spent hours in his rooms playing games in front of a long mirror, winding bits of cloth around themselves, posing for imaginary photographers" (385). The other children call Paul and Zena "the Siamese twins." When Jill calls them narcissistic, Paul counters, " 'But love is always narcissistic' " (386). His "absent sense of right and wrong" correlates with Jack's amoral values, while his chastity or asexuality belongs as much to the underside of things as Jack's prostitution racket (383). In Paul and Zena the narcissism implicit in the doubling phenomenon is wholly negative.

"Below Paul and Zena—Martha" (386). At this stage, Martha is rarely herself. She is the mother figure of the Coldridge collective, "never alone, always tired," always on call, always advising (387). "Even her room was not hers: it was always bursting open under the pressures of some demand" (387). When they want to make love, she and Mark move into his study. Whenever Martha wishes "she could slap Gwen" or upbraid Jill, she remembers her younger self: "That girl, shrill, violent, cruel, cold, using any weapon fair or foul to survive, as she had had to do, had been stripped off her, had gone away, was simply a character worn for a day or two, a week or two, a year, half a dozen years, by Gwen or Jill or anybody else" (387)—as, one might add, Martha had worn other personalities or Mrs. Van's or Lynda's coat. In this passage personality is not compartmentalized but variable and layered. Martha can watch a discarded part of the self without regret, without a sense of frustration or loss. Even the stripping or peeling figure faces two ways. Here it is descriptive, accepting; for Mark, during cold-war harassments, it defines the denuded self.

Below Martha are Mark and Mark's study; and below him, finally, are Lynda and the shadow world of the basement. Detailed description of Lynda's lower world has to be reserved until Martha can "see" it.

The lives of the wider Coldridge circle, although its members are not resident with the Coldridges, are brought into the house chapter. Phoebe, mother of Gwen and Jill and ex-wife of Arthur Coldridge; Margaret, mother of Mark, Colin, and Arthur, now married to John Patten; and Graham Patten, John's son—all have a place in it. This period, another "bad time," precipitates Martha's visit to Jack after years of separation. The chapter, a collective chapter, is followed by the climactic and most ambitious collective chapter in the novel, the 1961 antinuclear Aldermaston March.

One of the rhythms of the novel is the movement from individuals to groups. Sometimes Martha, the protagonist, is eclipsed; sometimes she is the sole actor in a chapter. The house also has its alternations. At the beginning of the novel, it is under seige because hostile reporters want to get in to contact the family of the defector, Colin Coldridge. No one leaves during this time. Later the house has an exactly opposite rhythm. Mark goes on an intense social whirl; he is never home. At another time, the house is itself the center of parties, meetings, and so on. Before the Aldermaston March we are told that "the house continued," although the individuals in it or close to it are in combat or breakdown. It has become an actor. When it goes, the individuals go and the novel ends. The house is "compulsorily purchased, or almost," to become "an office for the Rates or Town Planning or before it was demolished altogether" (564). During this period Martha's holding-it-all-together function ends, and Rita Maynard takes over the house (564, 587).

The uses of the house, so carefully layered and contrasted with "the house that Jack built," do not end here. The house contains another kind of doubling; Mark's study walls have their counterpoint in Lynda's walls. Hers are "the two walls visible and invisible" (486). Mark's are more familiar. They resemble the walls Anna papers with newspaper clippings. The red, black, and yellow flags on one wall are an interestingly inexact echo of Anna's colored notebooks. Mark begins with two walls, but by the time of the Aldermaston March all his walls and the ceiling are covered. His room looks like "a medieval tent or pavilion" with streamers connecting different items on different walls. The first two walls have information on atomic installations, germ and chemical warfare, already contaminated areas of the globe, and items under the labels War, Famine, Riots, Poverty, Prisons. Information on space travel covers the ceiling; Dorothy's letters and diary entries are on one wall. Much later, Mark adds a hinged wall with data on mental hospitals and patients, which signals his effort to understand the world of the now-joined Lynda/Martha. Mark's visible, public walls are at once "the place of the unconstituted committee" (297) and a kind of sourcebook for Francis and others to study.

Mark sees his fifth wall as one form of breakthrough, as representing "factor X; that absolutely obvious, out-in-the-open, therefor-anybody-to-see fact which nobody was seeing yet" (434). His public walls belong to the upper world, while Lynda's are perhaps too obviously placed in "the shadow world of the basement," that "separate, almost secret establishment" that is Lessing's heart of darkness positively imagined (221, 187). Lynda's lower world is the dangerous, fascinating, unknown interior of the self, the source of

strange powers telepathic and visionary. Its topographical description is delayed until Martha can take in its meaning (chapter 2, part
4). Lynda's physical environment reflects the self she presents to
the world: "Her flat wore the same aspect of guile or doublefacedness" (485). Its "Ideal Antique Flat" quality soothes, then vaguely
disturbs, visitors. Lynda's rooms and her two walls are another kind
of book. The odd placement of objects and furniture makes the
room "a place to get out of as fast as possible—either that, or a
place to study, to make sense of, to sink oneself into" (486). Martha
chooses to sink herself into Lynda's room; she wants Lynda's hermetic knowledge. Francis will later have to choose between two
kinds of knowledge, his father's and his two mothers'.

Lynda's furniture is arranged parallel to the walls of her room to
create an invisible wall. Lynda moves in "the space between the
walls visible and invisible," as though saying, Martha speculates,
"Can I get out?" (487). Lynda's invisible walls are analogues to the
walls of the mind, cages she tries to open. So she walks round and
round, "testing the walls for weakness, for a thin place" through
which she will one day "simply step outside free" (494). (Lynda's
image becomes actuality for the narrator of The Memoirs of a Survivor,
who does walk through a wall to another world.) Martha inherits
Lynda's quest.

The powerful and highly original house imagery probably has its
immediate inspiration in the commune movements of the 1960s,
for the groups Francis and Paul lead have the nonideological hope-
fulness of those movements.[12] Certainly Martha's "'there isn't any
family I've ever seen that doesn't seem to me all wrong'" is an
axiom of the novel (71). She dislikes the Coldridge family and the
physical house at first, but they come to define a unique family, in
fact, the most viable collective of Martha's life until she lives in the
survivor community of Faris. The Coldridge house breathes and
changes with its occupants—sometimes divided, "all a mass of
small separate things . . . a mass of fragments, a smashed mirror"
(353); sometimes layered "in atmospheres or climates" (375); more
often and more essentially organic like her room: "of a piece, a
totality; yet no one could set out to create a house like it. It had
grown like this" (106). Her room, "whose presence was so strong,
so confident," is a microcosm of the house (104). Although so nur-
turing—"nothing in this house believed in the possibility of de-

struction"—and so unlike Jack's, the house must come to destruction (104). It has sheltered several generations, including the leaders of civilization's next explosion into a new form. Its job is done.

Like the Coldridge house, *The Four-Gated City* is shaped with the layerings and juxtapositions of persons and places. The layering image is finally stronger than the splitting image. Or the self is more layered than divided, more like the talismanic thirteen layers of wallpaper Martha encounters so soon after her arrival in London. Martha can meet earlier selves, in Mark, Patty, Gwen, or Jill, without regret. These selves have been lived and shed. They cannot hurt or anger Martha's current selves.

Another interesting feature of the Martha/Mark/Lynda selves is their solution to the problem of "thirds" so much on Anna/Ella's mind in *The Golden Notebook*. To Anna, the "third" is "the woman altogether better than I was" (*Golden Notebook*, 637). Lynda, as wife, seer, and friend, is "better" than Martha in certain ways from an Anna point of view. She is a wife, who, furthermore, accepts the reality of Martha's function as her husband's lover, household manager, and collaborator. By her shadowy presence, her visionary abilities, her basement habitat, and her asexuality, she makes the perfect third. Lynda's unusual constellation of traits permits Martha to live her life as the other woman without the guilt from which Anna Wulf was never free.

Three, as noted in the introduction, is also the symbolic number for the family. As the addition to the parental two, three suggests Lessing's compulsion to repeat her own primal family composition, a man and two women. Considered from this perspective, Martha seems tied to the split woman, one the functional wife and mother, the other recessive and waiting for independence.

Considered from yet another perspective, the unorthodoxy of the Martha/Mark/Lynda trio is as deliberate a suggestion of a new family pattern as are the "houses" in the novel. It makes three a parental number; it mixes legal and nonlegal relationships to make parenting a reality outside marriage. Francis and Paul are not Martha's blood children, yet she is their functional mother.

Lessing is emphatic about the triple nature of the heads of the Coldridge household. Francis has had to fend off jokes about Martha's role all his life—Martha has always occasioned gossip from outsiders—but the triad continues and is in fact insisted upon the closer the reader comes to the end of the novel. When the three appear publicly at the Aldermaston March, their names are linked in varying arrangements: Martha/Lynda/Mark (408), Mark/Lynda/Martha (413), Martha/Lynda/Mark (416), Martha/Mark/Lynda (416). Later there are further variations: Lynda/Mark/Martha (546) and Mark/Martha/Lynda (547).[13] The changing order of the three names is a highly deliberate way of validating the triad and underlining the equality of its members. The threesome, therefore, seem to resolve certain obsessive personal needs and to postulate nontraditional family forms that fit the "houses" Lessing creates for them.

Lynda/Martha/Mark are collaborating selves. Selves and antiselves like Martha/Maynard, Martha/Jack, Francis/Paul, and Mark/Jimmy Wood represent a different order of doubling. Jack, Jimmy, and Paul represent destroyed persons to Martha. They belong to a time in her life when antiselves have a mythical, religious dimension, as they did not when Maynard was a functioning part of her life. Martha decides that the definition of Jack as body and Jimmy as mind is inadequate, yet she is certain both represent "the extremer purer type of something or some person" that helps us to understand the rest of us (a standard premise of abnormal psychology) (514). As expected, Lessing expresses the utility of definition by opposites.

When Mark at last realizes Jimmy Wood's amorality, he is astonished at his twenty years of not "seeing" what Jimmy stands for. Jimmy's latest invention of a machine that will enable governments to "destroy the brains of people . . . felt to be dangerous" and his current project, a machine to help governments artificially stimulate telepathic powers, flout everything Mark believes in.[14] Mark's inability "to put two and two together" about someone he has been so close to for so long is explicitly compared with Martha's inability to see "what was screaming out to be seen" about Lynda (534). Jimmy's bizarre moral vacuity shows in his popular science fiction, which he exploits without the slightest awareness of or interest in what he is saying. (The children at the Aldermaston March know his books, but not Mark's.) Jimmy's "newest book is about a human mutant quite invisible to ordinary humanity because he was apparently and outwardly normal. Yet his capacities were superhuman" (415). This imaginary mutant predicts/foreshadows the special children of Faris, who are everything Jimmy Wood is not (as, for example, Saul's appearance is predicted/foreshadowed in *The Golden Notebook* in the short story synopses in the Yellow Notebook).

These collaborating and antagonistic selves coexist with sets of environmental mirrors. The collaborating selves can be called ego and ego rather than ego and alter ego. Martha and Mark are equally "active" participants in their relationship. Furthermore, in the Martha/Mark couple Lessing moves Martha (and herself?) away from her bondage to the "male" and "female" characteristics she inherited from her A-named father and her M-named mother. Anna Freeman Wulf, as her male name suggests, can be described from one point of view as more tied to sexual stereotypes than Martha/Mark, Martha/Lynda, and Martha/Mark/Lynda, who surely represent the most complex and "free" conception of gender roles in the Martha/Anna novels.

Lessing's shaping is not the shaping of the modernist tradition, but it is a significant and compelling shaping. In the Martha/Anna novels Lessing's mind moves in complex patterns of opposition and collaboration between doubles and multiples as though she were, like a physicist, seeing matter and antimatter everywhere. Her novelistic strategies can be compared with Lynda's "guile and doublefacedness." They provide readers with an ordinary novel whose rather flat, long-winded mass of apparently documentary material goes slightly out of focus, like Lynda's room, to reveal unexpected pattern, precision, and strangeness. The ending of the novel proper has its own surprise, a lyrical quality rare in Lessing, one suggesting long, melodic arcs of time. The house about to dissolve, its occupants to disperse, Martha stands alone considering what was, what is, and what will be. She sees herself

> like a planet doomed always to be dark on one side . . . vision in front only, a myopic searchlight blind except for the tiny three-dimensional path open immediately before her eyes in which the outline of a tree, a rose, emerged, then submerged in dark. She thought, with the dove's voice of her solitude: Where? But *where* How? Who? No, but *where*, where . . . Then silence and the birth of a repetition: *Where*? Here. Here?
>
> Here, where else, you fool, you poor fool, where else has it been, ever . . . [591. The ellipses, except for the first, are Lessing's.]

So the novel proper ends, at the edge of an unknown new beginning with Martha firmly and eternally conscious of her dark and light side as a human being, her built-in blindness and vision, her double human self. The repetition slips in, signalling its place in the process of going on. The "ever" and "always" of these last lines present us with the eternal recurrence so paradoxically a corollary of the opposing imagery of walls, rooms, houses, cities, families, fictions, and selves.

Then the appendix takes a leap into a future that seems to recapitulate in more extreme form the apocalypse of World War II. The single ruined city that opens the novel turns plural at its end as ruined cities are everywhere and survivors again try to rebuild. The return to ruin is not quite circular, for the survival of the underground telepaths and the existence of the special children suggest that there can be change within circularity. These indicators of hope face new enemies and new underground activity. Recurrence and change are the permanent governors of human history, as "this powerful, prophetic, mysterious work" asserts (Oates, 48).

The novel somehow survives its didacticism and its long-winded, often compulsive documentation of the postwar fifties and sixties, which fragments into the ten documents of the appendix. These documents are a second ending to The Four-Gated City, a highly selective, abbreviated report on the final decades of our twentieth century. The Golden Notebook has a double ending: the Blue Notebook 4 and Free Women 5 sections contradict one another. The Four-Gated City has another kind of double ending. The appendix appears to extend the novel chronologically, and chronological extension does not seem to qualify as a double ending. Yet it does and it is. The appendix is inexactly defined as continuance. It is odd and disruptive in a number of ways. It breaks the format of the novel proper. It is wholly documentary. Its time frame is discontinuous. It lacks a central character. Above all, it depicts a world not essentially changed from the one before Catastrophe—the wrong people have the greater power—although the physical centers of political power have shifted and obvious racism has ended. When the novel concludes, the four-gated city is still in the title, not in the text.

6
Mothers and Daughters/
Aging and Dying

A faint warning voice from the well of fatality did remark that a girl child was in the direct line of matriarchy she so feared.

Doris Lessing, *A Proper Marriage*

"Imagine being old. Imagine when no one will turn to look at me. I'll be like that old woman there—an old grey sheep in a hair-net. It must be like being a ghost, moving among other people, and no one noticing you at all. Perhaps there's no one to care when she comes in and goes out. She lives in a room by herself, and if she died, no one would even notice it. Perhaps she doesn't know herself that she is alive?"

Doris Lessing, *Retreat to Innocence*

The loss of the daughter to the mother, the mother to the daughter, is the essential female tragedy.

Adrienne Rich, *Of Woman Born*

Julia Barr, the spoiled upper-class innocent of *Retreat to Innocence*, will not fare well in old age. We are meant to dislike her shallowness and her stereotypically female commitment to appearance. At age twenty-one she cannot imagine not being noticed by others. Old women are invisible. Julia's fear of invisibility and isolation are vividly captured in her unexpectedly original image of the old woman as "an old grey sheep in a hair-net."

Presumably other Doris Lessing characters will prove to have a finer, fuller appreciation of aging and aged women. In fact, Julia's fear of old age is duplicated in characters we are meant to judge positively. It initiates a fear of the aging process in Lessing protagonists that culminates in *The Diaries of Jane Somers*, published nearly thirty years after *Retreat to Innocence*, and that includes her five-volume *Canopus in Argos* series as well as her earlier five-volume *Children of Violence* series. It includes the unnamed narrator (she can be called the survivor) of *The Memoirs of a Survivor*, as well as Kate Brown of *The Summer before the Dark*. It should include Susan Rawlings of the short story "To Room Nineteen," for no discussion of Lessing's thinking about aging women can ignore her analysis of the mid-life crisis, one Lessing tends to fix in the early or mid-forties. Susan does not survive her crisis, but Kate Brown does. Kate Brown can, in fact, be described as Susan Rawlings positively reimagined. In Kate Brown's survival is writ the postulate that old age cannot be reached or successfully negotiated without a resolution of the mid-life crisis. But the problems of aging and dying, as Lessing addresses them, cannot be neatly placed within the simpler contemporary confines of the phrase "mid-life crisis."

There are many examples of women who nearly or actually break down or commit suicide in Lessing's fiction (e.g., Mary Turner in *Grass*; Susan Rawlings; Kate Brown; Anna Wulf in *The Golden Notebook*; Martha Quest, Lynda Coldridge, Dorothy Quentin, and Sarah/Sally Coldridge in *The Four-Gated City*). There are also examples of survival. Lynda Coldridge and Martha Quest are the most powerful. (Emily and her surrogate mother are also high on the survivor list.) Lynda Coldridge does more than survive a lifetime of bizarre treatment as a mental patient. In *Shikasta*, she collaborates with a doctor in training a new generation in the techniques of telepathy. Martha's life is conducive to our imagining a chapter called "Martha Quest: Sage and Survivor." But a little reflection shows how partial such an approach and such a chapter would finally be, how falsely upbeat in the face of Lessing's fundamental insistence on uncertainty and skepticism. Yes, Martha does become a sage, even a telepath, but her old age is more imagined than felt, more an afterthought in the appendix section to *The Four-Gated City* than a reality in the novel proper. Above all, to acclaim Martha and to ignore the most powerful portrait of the aging woman in all of Lessing's work until *The Diaries of Jane Somers* would be scandalous, especially when it occurs in the same novel. We cannot talk about Martha Quest in old age without talking about May Quest in old age.

Once May is mentioned the issue of the aging process in women becomes enormously complicated. We discover that it is impossible to talk about aging in women without talking about the mother-daughter relationship. In May and Martha the mother-daughter fulcrum is at its most intense and most negative. From Mary Turner's memories of her defeated, supposedly feminist, mother in *The Grass Is Singing* or Julia Barr's rivalry with her feminist and political mother, Jane Barr, to Jane (Janna) Somers's relationship with her surrogate mother, Maudie, or Alice Mellings's exploitation of her mother, Dorothy, in *The Good Terrorist*, Lessing restlessly works and reworks her vision of the mother-daughter relationship. That relationship is never resolved, unless we wish to call it resolution when mothers or daughters develop temporary working relationships with surrogate, nonbiological daughters or mothers, as the survivor and Emily Mary do in *Memoirs*, or as Kate and Maureen in *Summer* or Janna and Maudie in *Jane Somers* do. The mother-daughter tie is never dissociated from the process of growing and aging. Mothers—surrogate or otherwise—forever function as mirrors for their daughters. The complex circularity of daughters fighting mothers and then becoming mothers themselves both repeats and advances Lessing's themes and patterns.

I have not mentioned Anna Wulf in this connection. She is obviously exceptional in at least two ways. Her biological mother is absent (yet briefly present through the given name, May, she shares with Martha's mother). Instead she has the surrogate Mother Sugar whose role would be significantly diffused and defused if Anna's natural mother were also present. Anna is given a father and a unique single and professional life-style. She does have a daughter, Janet, who chooses boarding school, with its uniform dress code, in deliberate opposition to her mother's "free" style. Janet, who does not want to be like Anna, recalls Martha, who does not want to be like May. Janet's bourgeois longings are exaggerated in Janna Somers's glossy life-style. Janna Somers may also remind Lessing aficionados of the motherless Anna, as Maudie may remind them of Molly, Anna's other self. The echoic elements of Anna/Janet and Anna/Molly in Janna/Maudie do not destroy the integrity of the fictional characters in their respective works. The reverse is true. Their recurrence with variation opens small slits of light into authorial compulsions; the repetitions that lightly link novel to novel create special layers of meaning for the reader. The two women

Anna is, to use the phrasing of *The Golden Notebook*, seem indeed to have resurfaced in the figures of Janna and Maudie.

The media and Lessing herself were delighted with the deceptive game that presented Jane Somers instead of Doris Lessing to the public as the author of *The Diaries* (see Sprague and Tiger, introduction). Lessing claimed as her motive for the pseudonym her desire to expose the difficulties that face an unknown writer. Her altruism is suspect. Artistic deception is never that simple. The Jane Somers caper involved more profound personal and artistic needs. Through Jane/Janna Somers Lessing confronts more directly than she could in earlier novels or in the Canopus novels her own guilt and her own fears about aging and dying.

Thus problems of aging and dying in Lessing's work are unexpectedly localized in the always painful and always inescapable mother-daughter relationship. They are understandably located in women rather than in men both because Lessing is a woman and because women are on the whole more enslaved to physical appearance than men are. These problems are addressed fully and directly in *The Diaries of Jane Somers*, and less fully or directly in earlier works.

The Canopus novels consider the anguish of mortality from an indirect and species point of view. Here the problems of aging and dying seem to disappear, for Canopeans, Sirians, and Shammatans live for millennia. Yet the Canopean archives are an extremely painful record of the rise and fall of peoples and empires, of the collective suffering of inferior peoples like ourselves—inferior because they/we are so ridiculously short-lived and myopic, so impossibly greedy, corrupt, and victimized by hunger, poverty, disease, and racism. Finally and paradoxically, the world of the Canopean novels, its galactic stage and immortal foreground figures notwithstanding, is claustrophobic and filled with fatality.

There is a more pointed relationship between the fourth volume, *The Making of the Representative for Planet 8*, and Lessing's recent return to realism in *The Diaries of Jane Somers* and *The Good Terrorist*. The *Making of the Representative*, fabular and haunting as *Jane Somers* is not, can nonetheless be described as a dress rehearsal for the later novel. In *Making*, Lessing confronts species annihilation as a form of transcendence. Perhaps criticism of her space fiction adventures coalesced with her own need to return to earth and its smaller but more vivid problems of time and aging and dying. However we interpret the *Diaries*, their obverse relationship to *Making* is striking. Both works are concerned with coming to terms with mortality. But in the *Diaries* the universe is no longer abstract or galactic or remote. Ambien II's sexless androgyny disappears; the long millennial view is discarded. In the *Diaries* Lessing turns to the malodorous and incontinent world of ill and aged women, to their invisibility and isolation, to their imprisonment in state care in the form of Good Neighbours and Meals on Wheels, to the world that so terrified Julia Barr.

Making and *Diaries* form a paradoxical dialectical encounter with issues of aging and dying that reimagines the characteristic location of these problems in earlier mother-daughter dyads: May and Martha, Kate and Maureen, the survivor and Emily. The most recent dyad, Dorothy and Alice Mellings of *The Good Terrorist*, both reverses and sustains Lessing's earliest interpretation of the mother-daughter configuration. The rebellious, dependent daughter and the powerful mother are still there, but their psychic organization has undergone an ironic revolution. The daughter cannot escape her dependence, but the mother can. Dorothy abandons Alice instead of vice-versa. Furthermore, the mother figure is wholly sympathetic and the daughter figure wholly unsympathetic.

The temporal angst located in the mother-daughter relationship seems especially acute in the figures of Martha and May Quest in *The Four-Gated City* and in Jane Somers and Maudie Fowler in *The Diary of a Good Neighbour*. The angst in *The Making of the Representative for Planet 8* is related to the apparently unrelated earlier texts. The kinship between these temporal and transcendent novels asserts itself in unexpected ways.

Martha and May

Martha and May—the sounds of their names are close enough to suggest sisterhood and equality rather than the authority-dependency roles of the child-parent relationship. Both daughter and mother dread yet feel compelled to accomplish their final reunion in London. The novel is *The Four-Gated City*, the year approximately 1954; May is about sixty-four, Martha, thirty-five. May postpones her trip from Africa twice; Martha, terrified at the prospect of her mother's visit, turns in desperation to the medical establishment in the person of Dr. Lamb. Martha ironically perceives May's projected visit as an interruption of the excavation of her past that is her consuming project. That special excavation—Martha calls it "work"—is the indispensable precondition to mastery of the self. Martha makes no conscious connection between her interior analysis of the past and her mother's visit. The reader must make that connection and recognize a colossal irony: theoretical confrontation with the past is one thing, its materialization in the person of May Quest quite another. If the impending visit of mother to daughter can threaten breakdown and flight to the psychoanalyst, then Martha is still enslaved to her past and very far from the wholeness she so covets.

The central consciousness in The Four-Gated City and in its four predecessors is Martha Quest. There are times when that center shifts (as it does to Jimmy or to Mrs. Van in A Ripple from the Storm) or is diffused within a group of characters (as it is in the Aldermaston chapter of The Four-Gated City). But there is no shift so disruptive—even so violent, although the words and the scene are very quiet—in any of the novels as the one that transfers the point of view to May Quest in Cape Town in chapter 4, part 2, of The Four-Gated City. The omniscient opening line is a shock: "An old lady sat in a flower-crammed balcony high above the breathing sea" (247). The extraordinary narrative shift and the empathy displayed toward the lonely, limited, psychically imprisoned Mrs. Quest belong to the authorial voice, not to Martha Quest. It is a point of view brought in from outside as though the authorial voice were making up for what Martha cannot do. Its intrusion is so emphatic and disruptive that it proclaims an unresolved artistic problem and suggests an unresolved personal one.

May thinks more about her own girlhood than she does about Martha on her voyage to England. Her most haunting memory is of her first menses. Fittingly, that memory is triggered by a daughter figure aboard ship who bends over and dislodges and then tosses overboard "a little bloody swab." The generational contrast is painful. May remembers "a long story of humiliation and furtiveness, great soaking bloody clouts that rubbed and smelled, and which one was always secretly washing, or concealing, or trying to burn; headaches and backaches and all kinds of necessary tact with obtuse brothers and fathers; and then her breasts, her first sprouting breasts, about which the family had made jokes and she had blushed—but of course, had been a good sort" (268). May had earlier admired the athletic, healthy young woman of the 1950s, but her furtive act, occurring as if May were not present, and her casual remark, " 'Plenty of room in the sea' " (267), make May seethe, rage, suffer.

This episode and recall (probably a pastiche of her mother's stories and her own experiences) are typical of Lessing's immense sympathy with the older woman out of step with the mores of the younger generation. May Quest may not understand her subjections and her humiliations, but Lessing makes the reader understand them in ways that Martha cannot. Martha has typically taunted her mother with her sexuality and her intellect and will do so again both wittingly and unwittingly, affronting her with capacities traditionally denied to women, capacities May rejects in her daughter and in other women. Instead of criticizing Mrs. Quest for her obvious failures, as Martha has always done, Lessing makes the reader understand May's rage at having been cheated and her transference of that rage to the young woman and to Martha.

May's London visit is doomed to failure. Her racism, her anticommunism, her inability to understand Martha's sexual life with the man who is Lynda's husband in name only, make her do everything wrong. She cannot stop herself. Her reflex response of a lifetime—compulsive housecleaning—could not be more wrong. Martha's bottled rage and inability to act for herself sends her in turn to Dr. Lamb to act for her. He does Martha's dirty work. May returns home to wait for death, having been, in her last years, able to relate only to children—to white ones in England, black ones in Africa. Mrs. Quest does, in fact, as we later offhandedly learn, die less than a year later, an exemplar of Adrienne Rich's judgment that "the mother stands for the victim in ourselves, the unfree woman, the martyr" (Of Woman Born, 238). Mother and daughter are indeed, to use Rich's language, tragically lost to one another (240), unable to break the patterns of their shared past.

In 1958, when Martha is almost thirty-nine, she describes herself as a middle-aged woman, "a kind of special instrument sensitised to [the] mood and need and state" of each member of the family (352), "being the person who ran and managed and kept going" (354). She has become "her old antagonist, the competent middle-aged woman" (219), whom "she hated and feared more than any other" (360). Like Susan Rawlings of "To Room Nineteen," she looks forward to time alone; unlike Susan, she doesn't have to leave home to begin to understand her quest. (She discovers it through Lynda Coldridge in the basement rooms of the Coldridge house.) Later Martha graduates to her own room in the house of one of her nonbiological sons. Martha's relationship with her large, non-kin brood—one more like a commune than family—makes her movement in and out of the family more possible and less filled with anger and resentment than in her earlier kinship families. These, the one she is born into and the ones she makes by her own two marriages, are failures. They crack under strain. They lack the organic quality of the Coldridge house and brood, which are like the tree outside Martha's window in their ability to grow and change.

The double ending of The Four-Gated City needs to be insisted upon. The appendix should be kept separate from the novel proper. Martha's old age and death are reported in the appendix indirectly and fitfully in part of a letter written to Francis Coldridge in 1997. In it Martha says without anxiety or regret that she will die next winter. Her abilities as a "seer" and "hearer" enable her to know how and when she will die. The psychological meaning of her special knowledge has a sharp ironic edge, for ordinary humans have no foreknowledge of the time of their death. Such foreknowledge signifies exceptional power; it is a form of control denied to the rest of us. This element of control can be described as the underside of the calm readiness that defines Martha's acceptance of death. May Quest could not have gone quietly to her death. She had no knowledge and no power.

Martha's new community of all ages and colors is quite different from the communities Francis and Mark Coldridge manage. Their communities are, in essential ways, clones of our own, replete with corruption, mistrust, rigidities. Only racism seems significantly reduced in the post-Catastrophe world. The painful point is that there is no utopia after this catastrophe or any other catastrophe. The four-gated city belongs to the future. Martha's pastoral island community is exceptional and temporary, for after her death the outside world finds Faris and disperses its members.

Martha dies on an island community poor in material things but rich in survival and communal skills. In retrospect, the Coldridge household seems a fit preparation for Martha's post-holocaust collective. The little community on the island of Faris, north of Scotland, is the closest candidate for the ideal community—it is pointedly and significantly not a city—in all of Lessing's fiction until Lessing constructs her Canopean cities, which are, like her four-gated cities, mythic rather than actual. No one on Faris is marginal or nonfunctional. Martha shares her learning, her accumulated wisdom, with her peers and the younger members of her collective. The Faris community functions much like Francis's earliest commune, without rules yet with unstated understanding of communal roles and values. In a community brought together by the right shared ideology, aging seems to present no dangers. On Faris Martha escapes "the tyranny of the family" and the obsolescence of the elderly. In her old age, the time of her life that should be, as the clichés of our youth culture would have it, arid, imprisoned, and isolated, Martha is paradoxically freer than she has ever been, although she continues to perform typically female caretaker roles.

Janna and Maudie

Martha's idealized aging rewrites the kind of aging her mother experienced. It occurs in another world. The aging women in *The Diary of a Good Neighbour*, the first of the two novels in *The Diaries of Jane Somers*, belong to the Euroamerican world of today. (The second novel, *If the Old Could . . .*, belongs to the genre of self-parody.) They enter our consciousness through the remove of the newspaper headline and the television newscast. We see them, but we do not see them. Still, they are a presence. They are there, aggressively asserting their kinship to the Martha we knew before the appendix to *The Four-Gated City* shot her into the future. They share the twentieth-century world of war, poverty, racism, and madness that marks the *Children of Violence* series, although they come to fictional life later in time, directly after the five Canopus novels. Lessing's move from the world of Canopus to the world of Meals on Wheels represents a shocking reversal of gears. It's as though Lessing were saying to critics of the Canopus series: "You wanted me to go back to the 'real' world; well, here I am. Can you take it?"

The specific private failures that haunt Janna may well have haunted Lessing. Janna was unable to give solace to her dying mother and her dying husband. Martha Quest knows that sending her mother back to Africa will significantly shorten her life. She chooses to save herself rather than be kind to her mother. Martha never looks at her guilt; Janna, so to speak, does it for her. It seems reasonable to postulate that the death of Lessing's second husband deepened her already deepening concern with aging and death. (Peter Lessing, their son, was still living with his mother.) Furthermore, the manner of his death must have been a shock, for in 1979 Gottfried Anton Lessing, then ambassador for the German Democratic Republic, was murdered by Tanzanian troops in Uganda "while supporting, in accordance with official policy, Idi Amin."[1] It is reasonable to think that Janna's need to come to terms with her guilt about her failures of feeling and behavior toward her mother and her husband represents in part a distancing of Lessing's response to the deaths of her own mother and husband. These biographical parallels are in the background, as participants in the genesis of *Diaries* and Canopus.

Jane Somers, familiarly known as Janna, is a woman in need. Her perfectly groomed exterior hides an existential emptiness and guilt whose exorcism is the subject of the novel. The editor of a woman's magazine called *Lilith* (compare the name with *Home and Hearth*, the magazine Ella writes for in the Yellow Notebook—these names simultaneously suggest and parody the homebound 1950s woman and the feminist 1980s woman), Janna is also a successful romantic novelist and serious sociologist. She cannot manage life without daily baths and elegant clothing. Her glossy life-style jostles violently against the realities of Maudie Fowler's life. Maudie, over ninety, poor, alone, incontinent, dirty, is wholly dependent on the bureaucracy that has created Home Help, Meals on Wheels, and Good Neighbours. This Maudie, whose bodily deterioration is a constant affront, becomes Janna's living hairshirt.

The Janna-Maudie relationship revises earlier mother-daughter relationships. In this version of that key relationship the daughter has all the power. Janna wants independence if not control even before she chooses Maudie. This is pointedly asserted when Janna rejects a relationship with her seventy-year-old neighbor, Mrs. Penny, because "she would take over my life" (11). Liking what she sees of Maudie at the chemist's shop, Janna follows her home; she decides when to visit and when not to visit, when to shop for Maudie, when to clean her body, her rooms, her clothing. She decides the terms of their conversations, asking Maudie to retrieve her past, to recollect and relive it—"For all the time I am trying to get her life mapped, dated" (101)—treating Maudie as a living artifact who can reveal and preserve a vanished way of life. Like other writers, Janna will use this material; Maudie's life as a milliner becomes part of Janna's novel, *The Milliners of Marylebone*. (Could this title be a deliberate and ironic recall of George Eliot's "mind and millinery species"?) Maudie is Janna's responsibility, not the reverse. Janna functions as Maudie's mother.

The popular description of old age as a second childhood accords with this description of role reversal. Maudie even physically resembles a young girl in some ways, most vividly in "her crotch like a little girl's, no hair" (127). Maudie also acts out. In her dependency and her histrionic flair she does seem more like Molly of *The Golden Notebook*, whereas Janna, who manages everything so well, seems more like Anna. Despite the age difference between them, Janna and Maudie do share qualities with these names and characters that go back over twenty years.

These aspects of their characters may make Lessing's prefatory remarks about the genesis of Janna more understandable. She does not say the obvious, that Maudie derives from Lessing's mother, Emily Maude McVeagh. She says instead that thinking "about what my mother would be like if she lived now: that practical, efficient, energetic woman," went into the making of Janna Somers (viii). Her silence about what went into the making and the naming of Maudie Fowler is conspicuous. Maudie, described as "a fierce angry old woman," has something in common with May Quest and Emily Maude McVeagh Tayler.

At least one other woman went into the character of Maudie, although Lessing credits her with affecting the making of *Making* and perversely leaves her out of the picture in her preface to *The Diaries*. This ninety-two-year-old friend took "a long cold time to die, and she was hungry too, for she was refusing to eat and drink, so as to hurry things along" (144). This friend is, therefore, a source for two very different kinds of novels.

In a 1985 talk in San Francisco Lessing was more open and more detailed about the sources of her Jane and Maudie figures than she is in her preface. Maudie comes from Lessing's experiences with the old and their social services. Jane has at least three sources. She is in part based on a friend insulated from suffering and poverty who "joined the human race" after the death of her husband; this woman "changed completely" after two or three years. Another source for Jane is an "extremely beautiful" woman friend obsessed with the need to present a perfectly groomed self. Another source is a friend who writes for a magazine. These three women (Lessing's mother is not mentioned) or "these ideas went to form Jane Somers, who is efficient, practical, obsessively tidy, orderly, rather conservative, and to whom the darker sides of life come as a continual surprise" ("Doris Lessing Talks about Jane Somers," 5).[2]

Janna, functioning as both mother and daughter to Maudie, also has two sister selves, Joyce, her other self at Lilith, and Georgie, her biological sister. When yet another J figure is introduced in the person of Janna's niece Jill, the effect is almost comical. (The J's proliferate as Janna's family name turns out to be James, and Joyce is married to Jack.) Janna mediates between two generations, one quite young, the other quite old, as mentor to Jill and caretaker to Maudie. Her sister selves seem to be divided into stereotypical roles; Georgie has the children, Joyce the career. Joyce is, however, a more complicated figure, for she fights to keep her husband from leaving her for his younger mistress. Part of this fight involves giving up her job with Lilith to accompany her husband to America. Janna chose to have neither children nor an emotionally close relationship with her husband, Freddie.

Another aspect of the naming strategies in this novel almost acquires the status of an in-joke. The Lilith staff debates whether Lilith is right for the girl of "the difficult, anxious eighties." The name Martha is proposed: "Arguments for Martha. We need something more workaday, less of an incitement to envy, an image of willing, adaptable, intelligent service" (140). As a description of Martha Quest, this is tongue-in-cheek, yet essentially accurate. It is harder, odder, or more amusing to read Lilith as a name that represents glamor. Perhaps the omission of Lilith's role as the wife in the attic, the wife who preceded Eve, is deliberate, even slyly comic. The name Lilith may sound glamorous because it is exotic; but in her person Lilith was in fact radically disobedient. Or is that part of the comedy?

The name Lilith remains on the masthead, but the magazine changes. Under Janna's leadership, it begins to have articles about aged women, about alcoholism and other "hard" issues. The discarded Martha remains to amuse readers of the Martha Quest novels.

The world of Jane Somers is not a world concerned with transcendence or last things. Its discourse is not eschatological or religious. It is bare, flat, and without reverberation, yet Janna's relationship with Maudie vibrates with "higher" meanings, for Janna wants to do good and to be good; she wants to atone, to learn to feel, to give, and to love her fellow woman. Janna does change, but her changes are not dramatic. One could be cruel and say that instead of long soaks in her tub, she takes shorter ones and sometimes even skips a soak altogether. Her character, like the overall conception of the novel, has its parodic edge. Yet Janna does travel beyond dirt and smell to the person Maudie is, to the person she herself is.

Janna also learns to experience time differently, as the very young and the very old do. The examples are simple: sitting "on a wall, along a garden" watching birds, sitting at a café, looking, listening (165). This over-busy woman begins to experience pleasure. She can sit still; she no longer fears the old on streets or park benches; instead she waits "for when they trust me enough to tell me their tales, so full of history" (166). Janna can look past the physical impairment of others and understand the fragility of her own good health, of anyone's good health. She is another person, "not at all that Janna who refused to participate when her husband, her mother, were dying. I sit for hours near Maudie, ready to give what my mother, my husband, needed from me; my consciousness of what was happening, my participation in it" (218). The contrast with Martha Quest's behavior to May Quest is striking.

At ninety-two, Maudie still holds on to life—and to Janna. This "sullen, sulking furious old woman" is in constant rebellion against her physical destruction; she rages in her way against the ravages of time. To Janna, "her hand nevertheless speaks the language of our friendship" (220). Her bravery and her spirit of independence are remarkable. She is one of the futures Martha Quest might have had; she is a Lilith figure.

Janna does not abandon her; she stays with Maudie until she dies, for death is an end in this novel. There is no afterlife. Janna will, like Martha Quest and Anna Wulf, go on. Her newfound saintly/secular vocation as a good neighbor, not a Good Neighbour, will not end with Maudie's death. Some Lessing readers thought that Jane Somers was a social worker like themselves ("Doris Lessing Talks about Jane Somers," 4). This aspect of Jane Somers recalls Anna Wulf's years of nonprofessional mediation before she de-

cides, at the end of *The Golden Notebook*, to become a marriage counselor. In her self-appointed selfish/selfless role, Janna will befriend
other old women, probably Annie and Eliza, whose names, like
Maudie's, repeat earlier Lessing names. These repetitions are one
expression of the inevitability, perhaps even the desirability, of circularity in fiction and in life.

Alsi and the Representative(s)

The word "good" is not used ambiguously or ironically for Janna/
Jane Somers as it is for Alice Mellings of *The Good Terrorist*. But the
word is oddly redolent; it gives to these flatly realistic, often banal,
novels a hint of Lessing's larger moral and religious concerns, concerns she can bring to the surface more directly, more fully, and
more openly in her Canopus novels. *The Making of the Representative*
can be described as her most devotional novel as well as her most
eschatological one. It is a contemporary version of Job's struggle to
understand apparently arbitrary affliction. Lessing's parable transfers individual struggle to a planetary theater. Its parable elements
pointedly relate it to the second novel in the Canopus series, *The
Marriages between Zones Three, Four, and Five*, as Betsy Draine has co-
gently argued. The two are almost mirror images of one another,
Marriages being "light, warmth and optimism" and *Making* "dark,
cold, and pessimism" (Draine, *Substance under Pressure*, 174). The subject matter and time of composition also relate *Making* to the Jane
Somers novels in a different way. Both are concerned with last
things.

Making is "more elegiac than political," as one reviewer describes
it, only if political is narrowly defined (Lehmann-Haupt, 25). It is
certainly doctrinal. The elegiac tone is firmly grounded in a Canopean doctrine whose essentials exist in many religions.

Planet 8 is a lovely planet, almost as favored as Rohanda (Earth)
was before its fall. It has never known crime or winter or poverty. It
has been a model planet in complete harmony with its Canopean
mentors. It has been obedient and devout. Canopus descends and
tells the Planet 8 population that it must build a wall around the
planetary circumference. The people cannot comprehend its function: "A wall. A great black shining wall. A *useless* wall" (4). Yet Planet
8 performs its duty. The building of the wall takes the communal

effort of generations, almost as though it were a medieval cathedral. Doeg, the narrator, was an infant when its construction began. The gradual transformation of Planet 8 and its inhabitants that follows is existentially haunting. Temperate climate disappears; ice, snow, and darkness define the new dispensation; theft and murder destroy the Eden that was. At first the wall does hold back the snow and Canopus does airlift food and promise to airlift the population elsewhere at a later time, a not unreasonable solution, since Canopus is always busily shifting populations from planet to planet as part of its mysterious long-range plan for genetic improvement of the galaxy. The Planet 8 population is itself a product of such genetic manipulation; it is a mix descended from native and imported peoples from different planets.

Something goes wrong; Canopus cannot say what. It can only reveal itself as capable of error, as subject to another, greater power. Or is Canopus not entirely truthful? Does it participate in setting up the destruction of Planet 8 as a test of the devotion of its inhabitants? The apparently arbitrary suffering and destruction of the planet and its people inexorably proceed. The "benign" imperialism (Parrinder, 9) of Canopus proceeds on its malignant way. ("Our populations felt as if they were being punished . . . yet they had done no wrong" [36].) Those who survive long marches, starvation, unbearable cold, and premature aging achieve a final transcendence which suggests that all their trials have been stages in mystical experience. In effect, they become one with the cosmos. Doeg, Alsi, Marl, Masson, Klin, Bratch, Pedug, Rivalin—even Johor, the Canopean agent who has remained to share their suffering—break into molecular matter as Charles Watkins of *Briefing* yearned to do, as the survivor and Emily of *Memoirs* in effect do when they walk through their wall. Lynda and Mark were their predecessors; their efforts to break through four walls cannot quite be defined as a desire to break through the wall of phenomenality, but in their novel, *The Four-Gated City*, the compulsion to break boundaries does undergo a qualitative leap. It is fair to say that the desire to break through the boundaries of matter has been in Lessing's fiction for a long time, at least since 1969, and that this breakthrough has been most obviously demonstrated in *Memoirs of a Survivor* and in *Making*.

Another way to describe the explosion of the inhabitants of Planet 8 into the cosmos is to say that its "we-ness" at that point reaches its apogee. Johor has flatly announced, "You will not die out" (16), but he does not, of course, say what form the life of the people will take. Later, he says, changing yet imitating Genesis, you will return to the light (not to the dust) from which you came (59). The inhabitants have already traveled far toward we-ness when we meet them. They are all functional creatures. Doeg, the narrator, is the Memory Maker and Keeper of Records; Marl, the Keeper of the Herds; Bratch, the Physician; Klin, the Fruit Maker; Rivalin, the Guardian of the Lakes; and so on. These functions are not necessarily permanent, although Doeg feels that he is always essentially Doeg: "Though I have been Klin and Marl and Pedug and Masson, when needed. But Doeg is my nature, I suppose" (55). There are other Doegs as there were other Ambiens. When Klin, Marl, and Doeg return from a reconnaissance trip to Planet 10, "we were all Doeg" (54). At one point in the narrative three Marls appear.

Characters who duplicate each other, who "'break down' into each other, into other people," are not new in Lessing's fiction, as I have been arguing throughout this study (see the preface to The Golden Notebook, vii). In Making, shifting, multiple selves have become totally positive. The new element is the identification of the selves with a particular skill, as though we are all potentially poets, herdsmen, doctors, and farmers and can call these selves into existence when they are needed. The Martha Quest who picks at the thirteen layers of wallpaper she finds in a bombed-out house in postwar London announces personality as a thing of layers rather than fragments. In Making, societal mores encourage every inhabitant to become a layered entity. If there could be a deviant on Planet 8 in its Edenic phase, he would be a single personality.

Only Alsi's name does not stand for a function, probably because she is too young to have acquired a function. That Alsi (another Alis/Alice?) is the only woman among the several Representatives who are to become the single Representative is a shock for a number of reasons. That she is both the only woman and the only person without a functional name at the final transcendence is disturbing—especially since Lessing takes the trouble to note that the Scott expedition of 1910–13, cited in the afterword as a major source for the novel, had no women. "At that time," she goes on, "the women who were demanding rights were being beaten by policemen, forcibly fed in prisons, derided and jeered at by fine gentlemen, generally ill-treated and often enough by other women. It was simply not possible for women to be on expeditions . . . the idea would not have surfaced" (132). Yet women longed to participate in exploration; Lessing cites letters between women of the period who knew they could "'be as brave and resourceful'" as men, of women who lamented their exclusion with "'the bitter tears of unused and patronised and frustrated women'" (132). Lessing further notes that even the "frieze or backdrop" of women "—no, ladies—who stood elegantly about in their drooping fettering garments, smiling wistfully at these warriors of theirs ... did not always see things as their men did" (132). How remarkable that in dealing with a future society aeons away from our own, Lessing chose not to eradicate the exclusions of 1910–13. How remarkable that Lessing's sensitivity to these exclusions is recorded in an afterword and not in the novel proper. From this point of view Planet 8 seems atavistic rather than futurist.

Alsi begins and ends as a token woman even though she becomes a Doeg for a while. Her role as the keeper of the little snow animals who mysteriously and briefly come to life is more memorable than her stint as Doeg. Indeed, given the emphasis on interchanging and multiple personality in *Making*, the male character of the Representatives/Representative is overwhelming. Even the storyteller historian of Planet 8 is male, although he is imagined by a woman author.[3]

The concept of Representation is built into the social organization of Planet 8. Five Representatives govern the entire planet. But Representation means more than it does in our world; it seems to mean almost physical embodiment of those represented in the Five who represent. During one of his catechizing sessions with Doeg, Johor takes the planet's already far advanced we-ness to the point where Doeg, startled, asks: "'You cannot be saying to me that it does not matter if the populations of a whole planet have to die—a species?'" (55)—that is, can Representation be taken to the point where we shall continue to exist as some other form of matter even outside our planet? This concept goes far beyond the kind of essence in multiplicity that Doeg understands.

Doeg can speak of filling "a town with these variations of myself, then a city, then, in my mind, whole landscapes. Doeg, Doeg, Doeg again, and mentally I greeted these non-existent never-to-exist people ... all of whom resembled me more or less, closely or only slightly" (81). His words beautifully evoke the dense population of the artist's imagination, different yet overlapping, partaking of and dependent on the artist for existence, as much as they describe multiple existence. They validate the kind of repetition of names, characters, and events that Lessing's work demonstrates. Doeg is Doeg even though he has "used many names in my life" (81). Doeg, although I, is "the feeling of me that I share with my unknown friends, my other selves" (85). His words also give new shape to traditional mystical doctrines of the one and many.

Sometimes Representation becomes too narrowly, too simply, defined—when, for example, the change of name is merely a way of saying that for a brief time we change roles. When Alsi becomes Doeg, she takes "her turn to remember and to reproduce in words experiences that we all needed to have fixed and set so that our annals would be in order" (86). In the world of Planet 8, "we often enough changed our roles, did different kinds of work; becoming for those times the Representative for whatever it was that was needed" (86). So described, the change in personality seems superficial, too small to contain the larger metaphysical meanings and metaphors Lessing is reaching for. At these times, the proverbial change of hats would do as well as a name change.

Lessing's claim that her ninety-two-year-old friend went into the novel has a more specific referent than the general one that the friend and the novel were both confronting aging, suffering, and dying. Alsi, the only woman in the novel, is also the only figure to display the aging process that we are told all Planet 8 inhabitants are experiencing. She looks down at her body beneath the numberless layers that cover it to see "her rib cage, with the yellow skin stretched tight over it, each bone evident and—where were her breasts?" (88). She probes lower to find "two skinny bags depended, and these bags ended in small hard lumps, and on the skin that held the lumps were brown wrinkles—her nipples" (88). She becomes a kind of totemic figure as Doeg and Johor look at "the old, very old woman's body, shrivelled by starvation, . . . displayed there before us, . . . her face . . . bare to us—gaunt, sallow, with sunken black eyes" (88).

Surely this Alsi is Maudie. The specifics of her description belong to Maudie; they leap out of the page, the only nakedness Lessing chooses to reveal. If this connection is accepted, then the names, with their A/M pattern, leap out in another way, as versions of the first use of A and M introduced so many years ago in *Martha Quest* in the figures of Alfred and May Quest, who are repeated in the many female/female and female/male pairs: Martha/Marnie/Maisie/Alice/Marjorie; Martha/Anderson/Adolph/Anton; Anna/Molly/Mark; Al·Ith/Murti·; and so forth. The names of Marl and Masson also belong to this constellation. Names like Bratch, Pedug, and Rivalin are probably concoctions made to sound deliberately strange in the traditions of science fiction. Doeg is different; his is an Old Testament name, belonging to the Edomite chief of Saul's herdsmen who slaughtered eighty-five priests of Nob at Saul's command (1 Sam. 21–22). The parallels with Lessing's Doeg are sufficient to establish his ironic kinship with the biblical Doeg.

Another interesting fact about Alsi is that despite her aged body, "the hollows near the sockets" of her eyes show "vulnerability, something still fresh and youthful" (88). So Alsi seems to be simultaneously both a young girl and an old woman, experiencing that division differently yet in the same way as ordinary mortal women (like May Quest, for example), who find their old bodies in the mirror incompatible with their inner ageless selves.

Alsi's double self suggests another hypothesis. The two parts that constitute Alsi might also have been placed in different bodies, in the bodies we know as Janna and Maudie of *The Diary of a Good Neighbour*. Jane's nickname of Janna only slightly disguises her Anna name, confirming what is clear from her characterization, that she is both the independent *A* female and the *J* child. Thus Alsi resurfaces in somewhat different form in the mother and daughter figures in *Diary*, repeating and altering her character as it reappears in both Janna and Maudie. She does what the people of Planet 8 and its artists do all the time. Lessing functions like Doeg—making, repeating, participating in her creations. Of course, she also disguises and riddles. Her extraliterary hints about the creation of Maudie are in *Making*, not in the novel in which she appears. Her information that Janna is in part based on her mother is not very convincing; it is more convincing to see Janna as a piece of her own self made somewhat younger, as Lessing has often made characters based on her own life.

If the structure of *Marriages* can be described as mimicking "stages of consciousness" (Draine, *Substance under Pressure*, 143–44), then *Making* can be described as mimicking stages of mystical experience. By the end of the novel, Doeg and his people have an extraordinary experience of transcendence. They do not become, like shamans, "specialists in ecstasy" (Eliade, *Myths*, 73), but their single and final experience of ecstasy is unmistakably the apogee of mystical transport. Perhaps it is the unknowable and untranslatable experience that awaits Al·Ith of *Marriages* when or if she reaches Zone One. The Representative can also be described as having undergone "the symbolic return to chaos [that] is indispensable to any new creation" (Eliade, *Myths*, 80). Ecstasy, chaos, and death become almost interchangeable events; in Mircea Eliade's words, "Every 'trance' is another 'death' during which the soul leaves the body and voyages into all the cosmic regions" (*Memories*, 96). In *Making* the body is not left behind; it voyages with the soul. Death does indeed become the ultimate rite of passage (Eliade, *Myths*, 226).

Katherine Fishburn defines the mystical center of *Making* as peculiarly Eastern (Sufi primarily); she daringly argues that the novel must be seen through "the double lens of particle physics and Eastern mysticism" (122). Doeg's vocabulary does make this approach persuasive; words like "pulses," "atom," "molecules," and even "atomic structure" recur during the final explosion of body into cosmos. Furthermore, Lessing has elsewhere (in the preface to *The Sirian Experiments*, for example) indicated her attraction to the romance of the new physics, especially to its extraordinary vocabulary:

> What *of course* I would like to be writing is the story of the
> Red and White Dwarves and their Remembering Mirror, their
> space rocket (powered by anti-gravity), their attendant entities
> Hadron, Gluon, Pion, Lepton, and Muon, and the Charmed
> Quarks and the Coloured Quarks.
> But we can't all be physicists. [ix]

The new physics may finally be more a graft than an essence in *Making*, but its presence is unmistakably there to buttress older mystical thought and to give it new metaphors.

Let me add another suggestion, one that coexists with rather than excludes the other strands of Lessing's thought and strategies. The concept of the double has been considered both a protection against the fear of death and a sign of the fear of death. This apparent contradiction distinguishes all discourse about the phenomenon. The double appears to be at once one thing and its other. For one recent commentator, doubles fictions "impart experiences of duplication, division, dispersal, abeyance" (Karl Miller, 25). If this interpretation is accepted, the dispersal at the end of *Making* is as much a part of Lessing's doubles talk as her division of opposites and similars into figures like Alsi young and Alsi old, Janna and Maudie, or Martha and May Quest. The protean potential of doubling is amply demonstrated in *Making* and *The Diaries*, as it is in Lessing's entire body of work.[4]

Perhaps guilt is the shape goodness takes in the Martha/May dialectic. The Martha Quest novels were framed outside an ethos that considers questions of the good in traditional religious terms, but if we think of guilt as the negative pole of an ideal of filial and other behavior, then goodness is also at issue in the Martha Quest novels. The shift to direct confrontation with the question of goodness is a feature of Lessing's later novels. That question, applied on a galactic stage, is framed in religious, species terms that only temporarily or superficially resolve problems of mothers, daughters, and aging. These problems resurface in the Somers novels and in *The Good Terrorist*.

Making succeeds despite its central belief in obedience, a belief Lessing had constantly questioned when her gods were Marxist. Coming to terms with undeserved punishment is the framework of her latest parable, one inconceivable to the adolescent Lessing, who rejected her mother's adulation of one of the heroically fallen members of the Scott expedition with the wonderfully astringent retort, " 'But what else could he have done? And anyway, they were all in the dying business'" (afterword, 125). Now an older Lessing has become a reverent explorer of "the dying business."

"The dying business" as it is imagined in *Making* removes women from the center of Lessing's narrative. Yet women erupt even within this male-centered eschatological meditation. Their bodies force themselves into the narrative. Alsi's body, like Maudie's or May's or the young Martha's, acquires a haunting particularity rarely achieved or even sought for in the Canopean novels. Thus, though the mother/daughter dialectic appears to be buried or absent in *Making*, it is still there and still connected with questions of aging and dying. Lessing's mirror imperatives still display themselves in this novel about transcendence. Lessing need not envy the imaginative freedom of the new physics, for she has, in her novels about the aging and dying of mothers and daughters, created her own remembering mirrors.

Part III
Colonialism In and Out of Space

7

Radical Politics:
A Ripple from the Storm (1958)

The title *A Ripple from the Storm* has its double meanings, as do all the Martha Quest titles save the first. Its two-year time span is the briefest of the first four novels and contrasts sharply with the twenty-year time span permitted in *The Four-Gated City* (fifty if the appendix is added on). Yet *Ripple*, like *The Four-Gated City*, may be described as having a collective protagonist. The large cast of characters and the especial focus on Martha's left group recall the Coldridge household and, of course, the African group in the Black Notebook sections of *The Golden Notebook*, as well as the Sherban household in *Shikasta*. These two most densely packed years of Martha's political life, approximately 1941–43, coincide with the fiercest fighting on the Russian front during World War II and the turning back of the Germans from Stalingrad (renamed Volgograd in 1961) in February 1943, an event that marked the turning point of the war in Europe.

The storm in the title refers to the war as well as to the actual storm at the end of the novel. Zambesia is one ripple from the violence of the war. The title suggests both Zambesia's distance from major world events and its inescapable relation to those events. The title also refers to Martha's sense of being cut off from the "real" events of the world, her own sense of exile from history. The title of the next volume in the series, *Landlocked*, emphasizes in another way the limits of the country and the individual it imprisons. A waiting novel filled with love and death, *Landlocked* is also filled with the acceptance of feeling that the Martha of *Ripple* perversely continues to sabotage. *Landlocked* portrays Martha's withdrawal from the political immersion so total in *Ripple*. The first two novels in the series have a similar immersion/withdrawal rhythm:

in them Martha separates first from the family she was born into, then from the one she makes by marriage.

Many readers think of *Ripple* as a novel whose "narrative content embraces what seems like one endless Communist meeting" (Rubenstein, *Novelistic Vision*, 57). *Ripple* is, on the contrary, a superb political novel, an exploration at once satirical and painful of the contradiction between the surfaces of political discourse and the realities of political manipulation, between actual agendas and hidden agendas. The liberal, labor, and Communist meetings are significantly differentiated to exhibit power groups in conflict with themselves and others. Furthermore, the major political issues in the novel are not war and socialism, which seem uppermost to the group, but racism and sexism. The politics of race and sex are in fact anatomized in this novel as they are nowhere else in Lessing's novels.

The division between what seems and what is is wide and deep and painful in this novel. Martha's busy, sleepless life hides a misery only illness and dreams uncover on occasion. Her double life is not like Mrs. Van's consciously chosen double life, without which Mrs. Van could not have transcended traditional female roles. Martha, who thinks she is free and undivided, a unified woman who is both personally and politically radical, is more divided than ever and in the narrowest cage she has ever known by the end of the novel.

She has no inner measure. She feverishly checks herself against others, particularly against her most important "others," Maisie and Marjorie. These three M women recall the tripling in *A Proper Marriage*, where Martha, Stella, and Alice marry and have their first children at approximately the same time. The pairs Martha/Anton, Maisie/Andrew, and Marjorie/Colin (Maisie/Athen are a recessive fourth pair who succeed Maisie/Andrew) recall Martha/Douglas, Stella/Andrew, and Alice/Willie of the preceding novel. Anton, Andrew, and Athen are set against each other, while the women present cooperative rather than combative selves. These projections of the primary selves are signaled by Lessing's continued use of the A/M naming pattern initiated in the first two Martha Quest novels.

There are no antifictions in *Ripple* but other familiar Lessing patterns display themselves. The natural world proclaims its power even amid the urban claustrophobia of *Ripple*, as the actual storm in the title coincides with the group's disintegration. Like dreams, the storm as fact and symbol insists on erupting suppressed matter.

Nor can the dream of the ideal city be entirely suppressed. It breaks through the frantic, cluttered surface of Ripple to announce its presence and endurance. Thus Lessing bends the repetitive motifs and strategies of the earlier Martha Quest novels to this one: double and multiple selves intertwine with her unique naming pattern, for example. The human interaction with elemental natural facts is effectively reimagined. Echoic private dreams and the public dream of an ideal city persist beneath an inhospitable life-style.

Personal and political destinies in Ripple are densely interwoven despite the surface orthodoxy that Communists have no personal lives, that "a Communist must consider himself a dead man on leave" (30), as Anton says and Martha echoes. The opening epigraph, from Louis Aragon, a heroic figure for literary Communists, aptly captures the emotional tenor of the novel: "There is no passion for the absolute without the accompanying frenzy of the absolute." The interdependence of political passion and political frenzy is brilliantly uncovered in this much-undervalued novel.

The issue of the African Branch is the single significant political issue in the novel, and as postwar politics have taught the world community, what may have seemed to many a ripple, or local, issue is central and worldwide. Every other educational or political effort in the novel is exposed as misconceived or irrelevant and comic: a class on education in the Soviet Union, the condition of miners in Wales, the necessity for a Second Front, classes on the history of the Communist party of the Soviet Union, and—the ultimate absurdity—the furious debate over the details of a 150-page blueprint for the upcoming Communist rule of Zambesia. The jargon is grotesque. Only sections of The Golden Notebook rival Lessing's anatomy of left jargon in this novel. (The Sentimental Agents is simply not in the running.) Three meetings and a trial structure the novel. The opening Help Save Our Allies meeting shows Communist tactics in a popular-front organization. Lessing skillfully leads the novel toward the climactic Social Democratic meeting at which the African Branch issue is fully aired. This meeting and Jack Dobie's libel trial, which follows it, deserve to be compared with the trial of the white race in Shikasta. The group meeting that closes the novel is short and parodic, defining with its remaining three members the absurdity of Communist power at that time in what was then Southern Rhodesia.

Let us consider the African Branch issue.[1] An all-white labor or

Social Democratic party appears to be debating the nature of black participation in their unions. The fact that African participation should exist seems axiomatic. That theoretical position can be implemented in one of two ways. Labor can go for an integrated or a segregated black membership. The right wing of the Social Democratic party, led by Mr. McFarline—the man who made sexual advances to the teenage Martha—who is now still unmarried and still populating his compound with his half-caste children, insists that a segregated African Branch is undemocratic. His faction proposes the integration of Africans into the party. The other wing, led by Mrs. Van, proposes an African Branch as the only way to achieve black participation in a racist colony.

Communist theory and practical politics collide, as the innocent Tommy Brown sees. He cannot understand how Communists can support a segregationist position; at the same time he knows his upbringing will make it impossible for him to accept blacks as political equals. Mrs. Van observes that keeping blacks out has kept blacks unskilled and differentially paid. Such disparity might have been mitigated, if not avoided, she argues, had the trade unions accepted African Branches years ago. The leader of the six new members present, the swing vote, votes for the African Branch on the ground that, although undemocratic, it is practical. Integration, he asserts, will eliminate black participation entirely. He has put the grotesque paradox of the African Branch issue squarely and made clear why the Communists are supporting Mrs. Van. However, the leader of the six is sorry the issue ever arose. His quirky stand is later followed by his questioning of Jack Dobie and Johnny Lindsay for accepting Communist support. Mrs. Van wins her battle but loses the war, for the question of Communist support destroys her political career, makes the aging and ill Johnny Lindsay suffer, and loses Jack Dobie a union election. The issue of Communist support also leads to the newspaper attack on Jack Dobie that is the occasion for the farcical libel trial he also loses.

These complex political strands in all their paradoxicality are effectively ordered. The major paradox, that right-wing labor is for integration and Communists and left labor for segregation, could not be more outrageous. The practical politics of this issue require those who oppose segregation to support it.

Mr. Matushi and two other blacks sit through the discussion hearing themselves contradictorily described as either dangerous or childlike and unfit for political participation on either ground. Once the blacks leave, the talk gets "freer," meaning more openly racist. The meaning of "freer" in this context rings its paradoxical message loudly for the reader. The issue of the African Branch splinters the Social Democratic party, for after the African Branch is voted in, the opposition splits off to proclaim a lily-white entity called the Labour party. Both segments of course continue to claim a commitment to socialism.

What Lenin and Marxists called "the woman question" does not tear the party apart, but the sexism of socialists, Communists, and black males is fully and specifically exposed in *Ripple*. It is an issue as crucial as the African Branch issue, although more subterranean and not an action question on anyone's agenda. It cuts across color and party lines.

The feminism in this volume is forthright. Readers acquainted with Lessing's later frequent defensiveness about feminism may be surprised at Martha's awareness of the similarity between her bourgeois first husband, Douglas Knowell, and her Communist lover William Brown: "for a few moments, she had seen the men as one, and identical with the pompous, hypocritical and essentially male fabric of society" (19). Her observation is phrased in terms very like Virginia Woolf's. It is also another example of Lessing's ability to see correspondence between seeming opposites.

"The woman question" does come up at a left group self-criticism meeting. The atmosphere is absurdist: members asked to testify against each other's failings hear Jimmy Jones complain about women comrades wearing lipstick and nail polish. His question is somewhat dignified by Anton, the chair, who translates it into "the woman question." Martha approves of Anton's gesture but finds that it contradicts his treatment of his mistress, Toni Mandel, "the Austrian woman." Jasmine is defiant: "'I personally consider that all men, whether Communist or not, have remnants in them of middle-class ideas about women. Even Lenin. Even Lenin talked about greasy glasses'" (122). This "inner" meeting precedes two public "outer" meetings—the meeting in the Location, the first ever to bring black and white together, and the one following the executive committee discussion of the African Branch issue—at which supposedly liberated men expose their unliberated attitudes toward women.

At the Location meeting, pamphlets relating to women are untouched by black males. There are, of course, no black women present, as Mrs. Van energetically reminds her almost entirely black male audience. When Marie du Preez is as usual interrupted by her husband while she is addressing the meeting, she responds: "'Men! If there's one thing that teaches me there's no such thing as colour, [it] is that men are men, black and white'" (186). When Piet du Preez's response is laughter, the men take their cue from him. As at the Communist meeting, the men turn feminist issues into a joke. Marie goes on to express the hope that African women will start a movement of their own.

When the executive committee of the Social Democratic party concludes at midnight, with the McFarline faction temporarily defeated, McFarline says, so that Mrs. Van can overhear, that if she were "'the last woman left alive in the world he couldn't bring himself to f—— her'" (247). He raises his voice and continues his assault: "'Mrs. Van's without c—— or t—— for me and that's the truth'" (247). Soon another man says, "'If it's Communism to expect a woman who should be in bed to sit up at meetings till all hours in all this smoke and bad air, then Communism is not for me'" (247). Marjorie's normally "impulsive charm" is thoroughly eroded as she explodes: "'As far as I can see when we get socialism we'll have to fight another revolution against men'" (247). Colin, her husband, has that day told her he does not believe in women working after marriage. At different points in the novel Andrew and Anton join Colin in saying they do not want their wives, Maisie and Martha, working after marriage.

Professions of dedication to equality do not, for these men, contradict their private patriarchal behavior patterns. This "savage discrepancy," a phrase used to describe Martha in *Martha Quest* (72), fully applies to the complex of political and private intertwinings in *Ripple*. The discrepancy is the more savage as more characters, Martha herself and others, and especially the author-observer, openly point out its existence. Although the Communists and Mrs. Van and her followers should and do support an African Branch, somewhere Tommy Brown's innocent question is heard: How can socialists support segregation? Human realities constantly collide with and undercut ideals. How can McFarline and Anton be called socialists when their everyday life exploits women? Martha's awareness of discrepancy governs the novel. The political fights contain and illustrate personal discrepancy somewhat at a remove; the private lives contain and illustrate political discrepancy somewhat at a remove. Politics has a private dimension; private life has a political dimension.

The portraits of the group are so rich that it is tempting to think of *Ripple* as a collective Bildungsroman. (Perhaps the term, already applied to *The Four-Gated City*, belongs to the entire *Children of Violence* series.)[2] There are the Communist women: Martha, Marjorie, Maisie, Marie, Jasmine; the men: Anton Hesse, Andrew McGrew, Athen, and the more minor Colin, Piet, William Brown, Jackie Bolton, Tommy, Murdoch Mathews, Jimmy Jones; the older-generation Social Democrats: Mrs. Van, Johnny Lindsay, Jack Dobie, McFarline; the bourgeois parental figures: Maynard and his wife, Myra, Alfred and May Quest; the blacks: Elias Phiri, Mr. Matushi. The recessive blacks of the preceding novels here acquire a public political dimension, a dimension of possibility. They are, of course, still recessive; the novel is still a white novel. There are two heroic figures, Mrs. Van and Athen. Only Mrs. Van is given a credible past; we must assume that if Athen were given a detailed past, even he would have agonies and compromises comparable to Mrs. Van's.

Martha is the primary woman, Anton the primary man. "Savage discrepancy" does not overstate the gulf between what they want to be and what they are, between what they profess and what they do. Martha, measuring herself against other women, primarily against Maisie and Marjorie, asks herself as she notes Marjorie's dry, humorous tones in her own voice, "Why is it I listen for the echoes of other people in my voice and what I do all the time?" (260). When she becomes a couple with Anton, she measures the married Martha/Anton against other marrieds—Maisie/Andrew, Marjorie/Colin—and sometimes against the unmarried Maisie/Athen. She measures Anton against Andrew, Anton against Athen. These measurings are not ordinary measurings; they are signs of Martha's acute dissatisfaction with herself and her need for a model. Near the end of the novel, she laments, "The fact is, I'm not a person at all, I'm nothing yet—perhaps I never will be" (260).

Being a person is tied up with being a socialist and an individual within a group. No previous group has so fully and so intensely enlisted Martha's loyalties, not the family she was born into, not the Club, not the family she formed by her first marriage. Her loyalty to the group's principles and its life-style is heightened by the fact of war. Without the war, Martha would have had almost no contact with anyone outside Zambesia. The war brings men from the "storm," from various classes and countries—British airmen, Anton from Germany, Athen from Greece, later Thomas Stern from Poland and Israel—and an unheard-of receptivity to Soviet life and ideals. This receptivity explains Mrs. Van's willingness to accept Communist assistance and also accounts for the existence of many fringe organizations like Help Save Our Allies and Sympathizers of Russia. Yes, "the glories of Stalingrad had created inexhaustible stores of good will" (40) that will totally dissipate after the war. McGrath's ballroom, earlier the center of bourgeois frivolity, is now the center of left-wing solemnity in the form of political mass meetings.

Martha's loyalty to the group is deep and total. She is "conscious that the moment she left the group she felt as let down as if a physical support had been removed" (18). Outside criticism does not touch her because she feels "invisible to anyone but the group" (19). Once up until three or four in the morning dancing and drinking, she is now up until three or four at political meetings. Her work at the law office is barely mentioned, yet she is holding down a full-time job there and at the same time serving in various capacities in several organizations, in one of which she is responsible for the distribution (once the able Jasmine's job) of The Watchdog, the Communist newspaper published in Johannesburg.

The group is mother, father, sister, brother, children. Martha sees her father once in the novel, accidentally on the street. Mrs. Quest appears at rare ritual occasions, when Martha is ill, when she marries. (Her brother is an unreal, rarely present standard Mrs. Quest uses against Martha.) Lessing's realism is, of course, highly selective; she edits out material not in the forefront of Martha's consciousness—job and family, for example. Only Caroline can break through the surface of Martha's mind and that only at night, when Martha's wind-up behavior is wound down. Martha longs for her daughter, yet she consciously submerges her longing and her guilt, sternly pushing Caroline into "a region of her mind marked No Admittance. Yet as soon as she slept, Caroline emerged from this forbidden place and confronted Martha" (90).

Thus, beneath her frantic activity, the Martha of Ripple is much more aware than she is usually thought to be. In Martha Quest she describes herself as "not observant" (96), but in Ripple she is very observant. Her critical intelligence is constantly at work decoding hidden political and personal agendas, reading body language, even noting the seeds of group division. These insights have a life of their own beneath Martha's other life, which is harried and hurried. Martha never sleeps enough or eats enough. She is constantly in motion, always impatient for the future, less alone than she was in her first collective, the family, yet "in a fever to be alone" (222).

Martha instinctively denies Anton's view that Communists should have no personal lives when she brings Maisie's "problem" to the group. The response to that problem is a litmus test for the group that only Anton fails. In Maisie's problem and its resolution, Lessing projects an effective counterpoint to Martha's relationship with Anton.

Pregnant by Binkie Maynard, Maisie asks magistrate Maynard to arrange compassionate leave so she and Binkie can marry. He refuses. (Later, he will arrange a leave for Binkie in order to destroy Maisie's marriage to Andrew.) Maisie, still indolent, apolitical, and "natural" rather than intellectual, agrees to accept an unwanted abortion but refuses Maynard's payoff. At the group meeting, Anton's barely disguised contempt for Maisie does not affect the sympathy of the others, including the young Royal Air Force (RAF) men. Andrew McGrew recalls a similar situation at home in Scotland, which was resolved when one of the town boys married the girl. In effect, he nominates himself.

Andrew and Maisie are immediately attracted; they marry and love each other in a way that is a model to the group. When Athen, the storybook Greek partisan, hears of this act, he applauds it as socialist behavior. Only someone with Athen's impeccable credentials as a fighter for liberation from the Nazis could so commandingly counteract Anton's jabs at everyone else's political incorrectness and bourgeois life. Athen is the idealized Communist, humane and loving as well as ideologically sound.

When Athen places his imprimatur of approval upon the marriage and its baby, the group feels vindicated. They are right, after all, in caring about the "personal." Athen's "impressive gift of silence" effectively overcomes Anton's wordy ideological clichés. Tommy, who could not understand how Communists can support an African Branch, cannot understand why Andrew would marry a woman whose baby will not be his. Tommy's comment is the occasion for Athen's peroration about my, my, my and its temporary recessiveness in time of war: "'A baby is being born. A new human being. That's all, comrade'" (170). Athen reiterates a point of view endemic in Lessing's work, which in *Shikasta* is translated into the ponderous SOWF, for Substance of We Feeling. He continues, "'When a baby is born it is born to everyone—don't you see that? It's my child and your child and Martha's child'" (170).[3] The group's support of Maisie and its arranged marriage of Maisie and Andrew represent the high point of its "socialist" behavior.

Martha, continuing to measure herself against the Maisie who is also a projection of a freer part of her own self, thinks, "There's Maisie, in such a complicated mess, and she's quite happy—I never was. I never do anything right. I should have been happy when I was pregnant, but I was fighting everything" (168). Looking at the happiness of others induces in her a feeling of "being shut out of something beautiful and simple" (171). Maisie's happiness even makes Martha momentarily yearn for another baby. She notes the bond of feeling between the apolitical Maisie and the highly political Athen. When Athen strokes Maisie's mountainous belly, the scene is highly sexual and the unexpressed desire of the two for each other perhaps more powerful than if it had been put into words or realized in the sexual act.

Everyone is delighted that Maisie and Andrew marry. Marjorie remarks, "smiling dryly, 'The group is going to have a baby—but it's not my baby!'" (158). Marjorie, also pregnant, is another measuring mirror and a self Martha partly was, partly is, or might become. (Her dryness is, for example, becoming Martha's.) Marjorie's Colin is, like Martha's first husband, a civil servant. As Martha watches Colin's "proprietary hand" on Marjorie and her "stiff resenting forearm," she thinks, "disliking Marjorie, 'Why did she marry him? What for? She doesn't love him'" (164). Seeing Marjorie and Colin together is one of a number of mirror insights that make Martha decide to break off with Anton: "'I'll tell Anton today it's no good us going on'" (164). Later, as Marjorie's arm rests more contritely and affectionately on Colin's, Martha's cool analytic appraisal is, "She's feeling guilty, because she resents him so much . . . I really must talk to Anton tonight" (167). That evening Jasmine issues her indirect warning against Martha's marriage to Anton. The night Athen talks so feelingly about Maisie's baby as a "we" baby is the night Martha determines to break with Anton. It is the last mirror insight: "It was a moment of illumination, a flash of light: I don't know anything about anything yet. I must try to keep myself free and open, and try to think more, try not to drift into things" (172).

These three insights, from three of her many mirrors, Marjorie, Jasmine, and Athen, bring Martha to the decision she has wanted to make. The unbelievable happens. On the night that Martha plans to break with Anton she agrees to marry him. This reversal, superbly orchestrated by Lessing, is a brilliant example of the "savage discrepancy" that can rule private and political life. How is it accomplished?

Anton becomes a "personal" factor in Martha's life during the time of her illness, a time of special vulnerability. Part 1 of the four parts of the novel is almost wholly a group section. It nears its end with Martha "shivering spasmodically" and "thinking feebly that to get sick was an act of irresponsibility and disloyalty to the whole group" (83). When Anton arrives during her illness, Martha permits Anton to take on the parental role she has denied to her mother and her widowed landlady. After his first call to Dr. Stern for her, Martha has "an old feeling of being hemmed in and disposed of" (95). After the second call, she thinks, "Well, that means now Anton and I will be together" (96). Anton, who enters her life as a father figure rather than as a lover, will become more child than father and she more mother than child. At the outset of their "personal" relationship, Martha feels more "caged" than cared for by Anton. Yet she perversely feels (a not uncommon female response) that Anton's caring obligates her to repay him—with a sexual relationship.

The images of Anton remain contradictory. The revolutionary, "essentially masculine, powerful and brave" Anton does not go with the Anton in bed. Nor does the "logically right" Anton go with the "inhuman and wrong" Anton. The problem of fitting "these two features . . . together" is insurmountable (99). Martha admits to having experienced sexual pleasure with Douglas Knowell and William Brown, but neglects to mention the lack of it with Adolph King, her first lover, who is most like Anton in his mechanical lovemaking and in the way he manipulates her guilt feelings. Nonetheless, sexual incompatibility is enough to make Martha decide that she and Anton must stop seeing each other. Implementing that decision is another matter. The night she has come to the point of being able to say no, Anton confronts her with the only ploy that could make her change her mind.

The CID has told him that enemy aliens cannot have affairs with British subjects. "'And so if we analyze the position it is this,'" Anton characteristically begins: "'We must break this off, or we must get married. And that is not the lightest decision'" (174). Martha just might have accepted CID interference as a convenience to accomplish her end. But when Anton presses his advantage and interprets the CID visit as a scarcely disguised warning against his left-wing activity, Martha succumbs easily and fully. Marrying Anton suddenly becomes both a political and a compassionate act of the kind already sanctioned by the group in the merely compassionate marriage of Maisie and Andrew.

The authorial voice guides the reader to reject Martha's reasoning: "Andrew could marry Maisie to help her out—that was a good thing to do; everyone feels it. (She did not remind herself now that everyone felt it except Anton.) And if I marry Anton, and it's nothing but a formality after all, it will make things easy for him" (174). Martha's self-deception is gargantuan—and credible. She will marry to help Anton. Her own needs do not get a hearing. She cannot practice socialist equality in her private life. Although she resents her decision to marry Anton, she is incapable of reversing it. Instead she shows her anger at her compliance in major denial and in trivial acts of subversion. She does not tell her mother she is getting married; she does not tell Mrs. Van. She refuses a celebration of any kind; she will not interrupt her daily routine. She diminishes the civil ceremony by sandwiching it in between day-long meetings, including the important Location meeting. Her body, as usual, as good a register as dreams, rejects what her intellect has forced upon it. She is in her typical "fever of anxiety, the familiar strained irritation" (178). As she looks for an unwrinkled dress to wear, she wonders, "Why should I bother? . . . It's nothing but a formality for both of us" (178). Jasmine, clearly disapproving of both the marriage and Martha's attitude toward the ceremony, later tartly remarks, "'That's right, Matty's back on duty, wedding or no wedding'" (179). (Jasmine will make the only true marriage of convenience in the series when she marries to acquire South African citizenship; she and her husband meet for the ceremony and separate forever directly after it.)

Mrs. Quest appears at the nonparty wedding party of Communists and socialists with a sheaf of news clippings about kaffirs from readers signed "White Settler," "Old Hand," and the like. Mrs. Van defuses the situation by taking the clippings from her to add them, as she says, to her collection. What Mrs. Van does not say is that the letters will go into a file headed "White Settler Imbecilities" (207). The absurdist character of Martha's wedding "reception" surely comes to a climax with these letters and their disposition. Mrs. Van, Jack Dobie, and Johnny Lindsay soon leave. They are socialists who disagree "totally with an ethic which allowed a young woman to spend her wedding night at a political meeting" (203).

Nowhere in the novels of Doris Lessing is the courtship and marriage plot of nineteenth-century fiction so painfully exploded. Martha looks forward to the dissolution of her second marriage before it begins. If her first marriage was based on the illusion of love, her second is based on a conscious decision to circumvent feeling. The pain of repetition is at its worst as Martha voluntarily and knowingly reenters the cage of a wrong marriage. (Jasmine wonders— and the burden of Lessing's work echoes her wonder—if there can ever be a right one.)

Martha has known only the public Anton, the harshly self-righteous keeper of his brand of communism, and the Anton of a brief "courtship" period. She has yet to know the privately bourgeois male chauvinist who prefers his wife more hausfrau than political comrade. This Communist pillar resents the time Martha gives to her meetings and is willing to use Maisie's need for Martha when she is alone and close to term as a pretext to keep Martha with him and away from the critical council meeting at the end of the novel. The paradoxes multiply. Anton, "so bitterly proletarian," turns out to have "a sense of property which Martha had not," yet he always condemns "her middle-class attitudes" (230–31). He spends all his savings on furnishings, while Martha would prefer Maisie's style: "a bare living room, a place to camp in, furnished with the help of friends and ingenuity" (222–23). The bourgeois Anton rejects Maisie's natural immunity to bourgeois standards as bohemian.

In truth, Martha keeps herself a nonparticipant or a passive partner in the marriage in both inner and outer ways. She accepts a ceremony she never wanted: "I wish we could have done like Marjorie and Colin, and Andrew and Maisie—they got married and told us about it afterwards" (182). She permits the apartment to have Anton's personality, not hers. She almost welcomes its use as a communal crash pad. Above all, she will not see (nor does Lessing tell us) that in crucial ways Anton is a descendant of Alfred Quest: he begins as a soldier and ends as a patient. Although he appears to be forceful and capable, he tells Martha that she is the capable one—which means she must find their apartment, arrange their move, and so on. Anton is quite content to be done for, Martha not content to do for; yet in some deeper recess of her being Martha has connived to repeat Alfred and May's relationship.

After a pointless argument in which Martha irreverently calls Comrade Stalin "Uncle Joe," the humorless Anton refuses to speak to her. To joke about a sacred figure is impermissible. The more than month-long silence between the two recalls the silences in the Turner household in The Grass Is Singing. Martha knows exactly how she is supposed to end the freeze. She must "put her arms around him and apologize. But she was fighting against the final collapse of her conception of him" (255). On some levels Anton does like to play father; he wants the rebirth in Martha of the "capricious, charming, filial" creature. To "this compliant little girl Anton would be kind—and patronizing" (255). The paradox of Anton as both parental and filial hangs together for Martha, who evaluates his strong surface as "a mask for his being dependent on her; she would be his child, not he hers" (255). Martha's anger at childish males has its ironies, given the incestuous elements in her own background and behavior and her belief that the right man will make her whole. Anton is a failure because he presents her with needs rather than solutions.

Sexual relations between Anton and Martha never improve. After consulting one of Marjorie's books, Martha discovers that Anton is suffering from premature ejaculation. She can never tell him. Their inadequate lovemaking is contrasted with Maisie's and Andrew's: "They had made love easily since the beginning, adjusting themselves without thinking to her altering shape"(221). Martha, who seems to have made a free choice, is finally and ironically more bound in her socialist marriage than she was in her bourgeois marriage.

The Martha/Anton marriage begins badly and is doomed to get worse. The less predictable deterioration of the Maisie/Andrew marriage is especially painful because their marriage of convenience, perhaps the group's only positive achievement, has become a love match and a touchstone. Maisie and Andrew live in the flat below Martha and Anton, an interesting earlier version of the complex layerings of the Coldridge house in *The Four-Gated City*. From the moment the Maynards engineer their son's leave in order to separate Maisie and Andrew, the group touchstone begins to fall apart. Maisie and Andrew both discover that socialism in one family, like socialism in one country, is unlikely to work. Neither is immune from the disease of ownership. The impending appearance of the natural father of the child Maisie is carrying sows seeds of destruction. Andrew suddenly finds Maisie's body ugly and misshapen. Maisie is also affected, thinking conventionally that the father of her child is coming. That night for the first time Maisie and Andrew do not share a bed. Soon they have agreed to a divorce, and Andrew is transferred as a result of Maynardian machinations. Maisie, who rejects Binkie, continues to live below Martha and Anton, awaiting the birth of her child, again alone, again a casualty.

The touchstone significance of the McGrew marriage is so important to Martha she is "unable to face the thought that Maisie's and Andrew's love was at an end" (240). The death of their love induces a "mourning as if a happiness of her own had collapsed" (256). "Various aspects" of Lessing's self are as "parcelled out" in *Ripple* and in the other Martha Quest novels as they are in *The Four-Gated City* (Bertelsen, "Interview," 109). A "happiness of her own" has indeed collapsed for Martha, since Maisie is one of her other selves.

The collapse of the group-sponsored marriage foreshadows the disintegration of the group itself. Men are transferred ("posted"); others leave. Even Jasmine announces her upcoming departure for South Africa and does so without applying for permission, as party discipline requires. Anton, Martha, and Marjorie are the only three left of the group at the end of the novel.

The only woman, the only person, who seems able to work within the limits of social and psychological realities is Mrs. Van. Her legacy to Martha is as important as Thomas Stern's. When Martha leaves for England, she carries with her Mrs. Van's winter coat and Thomas Stern's manuscript. Mrs. Van is the most important of Martha's parental mirrors, as the novel's exceptional wrench away from Martha's point of view to Mrs. Van's underscores. In a retrospective, rather undigested lump of narrative, Mrs. Van der Bylt's entire life is laid before the reader even more fully than is May

Quest's in *The Four-Gated City*. A line from Olive Schreiner, the liberating force in Mrs. Van's life, serves as an epigraph to this section: "My friendship for him began by my being struck by the stand he took on certain political questions" (151). This line connects female and male, the political and the personal. In fact, Mrs. Van is the only woman in the novel to have profoundly close nonsexual friendships with men. Martha's teenage friendship with the Cohen boys could have become such a friendship but did not. (In *Ripple* Joss is in the armed forces and Solly an enemy labeled Trotskyist.)

Mrs. Van's life is a major contrasting mirror to Martha's. It is worth a review. Schreiner's *Story of an African Farm* was the source of the two major illuminations of Mrs. Van's life. Her reading of it at age eighteen started "an intellectual revolution in her" that she deliberately hides. Like Olive Schreiner, she devoured suffragist and socialist newspapers. For Mrs. Van, socialism was from the beginning inseparable from feminism. "The year was 1913" (193), which means that Mrs. Van's significant growth occurred during World War I, a timing that makes her another child of violence. On her premarital European trip she concluded that she knew nothing and that "all these exciting European currents" were not where she belonged (193). She chose marriage and her apparently peripheral country: "'When I'm married and independent I shall educate myself'" (193).

Her second realization, that her husband was not her equal and that their relationship would be an emotional and intellectual failure, brought her to the conscious decision to lead a double life. She has one life at home and another outside her home. She is the mother of seven children, the wife of a weathy lawyer, and at the same time, "an atheist, a socialist, and a believer in racial equality—this last was the hardest because of the way she had been brought up" (194).

Despite the emotional deprivations she has suffered, despite the grotesque split in her life, she is described as "a happy woman" (194). Here is an older woman who accomplishes her extraordinary political goals in a marriage without love, raises happy children, and is surrounded by nine grandchildren, none of whom shares her political ideals. What a contrasting mirror for the Martha who has left one husband and refused her child, is in a disastrous second marriage, and does not know who or what she wants to be.

When Mrs. Van made her decision to live her double life, her husband was privately relieved, as he could now make his filial claims upon her without guilt. For Mr. Van, like Anton, expected to be taken care of. When Mrs. Van arrives home with her bad back on the day of Martha's marriage, the day her flashback narrative begins, she attends to her husband's demands first, although Mrs. Maynard is waiting to see her.

Lessing manipulates the narrative so that the three mother figures, Mrs. Van, Myra Maynard, and May Quest, appear together on this important day. Mrs. Maynard wants Mrs. Van to separate Maisie and Andrew so that Maisie can marry Binkie and give the Maynards a grandchild. Mrs. Quest, a second visitor, wants Mrs. Van somehow to right the wrong of her not having been told of Martha's marriage that morning. Both women appeal to the Mrs. Van who has the respect of Martha that neither can command. Mrs. Van is politically radical and personally conservative; Mrs. Maynard "conservative by conviction, unegalitarian, aristocratic. Yet surely there was something romantically anarchistic in her that was shown by her cabinet of wire-pulling ladies, and her passion for intrigue and even her handsome husband with his discreet but of course gossiped-about liaisons" (196). By contrast with Mrs. Van, she has one "unsatisfactory" son and no grandchildren. Mrs. Van will not respond to Mrs. Maynard's repeated efforts to get her to pull strings and intrigue, for Mrs. Van's politics are all public. This leader of a double life hates duplicity in politics. The contradiction between the two women makes them "watch each other and reflect about themselves" (196). Mrs. Quest is clearly out of her league in the company of two matriarchs like Mrs. Van and Mrs. Maynard.

Myra Maynard brings the news that Martha and Anton have married that morning. Mrs. Van, touched yet disapproving that Martha should have come to a meeting directly after her wedding, is critical of Martha's past behavior: "To leave a husband was pardonable although—as she had herself proved—hardly necessary. To leave a child was unforgivable" (197–98). Yet Martha is as much a mirror for her as she is for Martha. When she sees Martha back away from Anton that night, then give a false smile, she recalls the first night of her own marriage. That recall is like footage from a film, perhaps like one of the scenes behind the wall in *Memoirs*. Unlike Martha, who does not cry and who should cry, Mrs. Van believes, the just-married Mrs. Van had cried soundlessly: "The cold tears had run down over her cheeks all night" (204); these tears sealed an emotional refusal of her husband: "and so the sword had not stabbed into her, never again, the soft dark painful place which she felt to be somewhere under her heart had remained untouched. She had remained herself" (204–5). Her husband's failure in perception makes him think of her as "a cold and unpassionate woman" (195). But Mrs. Van has kept herself intact and put her passion into her children and her politics.

Martha is deeply affected by Mrs. Van's coolness toward her after her wedding day. Equally uneasy about her desire to cry and her desire to engage in her usual self-parody, Martha nonetheless keeps Mrs. Van's roses "long after they should have been thrown away" (226). Mrs. Van's coolness abates only after Martha has made the decision to forego the council meeting in order to care for Maisie. For this "cold and unpassionate woman," the personal is always a part of the political life. She will support Jack Dobie at his libel trial, although her husband is his libeler's attorney.

Lessing's characteristic naming patterns recur. A striking number of A and M names suggest the kinship of all the figures and their function as doubles of Martha. The A names continue to be predominantly male and the M names predominantly female, as they were in the first two Martha Quest novels. The M names flood the novel: Martha, Maisie McGrew, Marjorie, Marie, Myra Maynard, May Quest, Toni Mandel (compare Tony Marston of The Grass Is Singing), and, for males, Mr. Maynard, McFarline, Matushi, Murdoch Mathews. The A names are far fewer and entirely male: Anton, Andrew McGrew, Athen, Alfred Quest. The novel also exhibits the secondary repetition of J names: Jasmine Cohen, Jackie Bolton, Jack Dobie, Johnny Lindsay, Jimmy Jones, Jan Van der Bylt. There are also William Brown and William (Bill) Bluett, variations on the M pattern.

These familiar A's, M's, and J's are more fully discussed elsewhere in this volume. Their fairly sharp definition as male or female contrasts significantly with the unique androgynous appeal of Grete, Anton's dead wife. Grete exists more as Martha imagines her than as Anton describes her, especially since Anton uses Grete as an invidious exemplar to make Martha feel unworthy. Martha nonetheless feels "drawn to this woman" whose photograph is in Anton's handkerchief drawer. (Maisie, by contrast, openly displays photographs of her two dead husbands.) Martha both respects and resents the dead Grete, whose "dark hair was cut like a man's," though "she was not masculine" (229). This androgynous figure who gave herself totally to the revolution and died in a concentration camp is someone Martha cannot "for the life of her" connect with Anton (229). Martha hears Grete described as a "fine public speaker," a woman with "great physical bravery . . . and 'a mind like a man's'" (229). The last remark says "a good deal about Anton," Martha realizes (229). She restores her own sense of wholeness by imagining a man for herself "perhaps rather in the line of a masculine counterpart to Grete" (230).

Grete is hardly a freestanding figure. She is Martha's ideal self: androgynous, both emotive and active, warm and powerful; perhaps a displacement of Martha's own homosexual desires, perhaps hermaphroditic more than androgynous or homosexual, as though the parts of a single self could join and be self-propagating and therefore all-powerful.

We know that Martha assumes men choose the same woman again and again, as women choose the same man—Lessing's repetitive naming pattern is one way of telling us this happens. Consider Anton's Austrian mistress, Toni Mandel, for example, whom Martha displaces. About her Martha thinks, "If he's interested in me . . . then perhaps I have something in common with her" (50). She must also have something in common with the Grete she so admires. If I die, she muses, then Grete and I will be a ghostly duet for Anton's next woman or wife to cope with, "propositions, bits of property from Anton's past" (230).

Martha's projection of her ideal man as a masculine Grete is also a way of describing her dissatisfaction with the men she has known: Anderson, Adolph, Douglas, William Brown, Anton, and those who have not been her lovers, Maynard, Piet, and others. Grete's name and Lynda Coldridge's name are outside the repetitive naming pattern. Like Lynda, Grete is a crucial register of where Martha is not—of her incompleteness, her misery (the Aragon epigraph concludes: "the passion for the absolute is the same as a passion for unhappiness"), and her inability to accept and develop her own femaleness against the cultural stereotypes of the group. Martha, like her group, is not feminist except incipiently, in her perceptions of Anton's sexism and in her construction of a male Grete.

Martha's ideal city exists in *Ripple* in two ways, as the nonracist ideal of her teenage years and as the Soviet Union, the first state in history to define itself as socialist. Martha's vision of the ideal city is most powerfully embodied in one she shares with Jasmine. Like her earliest dream of the city, this one is triggered by an actual black child. The two women see "a small ragged, barefooted black child, pot-bellied with malnutrition" (27). Their dream seemed "just around the corner; they could almost touch it. Each saw an ideal town, clean, noble, and beautiful, soaring up over the actual town they saw ... The ragged child was already a citizen of this ideal town, co-citizens with themselves" (27). But visions soon take second place in *Ripple* to day-to-day political activity.

Martha's utopia does coincide at times with her daily life and with the actual Soviet Union, for the socialist ideal in *Ripple* is touched with a mystical "holy fire" (31). This "holy fire" is sometimes lighted at meetings and even at rare moments linked with "those parts of her childhood she still owned, the moments of experience which seemed to her enduring and true; the moments of illumination and belief" (54). These moments are not at all like the discussion of the 150-page blueprint for a Communist Zambesia that only Maisie has the courage to question.

They are also a contrast to the horrible dreams Martha has, which are an internal register of her true or inner state. In a novel drenched in actualities dreams rarely surface. When they do, they are terrifying indicators of self-division: "For the cold salt-sprayed shores and the deep sullen pit seemed to have nothing in common, not to be connected, and their lack of connection was a danger" (85). The mysteriously opposed and seemingly unconnected dreams of sea and pit are a metaphor for her own deep division. Another dream finds Martha among "hordes of war-crushed people for whom she was responsible" (87). These images seem a prediction of the catastrophe of the 1970s detailed in the appendix section of *The Four-Gated City*. In them sea and shore are negative images, although on the surface of Martha's life, especially in *Landlocked*, water is always liberating.

The dream about Maisie has a more familiar imagery, but its message is the same. Martha is with Maisie (she really *is* Maisie) when her baby is due, "hurrying from door to door trying to find a house which would take her in. But the doors remained shut against them both" (175)—as, of course, they were shut against the Mary about to bear Jesus of Nazareth. Maisie's function as a displaced part of Martha in this dream would be hard to deny. It can be postulated that

Maisie is having the second child the fictional Martha rejects and the living Lessing did not. Martha, the active primary figure, classically overwhelmed with the anxiety of her frustrating responsibilities, seems a version of the frantically sweeping narrator behind the wall in *The Memoirs of a Survivor*.

Dreams define the true nature of *Ripple*, whose surface seems to speak to energetic daily political activity but whose inner life is parodic, absurdist, and desperate. The "well of desperation slowly filling below the attitude represented by a shrug of the shoulders" (230) perfectly defines the emotive reality of the novel. Beneath the feverish activity is a deadness, a wasteland as arid as the wasteland topography and imagery in *The Grass Is Singing*. The natural landscape seems wholly absent in the urban indoor landscapes of *Ripple*. In fact, Lessing builds to a climax of storm and rain that gives a literal meaning to the title of the novel. The feverish talk correlates with the dry season of the last section in the book. The land and the people waiting for rain are explicitly contrasted with the ice and snow of the Russian front. "The barren thunder, split with dry lightning" (229–30), coincides with the widening fissures within the Communist group and the Social Democratic group.[4]

Storms excite Martha sexually, but her desire will remain unslaked. Marjorie, beaded with sweat, reads the words, "Cold Snow Blizzard Death," while she, like Maisie, continually moves "her big body ... into easier positions" and thinks how welcome cold would be in Zambesia (212). On that night of dry thunder, Anton and Martha have their fight about Uncle Joe. Their room is "now continuously and irregularly illuminated by lightning. It's like the light from gunfire, Martha thought, her imagination returning to the Eastern front" (233). More dismayed than guilty because of the pettiness of her life, she thinks of herself "thousands of miles away from where the future of the world was decided" (233). The storm in the title of the novel is in this passage explicitly identified as the European front of World War II.[5]

That identification recurs and is extended, for when the group disintegrates, Martha feels herself cut off "from everything that had fed her imagination. Until this moment she had been part of the grandeur of the struggle in Europe, part of the Red Army, the guerrillas in China, the French underground and the partisans in Italy, Yugoslavia and Greece" (259). This identification recurs in other Lessing novels; it is Saul Green's Algerian story in *The Golden Note-*

book, Charles Watkins's Yugoslav partisan story in *Briefing*, and the sections in the Canopus novels that use and reuse the experience of World War II.

The rains at the end of the novel, which come down after Maisie's and Andrew's love has collapsed and just before the all-day meeting on the African Branch that Martha does not attend, enclose the town "in a hot downpour" (240). The "hot downpour" does not suggest relief. The pattern of dry, then hot, storm represents a very effective use of weather. Martha, now cut off from group sustenance, must listen to Anton talk about "'the objective political situation'" and the need to make "'a fresh analysis of the situation'" (261–62). She feels "overwhelmed by futility" as she slides "into sleep like a diver weighted with lead" (262), carried by waves of "a powerful driving exhaustion" (254) that make her fear deep sleep throughout this novel. Her inner state is very much like the dry, sterile thunder she hears, a state redolent of Eliot's *Waste Land* and Lessing's more direct use of that poem in her earlier *Grass* and *Retreat*.

Although the novel closes with Martha and Anton in bed, Martha is an isolated figure at the end, a woman imprisoned in an emotional wasteland that she recognizes but cannot alter. She is repeating more intensely and painfully the claustrophobia of the Quest home and her Sports Club life. The Martha who is more aware is also very unaware. She imagines release in the form of a "faceless man who waited in the wings of the future, waiting to free the Martha who was in cold storage" (230). The Martha who is aware that "she was becoming the most accomplished of sexual liars" is unaware of the discrepancy between her dream of a man as her heroic deliverer and her own feminism.

This Martha evaluates the last two years of her life positively: "That's another two years of my life gone. The phrase two years seemed meaningless: they had been years of so much hard work, excitement, happiness and learning that they seemed more important than all the time she had lived before" (261). The other face of these two years is desperate, frantic. Martha's "passion for the absolute" is fully played out in this novel; her insight and her blindness are richly and ironically apparent. The dialectic that she and Anton play out is brilliantly presented. Anton's portrait just misses caricature. Each partner in this new projection of a marriage of opposites excites the other to her or his worst extremes. Martha, who has for a second time lost her Questing name, becomes more self-critical and self-parodying (traits she shares with Anna Wulf) than ever and Anton more rigid and more solemn.

"The passion for the absolute" seems a rephrasing of the longing for the infinite that absorbed so many nineteenth-century romantic writers. Mrs. Van is the only character who can describe institutions—marriage is one of them—as a "question of compromise" and "tolerance" (228). Unlike Mrs. Van, Martha is consumed by the disparity between theory and practice, ideal and actuality. She discovers in *Ripple* that Communists and communism are like other people and other belief systems. Anton is not, like McFarline, a quintessential racist and sexist, but he is very badly flawed. So is the Martha who claims she wants freedom and chooses cages.

Martha's first freely chosen collective disintegrates. There will be others, for Lessing's fictional journey could be described as a search for satisfying, freely chosen collectives to replace the inherited and very unfree family collective. As a novel, *Ripple* has a new face if its political dimension is understood and the desperation under its frenzied motion is permitted to surface. No other English novel captures the absurdist element in politics so well—and so unsentimentally and meticulously illustrates the gap between theory and practice in private and public life. If the bush avenges itself in *Grass*, then the storm in *Ripple* rages against the "savage discrepancy" that is its subject.

8

From Mud Houses to Sacred Cities: Martha Quest to Ambien II

EB: I want to pursue the "Quest" story, although you rebuke me, and say I'm finding artificial constructs binding the books together . . . like the Ideal City image which occurs throughout the whole series. When Martha first has this vision in the veld in *Martha Quest* it seems to be very much like a Marxist vision of a classless society. Then it moves through being a symbol of personal harmony in those middle books. And by the time we get to the end, we've got London as a final "false city" and Faris Island with the pure notes of the flute being almost a mandala of mystic harmony. That one image both binds the books and changes quite a lot. Would you agree with that?

DL: Not particularly. The first one certainly couldn't have been Marxist. You know that Marxism took over a lot of Utopian ideas. Marxism didn't *create* these ideas of harmony and happiness and equality. It comes from religion. Utopias long predate Marxism. The idea of paradise and heaven comes from Christianity, not from Marxism. It's a Christian idea which Marxism has taken over. So Marxism is in fact structured like Christianity with Heaven and Hell—Hell being capitalism . . . It's exactly the same structure. And the idea of paradise is the classless society. It predates even Christianity. It's the old Golden Age theme.[1]

Bertelsen, "Interview"

And the city lieth foursquare.

Rev. 21:16

Although all artists are architects in the larger metaphoric sense, few have been builders of imagined cities. Fewer still have become involved in architectural pattern. Nasar's description of himself in *The Sirian Experiments* as "'an architect among other things'" (283) is also a description of his maker, Doris Lessing, who has, "among other things," been building houses and cities throughout her long career.

The city Martha Quest dreams about when she is fifteen is a leitmotiv in the five novels that she inhabits until she dies in 1997. The earliest image of the ideal city is triggered by Martha's leap from the reality of racism to her dream of a city in which "black and white and brown" parental figures smile approvingly at "the many-fathered children" who play together (*Martha Quest*, 11). Unexpectedly, this city is not in the future but in the past, for it is described as "fabulous and ancient." Other details also suggest an older edenic time from which humankind has fallen away: "colonnaded," fountains and flutes, "flower-bordered terraces," elders, golden. Martha's dream of this four-gated city is explicitly described as "Martha's version of the golden age" (11). Thus in *Martha Quest*, the very first volume of the *Children of Violence* series, Martha's dream of the ideal city is nostalgic and therefore implicitly ironic. It is also exclusionary, for "a stern and remorseless Martha" stands at the gate keeping out the unworthy, that is, her parents and other English and Afrikaners in the district.

On the private level, Martha's vision of the city at this stage in her life can be described as an adolescent revenge fantasy or as a "familiar daydream," to use Lessing's own words (*Martha Quest*, 10). On the public level, Martha's golden city is remarkable for its nostalgic quality. For a young girl already more than casually interested in the socialist ideal, her dream is notable for its assignment of racial equality to the past instead of to the socialist future, where it belongs. What seem conflated in embryo here are the edenic past and the utopian future. The location of the golden age in the past as well as in the future has often characterized human dreams of the earthly paradise. Indeed, a past utopia has often justified hopes for a radical future (Manuel and Manuel, 5; Eliade, *Cosmos and History*). Martha cannot know how archetypal her daydream is, how much "the nostalgic mode has been an auxiliary of utopia" (Manuel and Manuel, 5).

The interconnection between the paradisaic past and the paradisaic future must be established and accepted. Both modes run deep in human history and consciousness. The socialist utopia, intertwined as it is with the idea of progress, inevitably turns toward the future. Lessing's ironic distance from her adolescent protagonist is a critical comment on Martha's naive, romanticized construction of the four-gated city and an indication of Lessing's own commitment at this time to a socialist future: the socialist future is an earthly paradise, a realizable victory over inequality, racism, and war.

But Martha's early earthly paradise is not the same as the city she dreams of in The Four-Gated City. That later city is an archetypal one, in fact, a rigid, over-ordered city in violent contrast to the living, volatile London that has such different faces in the 1950s and 1960s. That London in all its phases engages authorial and reader sympathy as its equivalents in the Canopus novels do not. The cities in the appendix to The Four-Gated City are in a different category; they are closer to the degenerated cities of Shikasta. Between the Canopean cities and those of The Four-Gated City fall the cities of Briefing for a Descent into Hell and The Memoirs of a Survivor. In these two novels, Lessing tilts her emphasis toward the symbolic and the archetypal, rejecting the flawed but living cities of her earlier novels.

"She could have drawn a plan of that city," we are told of the sixteen-year-old Martha. These words are almost exactly repeated when Martha and Mark discuss their city in The Four-Gated City. Their shared dream of the "mythical," "hierarchic," "archetypal" city is so detailed it is "as good as a blueprint to build" (139). Its four gates, set to point north, south, east, and west, become a square containing arcs and circling streets. The shadow city that grows up around it ultimately engulfs the perfect inner city (an ironic reversal of the meaning of inner city for American readers). The over-ordered city breaks into inner and outer, into inner perfection and outer degeneration, into permanence and change, for while Martha and Mark discuss their mythical city, the real London is growing and changing away from the gracelessness and deprivation of its postwar state. In the late 1950s, "the dirty, ruinous, war-soaked city" (301–2) is quite changed. Martha keeps "that other" city "in her mind" as she walks through the new London, so that "that other" postwar city exists side by side with the present London of the 1950s (302).

These two real Londons, the London of the present and that of the past, are contrasted with the mythical four-gated city that is "an idea of a city. A City, rather!" (302). The capitalized City is changeless, "a solid, slow-moving thing" with known landmarks genera-

"The symbolic city as centre of the earth, its four walls laid out in a square." From Maier, Viatorium, reproduced in C. J. Jung's Collected Works, vol. 12, p. 82. (Courtesy Princeton University Press)

tions can refer to. But the real city has more vitality, excitement, fluidity. Listen to this description of the actual city: "But London heaved up and down, houses changed shape, collapsed, whole streets were vanishing into rubble, and arrow shapes in cement reached up into the clouds. Even the street surfaces were never level: they were always 'up,' being altered, dug into, pitted, while men rooted in them to find tangled pipes in wet earth" (302). This extraordinary flux makes London "exhilarating" for Martha. It almost erodes her dream of the ordered, hierarchic city: "It seemed as if the idea of a city or town as something slow-changing, almost permanent, belonged to the past when one had not needed so many pipes, cables, runnels, and types of machinery to keep it going. If time were slightly speeded up, then a city must now look like fountains of rubble cascading among great machines, while buildings momentarily form, change colour like vegetation, dissolve, re-form" (302). This new London, explicitly connected with the house on Radlett Street, survives war and other erosions. Its rebuilding is exuberant, energetic. This London does not dissipate the archetypal image for Martha, but "the old city all movement" surely commands greater reader loyalty than the hierarchic city at which Mark now laughs. The real city is closer to the process that the novel celebrates. The living, changing London is organic and stimulating. It seems almost like the tree whose organic nature is a celebratory motif throughout the series (Rose, Tree).

I am therefore doubtful that Lessing's "picture of the four-gated city has embodied harmony, reconciliation, integration" throughout the series (Stimpson, 205). Racial integration is its earliest and most durable, most positive feature. Because it reflects Martha's own changing consciousness, its meaning is variable, even ironic and limited. The ideal city contrasts with the disorder and variety of the Coldridge house. It is a blueprint without the human figure. It stands still. Our houses and lives do not.

The celebration of process in the novel is particularly evident in the depiction of the younger generation. Lessing is immensely sympathetic to the sixties ethos. Francis Coldridge stands for the best in that generation; he inherits the special skills and insights of his father, Mark, and of his two mothers, Martha and Lynda. His generation, skeptical of formal schooling, looks elsewhere for its education. It contains brave noncareerists who explore what Richard Sennett calls "the uses of disorder." Martha Quest herself chooses the apparently traditional female life as housemother, but the surface ordinariness of that life hides a radical inquiry into the nature of value. The hierarchical, stabilized city seems a highly unsuitable design for Martha's ethos. Its depiction represents a regressive longing for security, one that collides with a major lesson of the novel that speaks to risk and experiment and "painful unknowns" (Sennett, 66).

In Briefing for a Descent into Hell the real city has no attractions. The protagonist's return to it represents total and unambiguous defeat. Only the archetypal city in Charles Watkins's inner journey and the preindustrial villages of the river people Frederick Larson describes are meant to capture reader acceptance. One city exists in the "deviant" reality the novel evaluates positively; the other exists in the "normal" reality the novel evaluates negatively.

The houses in The Four-Gated City are mirrors of psychological reality. They do, however, have a physical reality of their own. In Briefing Lessing moves dangerously close to a solipsistic version of experience and reality. The strange, sacred city Charles encounters in his psychic journey physically reflects his inner state. When an animal dies, Charles says that it dies because his own thoughts were evil. When the empty, roofless stone city becomes inhabited by dog-rats or rat-dogs who then ferociously war with invading monkeys, we must assume that these warring creatures are projections of Charles's mind. These warring animals make it impossible for Charles to keep the sacred center of the city clean in preparation for the landing of the Crystal (we are again in the presence of a square city with a sacred circle at its center that functions as a kind of altar). This first empty, then overcrowded, city can be described as the theater of Charles's psyche. Within it Charles experiences his own creation myth, his own fall and redemption.

The roofless city with stone foundations makes Charles wonder, for "what stone city of such size and magnificence ever has had thatched roofs?" (50). Subsequently he postulates that the roofless city must have had tile roofs that wore away in heavy rains or buffeting winds. He decides to leave the roofs as they are, makes a bed of leaves, lies down with his leopard, and times his sleep by the moon, thus duplicating many elements of pastoral perfection.

Charles's questions reflect the standard prejudices of current archaeologists and anthropologists. The question resurfaces in connection with Frederick Larson, the anthropologist who inhabits the outer or "normal" world of *Briefing*. Rosemary Baines presents his case history in a letter to Charles as an encouraging mirror of the development she assumes Charles is himself undergoing. Charles and Frederick are doppelgänger figures: both are scholars—one in classics, the other in anthropology—who have had psychic and professional crises of faith. Charles is defeated, but like Lynda Coldridge, Frederick becomes what in *Shikasta* is called a "link" individual between ordinary reality and superreality.

Frederick's encounter with an African tribe whose life is based on the movements of a river profoundly shakes his already shaken anthropological assumptions. When the plain the tribe lives on floods, as it does annually, the tribe moves to a new shoreline until the waters subside. What would happen, Frederick asks himself, if the tribe were to move permanently to another site one year because the waters stayed too high? "It would be impossible to know that human beings had lived there. The huts were of wood and earth. The roofs of thatch. Most of the vessels were of wood. The earthenware was not fired, but sun-dried and made to be used and thrown easily away" (179). The point is that such a culture would leave no record of its existence. It stands as an indictment of anthropological dependence on artifacts. Yet Frederick maintains that this culture is "high" if judged by standards of harmony, responsibility, and peaceableness. Furthermore, its life is "more integrated with Nature than any he could remember," "very highly ritualised" as it is "around the seasons, the winds, the sun, the moon, the earth," as well as the river (179–80).

Frederick understands that there is "no way of knowing an ancient society's ideas except through the barrier of our own" (180). Another key event occurs for him when an Oxford professor assumes that the existence of certain trenches indicates a stone-building culture until a student tells him that African tribes used just such trenches for their huts of poles, mud plaster, and thatch. The accident of this student's presence forces the professor to modify his position. Frederick is certain that had the student not been present, the professor would have categorically asserted that the trench was built for a stone house.

Frederick undertakes a series of subversive exercises. He makes out a case for Arabs, Moors, and Saracens as the parents of Western civilization, rather than the Greeks and Romans. He concocts papers for his amusement that see the civilization he is unearthing from a different culture's perspective—the Roman, the Greek, the Aztec, and so on. When what he calls his Victorian crisis is over, he continues to have grave doubts about archaeology's "bases, premises, methods, and above all, its unconscious biases" (185).

Neither the deviant nor the normal world of Briefing is very successfully presented. Lessing seems uncomfortable with the allusive freight she loads on the novel. However much that freight is presumably naturalized in the person of its classics professor protagonist, the baggage is heavy, strained, and overly didactic. The double perspective is more successfully structured in The Memoirs of a Survivor. But Briefing remains extremely interesting for a variety of reasons: its male protagonist, its scholarly baggage, its attack on the psychiatric establishment, and the transparency of Lessing's new interest in mysticism of all kinds. For example, Watkins's expertise as a classicist provides decent cover for Lessing's uncharacteristic display of erudition in this novel, which alludes generously to many fields, among them mythology, philosophy, anthropology, archaeology, poetry, and hermetic literature. The prolix allusions could have come from Jimmy Wood's "potted library" in The Four-Gated City, which contains books on Rosicrucianism, alchemy, Buddhism, the many varieties of yoga, Zoroastrianism, esoteric Christianity, "tracts of the I Ching; Zen, witchcraft, magic, astrology and vampirism," Sufism, Christian mysticism—in short, "everything rejected by official culture and scholarship" (513).

The colored world of earth encased in pulsing light that Charles sees from a distant point in space could be as indebted to Shelleyan imagery (earthly color stains "the white radiance of eternity" in "Adonais") as to the eclectic literature of Neoplatonic and other mysticisms from which Shelley himself fed. (Martha Quest feeds on dissident poets like Blake, Shelley, and Whitman.) Even Wordsworth is a direct source here; Rosemary Baines talks of "prison shades" closing around the young (165). The "Immortality" ode is behind Briefing as surely as "Adonais" is. The Neoplatonic recycling of souls Lessing finds so attractive is used again in Shikasta, where souls reenter Earth from a miasmic Zone 6. In Briefing, the figure of Mercury, who as Hermes gave his name to the hermetic thought that has engaged Lessing for some twenty years, presides over the souls waiting to be born. (See Yates, 48 and passim.) Charles names his other appearances Thoth, Enoch, Buddha, Idris, and Hermes, accepting Mercury as "the carrier of news, or information from the Sun, the disseminator of laws from God's singing centre" (106).

The eclectic, syncretic lore that surrounds Mercury can be assumed to lie in the background of Lessing's conception of the sacred city. Ellen Cronan Rose has in an exciting and original article excavated Lessing's indebtedness to this rich amalgam of medieval and Renaissance thought for her conception of the four-gated city. Although this city and the African mud village intersect in their implicit criticism of the real cities of our time, they are more different than they are alike. Their juxtaposition in *Briefing* duplicates the juxtaposition of the sacred and the real cities in *The Four-Gated City*. The mud village is all change; if its closeness to nature has a sacramental quality, that quality is not visibly codified in complex rituals such as the ones we watch Charles perform in his inner city.

Frederick Larson's mud village is the mud house of Martha's childhood writ large, the houses of the Turner field hands in *The Grass Is Singing*, the house to whose site Doris Lessing returned in *Going Home*. Frederick brings the self-consciousness of the historical observer to bear on his mud village. The mud houses of Lessing's earlier fictions come out of the present time and her direct personal experience. For Martha, mud is the African bush, grass, sky, earth. It is sensual: "this frank embrace between the lifting breast of the land and the deep blue warmth of the sky is what exiles from Africa dream of" (*Martha Quest*, 230). Although the critical, rebellious adolescent Martha defines the native-style Quest house "as disgracefully shabby, even sordid"—its roof sags, its walls are patched and spotted—she does call it original (*Martha Quest*, 15). For this house, planned in white settler style for "bricks and proper roofing," was built with "grass and mud and stamped dung" (14). When Martha puts her ear to the central pole, she can hear "myriad tiny jaws at work" (14).

In *A Proper Marriage*, the middle-class and very pregnant Martha and Alice perform an almost orgiastic rite. They strip naked and plunge into a pothole. Martha stands "to her knees in heavy mud, the red, thick water closed below her shoulders" (134). When the symbolic snake intrudes, it is quite unthreatening: "It slid down over the red pulpy mud, and, clinging with its tail to a clutch of grass, it allowed itself to lie on the surface, swaying its vivid head just above the water" (135). This celebration of fecundity and union, so obviously prelapsarian, contains an ebullience and abandonment rarely found in Lessing.

The Turner house in *The Grass Is Singing*, with its brick walls and corrugated tin roof (destined for a "proper roof" it never gets), is, like Mary, out of place in the wilderness. The native houses are very different. Their huts of grass, poles, and mud collapse back into the earth when the workers leave for another job: "So there were always new huts, and always empty old ones" (152). These huts look "like natural growths from the ground, rather than man-made dwellings." Lessing continues: "It was as though a giant black hand had reached down from the sky, picked up a handful of sticks and grass, and dropped them magically on the earth in the form of huts" (152). Their qualities of spontaneity and naturalness make these mud huts the antipodes of Lessing's magical cities—the four-gated city, the inner city of *Briefing*, and the geometrical cities of *Shikasta*.

Lessing's image of the mud house has a central place in her iconography, one that perhaps only Nicole Ward Jouve has effectively isolated and analyzed. She describes Lessing's journey from *Martha Quest* to *The Four-Gated City* as a journey from mud to the void. Clearly unsympathetic to Lessing's abdication of earth for space, Jouve tracks Lessing's progressive move toward the remote and the abstract. A parallel mode marks Lessing's architectural journey, but as I have been suggesting, the journey is not a simple one, for the mud house is not a viable reality for Martha Quest or Doris Lessing. Martha, like Lessing, longs for the London in her mind, but accepts the actual London she finds.

When Doris Lessing visited Rhodesia after six years of living in London, she described her sense of homelessness: "The fact is I don't live anywhere; I never have since I left that first house on the kopje" (*Going Home*, 34–35). That first house pervades her imagination, although, as she reports, "it crumbled long ago, returned to the soil, was swallowed by the bush" (35)—like the huts and the Turner house in *The Grass Is Singing*, like the Quest house, and, of course, like the huts of the river people in *Briefing*. That first house was "a living thing, responsive to every mood of the weather," as stone houses emphatically are not (*Going Home*, 38). Lessing recalls that when it rained, "it was as if the house was enclosed by a light waterfall" (43). This image and Lessing's description of the field of mealies outside her window "as a hundred acres of smooth, clear apple-green that shimmered and rippled under the hot sun," or "in the moonlight, looking down, . . . a dim green sea, moving with light" (*Going Home*, 43), must remind the reader of the lush imagery Lessing uses to describe the green light-filled bower in which Martha Quest and Thomas Stern live and love in *Landlocked*.

There is one city that has yet to enter fully into Lessing scholarship. It is outside the European tradition, outside Jimmy Wood's "potted library," yet very much inside Lessing's life and psyche. Its existence destroys the binary opposition between the mud house and the geometrical city. That old stone city is today known as the Great Zimbabwe Ruins. Its grand stone ruins, assumed by Europeans to be beyond the skill of local peoples to build, have been variously attributed to ancient Phoenicians, Persians, Arabs, and Portuguese. The hill ruin was even once thought to be a copy of Solomon's Temple.[2] An organization named Rhodesian Ancient Ruins Limited was licensed to look for gold amid the ruins in the nineteenth century. This abbreviated history must have been known to Doris Lessing as she was growing up; she very likely visited the site, as it is in Shona country not very far from the Quest/Tayler house. Today these ruins, "comprising 12 separate clusters of buildings spread over 40 hectares," are attributed to ancestors of the present-day Shona and are thought to date back to the late twelfth century (Wannenburgh and Murphy, n.p.). The structures sport names like the Elliptical Enclosure, the Conical or Oval Tower, the Acropolis. The so-called Elliptical Temple is surrounded by a wall fourteen feet wide and up to thirty feet high in places. The Acropolis houses a structure that, like the Elliptical Temple, seems to follow the contour of the land rather than the imposed order of geometrical shapes. Deliberately irregular, deliberately planned to accommodate to the curve of the land rather than to the mathematician's instruments, these structures seem to be at once "natural" and mathematical.

The story of the discovery and interpretation of the Great Zimbabwe Ruins is replete with "unconscious biases" that could not have been lost on Doris Tayler. She did not need to be a professional archaeologist to relish the ironies of European response to the ruins. The ironies are not over, for today a nine-hole golf course covers the land on which Mashona battles were fought, and "drumbeats summon the guests to meals at a nearby hotel" (Wannenburgh and Murphy). Tourists may shop at a souvenir kiosk and

The Conical Tower of the Great Zimbabwe Ruins.
(Courtesy Ian Murphy)

inspect the replica of a karanga village that sits between a tea garden and the Elliptical Enclosure.

Many ancient cities known in Europe had stone centers and stone temples. However, the stone foundations and the stone center of Charles Watkins's inner city, as well as the stone cities of the First Time in *Shikasta*, surely owe at least as much to the Zimbabwe Ruins as they do to European examples. It is of some interest to learn that the word "zimbabwe" probably derives from the Bantu "zimba" for houses and "magbi" for stone. For many reasons, Zimbabwe is a suitable name for the country that was called Southern Rhodesia until independence in 1979. In *The Grass Is Singing*, Lessing uses the name "Rhodesia" for her southern African setting, but in *Martha Quest* she permanently changes that name to "Zambesia," probably after the Zambesi River. That name change is significant. It demonstrates Lessing's discomfort with the English-imposed "Rhodesia." So over thirty years before Africans repossessed the name of their land, Lessing symbolically repossessed it for them.

The double worlds of *Memoirs of a Survivor* have a special complexity. A different kind of reality exists on either side of a wall. It is as if, the nameless narrator tells us, "two ways of life, two lives, two worlds, lay side by side . . . closely connected" yet mutually and forever exclusive (25). On one side the nameless woman lives in a room that belongs to the "real" world; on the other side she moves through walls aptly said to be as "impermanent as theatre sets" (40). The other or inner side of the wall is not confined to ordinary reality. Objects can be displaced, time can go backward, in that other realm that begins as the realm of the psyche. This fundamental projection of an inner world and an outer world is familiar. The four-gated city is an inner city surrounded by a corrupt city; Charles Watkins undergoes an inner voyage within a corrupt outer framework. *Memoirs* also contains Lessing's familiar walls and rooms, but the walls and rooms that bind Mary Turner or Martha Quest or Lynda Coldridge are porous in this novel.

The nameless narrator's room is in a house on a block in a disintegrating city. What happens to the room, the house, the block, and the people who inhabit these spaces in this apocalyptic fable presents readers with a special leap in Lessing architechtonics. Collective life is painfully reduced to a room with a window that looks out on the street. The larger forms of collective political life are never visible. As services associated with the city and technology disappear—heat, light, food, stores, water—people leave, children become amoral. Cannibalism ultimately becomes acceptable even, or especially, to Hobbesian four-year-olds.[3] The apartment house becomes a miniature city. In the market, safely removed to the upper floors of the narrator's building, barter has replaced money. Small farms, gardens, and domestic animals flourish in those upper regions. Lessing's vertical restructuring of the apartment house brilliantly reimagines the ordinary as grotesque. Her "gift for combining prophecy and prosaic detail" makes her depiction of the death of the city credible (Dinnage, 39).

The square patch outside, where refugees gather to plot next moves and to socialize, seems a travesty of the sacred center Charles Watkins tries so desperately to keep clean. The dream of a terrestrial paradise is quite exploded in this "future speculation disguised as past reflection" (Dassin, 4). The worlds on both sides of the wall undergo radical change. On the outer side, Emily, the narrator's charge and other self, is middle-aged at fourteen and without illusion. She is forced to accept the impossibility of ever having a world without "'a pecking order'" (132). The destruction of property values and sexual taboos has not brought about a better world, a fact that undercuts those theories of progress which believe in destruction as a precondition to creation. Indeed, from one perspective, Memoirs can be described as a failed creation myth. Certainly Emily and Gerald believed that they were making a new start: "Free. Free, at least from what was left of 'civilisation' and its burdens" (167). They were a new Adam and Eve. Like their mythic predecessors, they failed, yet they are unaccountably granted the gift of moving outside time.

The space on the other side of the wall in the shape of rooms becomes something else at the end of the novel, as the narrator, not Emily, takes on the role of savior. She leads the few survivors—herself, Emily, Gerald, and some of the Hobbesian children—through her wall into an inner reality that has become more real than the disintegrated city.

The Canopus novels can be described as the world on the other side of the wall. Rosemary Dinnage's description of the two cities in The Four-Gated City serves the Shikastan model even better: "The paradisal, archetypically lost city," well described as "the dying city's mirror image" (38), has a mythic force and formal clarity in Shikasta that was missing in The Four-Gated City.

The "archetypically lost city" is also in the background of *The Sirian Experiments*; it haunts the imagination of Ambien II, who records her galactic monitoring on Shikasta and other planets. Of the five Canopus novels so far published, these two, the first and the third, are suffused with images of the city as the quintessential locus of human life and achievement. The degenerated city is always a reminder of the ideal city, of what Ellen Cronan Rose calls the *città felice* and Rosemary Dinnage calls the paradisal city. The city has, in fact, been historically associated with ambivalence, with both the corrupt and the perfect (Pike, xiii and passim).

The ideal city can also be called the sacred city, for in her conception of the ideal city in the Canopus novels, Lessing unquestionably projects a religious conception of the city, one that incorporates cross-cultural ancient, medieval, and Renaissance conceptions of the sacred city. Her "scriptural voice" dominates the series (Parrinder, 6).

In the preface to *Cosmos and History: The Myth of the Eternal Return*, Mircea Eliade describes archaic man as feeling "himself indissolubly connected with the cosmos and cosmic rhythms," while modern man insists that he is connected only with History" (vii). There are times when Lessing's *Shikasta* seems a fictional working out of the major ideas in Eliade's work. For one thing, Lessing accepts Eliade's basic formulation of the distinction between archaic and modern life, between sacred and temporal time. History in *Shikasta* becomes a religious unfolding of events that either deny or affirm the divine telos. Canopean emissaries stand in tutelary relationship to earthlings, trying to guide a fallen race back to connection with the cosmos. At its end, *Shikasta* is back at its beginning, back to what Lessing usually calls the First Time; once, like Eliade, she calls it the Great Time. She develops a myth of two Falls, the first being the fall from the First Time of the Giants; the second, the catastrophe of our time, the unfolding of our Century of Destruction.

The repetition that plagues Martha Quest is sacramental and desirable in the world of *Shikasta*. The city, the temple, the sacred stones, the globe itself, seem a duplicate of some celestial archetype. Every element of the Mathematical Cities seems an earthly imitation of celestial models. Like the inner city in *Briefing*, the Mathematical Cities have a sacred center. The Lock that is established between Canopus and the Giants depends on certain harmonic arrangements. Rituals and ritualistic objects have divine models. The future "will regenerate time; that is, will restore its original purity and integrity" (Eliade, *Cosmos and History*, 106). Thus the return of the Mathematical Cities at the end of the novel asserts the regenerating power of cyclical time. Linear time has little interest for Lessing in her Canopus novels; repetition, cycle, archetype—these nonlinear rhythms are valorized in her space fictions.

Perhaps her most startling borrowing from the "archaic" formulations of Babylonian and Iranian sources that entered Western thought via Pythagoras and Plato is her endorsement of the doctrine of astrological fatalism. A cosmic accident causes both Shikastan falls, as it causes the extermination of Planet 8 in *The Making of the Representative for Planet 8*. These apparently arbitrary events are in fact not arbitrary, for in the divine scheme of things, no historical catastrophe is arbitrary. When Canopus errs, as does happen, we must believe that a higher power even than Canopus understands the meaning of the particular catastrophe. Christianity sought "to liberate history from astral destiny" (Eliade, *Cosmos and History*, 136), but Lessing's astral determinism seems to shackle human destiny. She is, of course, connected with what Eliade perceives to be a movement away from belief in historical time. He cites Eliot and Joyce as examples of modern writers who are "saturated with nostalgia for the myth of eternal return, and, in the last analysis, for the abolition of time" (*Cosmos and History*, 153). This saturation is, finally, more crucial than whether Lessing or Eliot or Joyce or Yeats "believes" in the system each one has created.

Eliade concludes *Cosmos and History* with a line that can stand as an epigraph to *Shikasta*: "History and progress are a fall, both implying the final abandonment of the paradise of archetypes and repetition" (162). Sirius, enslaved to history and technology, sets spies against Canopus to try to discover how its agents travel, how they communicate without a visible technology. Highly evolved or godlike creatures can discard technology, can, in effect, return to nature, can establish rapport with cosmic forces and rhythms that technology loses. Humans closest to Canopus can talk with animals and know how to perform religious rituals perfectly. (The slightest deviation from the prescribed rituals is a sign of Degenerative Disease.) There is no progress; there is only an effort to return to primordial connection with the cosmos. We return to archetypes by repeating in ritual, in behavior, and in building patterns what was originally valid. According to Eliade, only repetitive connection with archetypal forms can relieve us from "the terror of history" (*Cosmos and History*, chap. 4). Lessing, who once seemed the quintessential believer in historical time, now seems a firm proselytizer for archaic time. John Leonard was not alone in lamenting Lessing's departure from historical time: "History is our dance. She leaves too early and we miss her" (35).

Of the available contemporary historical systems, the one that engaged Doris Lessing for so long, the Marxist, paradoxically permits, as Eliade is aware, an elimination of the terror of history. For "at the end of the Marxist philosophy of history lies the age of gold of the archaic eschatologies" (*Cosmos and History*, 149). Furthermore, in primitive communism there is also an age of gold at the beginning of time. In both the Communist future and the primitive communism of prehistory, therefore, there is a classless society and a secularized equivalent of the Garden of Eden and the City of God. Marxism is rightly described as a secularization of medieval and Renaissance millennial dreams.

Lessing's lifelong exploration of the city in fact and symbol reflects an indebtedness to the millennial aspirations that developed in the medieval period. Although the heavenly and the terrestrial cities are theoretically separate, they do in fact interconnect historically, as well as in Lessing's own work. These two cities are not, as I have been arguing, clearly separable before *Briefing*. They were certainly not separable during the several historical centuries of feverish millennial agitation.

It is perhaps both inevitable and paradoxical that millenarian thought should have surfaced in a church and within an ethos that had characteristically preached the postponement of earthly felicity until the afterlife. The "yet another kind of eschatology" that surfaced in the work of Joachim of Fiore (1145–1202) has been called "the most influential one known to Europe until the appearance of Marxism" (Cohn, 99). Marxism and the other socialist theories of the nineteenth century secularized that version of the earthly paradise announced by Joachim that became so diffused and radicalized between the end of the eleventh century and the middle of the sixteenth: "Within those centuries, it repeatedly happened in Europe that the desire of the poor to improve the material conditions of their lives became transfused with phantasies of a new Paradise on earth, a world purged of suffering and sin, a Kingdom of the Saints" (Cohn, xiii).

Medieval millenarianism promised terrestrial and collective salvation. Cataclysmic events were a precondition—indeed, a sign—that the end of the world in its corrupt form was imminent. Although the juxtaposition of the social thought of two such widely separated centuries as the thirteenth or fourteenth and the twentieth may be facile (as are the equivalences made today between communism and fascism), certain similarities do strike twentieth-century thinkers as justifiable. For example, Lessing's fictional Communists do see themselves as a chosen people (the vanguard of the working class) able to forge a terrestrial paradise. Communist theory predicts a final struggle with capitalism that will usher in that paradise. Like the theorists of the Middle Ages, Communists look forward to the perfect communal classless society. Communism shares with its medieval predecessors (one of them, Thomas Muntzer, is a Communist hero) a special sense of destiny. Though these commitments and emotional attitudes do not always acquire Lessing's authorial blessings, they are displayed in her work. Martha Quest's vision of the four-gated city has millennial force. It embodies her dreams of social justice and racial equality and reflects the power of Marxism as a revolutionary movement to endow its doctrines with transcendental meaning. The transcendent imperative is a constant in Lessing's work.[4] Its force and durability should not be underestimated.

Lessing's dreams of political salvation become dreams of religious salvation, but the dream of perfection remains. The over-ordered, hierarchical, mathematical cities represent the perfection human life cannot achieve. Yet Lessing imagines their existence in Shikasta in the near future as well as in the past of prehistory. We can, the end of Shikasta tells us conclusively (the double conclusion to The Four-Gated City is less conclusive), move toward beatitude. We can recreate the earthly paradise.

The origins of these Shikastan cities have uncomfortable parallels with modern colonial realities (Kaplan, "Britain's Imperial Past"). They were built by the Giants, people imported from Colony 10 by the Canopeans not to intermix with the Natives, the ancestors of Homo sapiens, but to stand in tutelary relation to them. (Intermixing of the two species occurs only after the Fall and is a sign of debasement.) There are hordes of natives and very few Giants—a million and a half to sixty thousand—as there were hordes of blacks and few whites in the Rhodesia Lessing grew up in. From another perspective, there is some wit in this vision of the human race and of Lessing's predominantly white audience as requiring tutelage. Its mythic basis, that there were giants in those days, is of course widespread and easily assimilable. The postulate of Giants and Natives becomes uncomfortable, however, when seen against colonialism and historical time. The colonial parallels are unavoidable as three galactic empires, Canopus, Sirius, and Shammat, exert their power over inferior peoples.

Despite this superior-inferior construction, the story of the Giants and the Natives has a mythic and narrative power unmatched by the rest of the novel. The cities in their final form are "of stone, . . . linked with the stone patterns as part of the transmitting system" that connects the planet with Canopus (25). If the Natives are able to manage the rigors of keeping "the stones aligned and moving as the forces moved and waxed and waned, and if the cities were kept up according to the laws of the Necessity," then "these little inhabitants of Rohanda who had been no more than scurrying monkeys . . . could expect to become men" able to take care of themselves (25–26). Then, "the work of the symbiosis complete" (26), the Giants can be airlifted elsewhere to perform other Canopean chores.

The temperaments of people are variously attuned to the different geometric shapes of the cities: Round, Square, Oval, Crescent, Rhomboid, Hexagonal, Circular, Triangular, and so on. The science of discovering who should go where is of course perfected. An existence dependent on "voluntary submission to the great Whole" is "not serfdom or slavery" but the source of health and progress (26). As in the Book of Genesis, disobedience is the primal sin.

The mix of mathematical and mystical rigidities in Lessing's architectural design is familiar to "potted library" readers: "Of course the shape of the city was as rigidly controlled upwards as it was in area, for roundness, or the hexagonal, or the spirit of Four or Five, was expressed as much in the upper parts as it was by what was experienced where the patterns of stone in building enmeshed with the earth" (26). The Round City is Lessing's most ecstatic example of devotional perfection. Everything in it is round; even roofs are "all domes and cupolas, and their colours were delicate pastel shades, creams, light pinks and soft blues, yellows and greens, and these glowed under the sunny sky" (31–32). The music, reflecting the inner self, holds "the whole city safe in its harmonies" (32). This time of perfection, "this precise and expert exchange of emanations" furthers "the prime object and aim of the galaxy . . . the creation of ever-evolving Sons and Daughters of the Purpose" (35). The point of existence is wholly devotional, to keep "the proper levels of transmission between the planet and Canopus" (27).

Everything is in its place in Lessing's world; the harmony of the cosmos is so finely and perfectly adjusted that untuning a single string brings discord. Both Shammat and Canopus untune that string, Canopus by permitting the Giants to be so innocent that they have no awareness of evil, Shammat by seeing this deficiency and exploiting it. Since that experience, Canopus has learned to inbuild "a certain amount of stress, of danger," in the lives of its children (23).

Literal discord follows Shammat's inner invasion. The discordant music of the stones soon drives inhabitants mad, some to suicide, and all finally to abandon the cities. Those Giants who refuse to be airlifted from Shikasta flee into the interior. At one point, Natives move into buildings formerly inhabited by the Giants. This, of course, will not do; it "was not good for the exact dispositions of the Round City. I told them this" (49). The species deteriorates; its life-span is shorter; its eugenic instincts disappear; mating becomes haphazard.[5] Efforts to imitate the cities result in what looks like "an act of impaired memory" (58). Shapes are incomplete, crooked, erratic.

When Johor returns to Earth thirty thousand years later, historical time has begun. Mating is haphazard still; on the site of the Round City stands "an agglomeration of streets, buildings, markets, put up anyhow, anywhere, without skills or symmetry or mastery" (105–6). These structures mirror the cheating, warring, treachery, theft, and slavery now the lot of the descendants of the Natives. We are in the time of the "Davidic stock" (David and Sais were two Natives in the First Time who helped Johor), the tribes of Israel who make a new covenant with God.

Between this era and the return of the cities at the end of the Century of Destruction, there is one significant structure—the Moroccan mud house the Sherbans live in. The Sherbans are the holy family of their (that is, our) time, for George is Johor, who has descended to Earth to implement the will of Canopus.[6] Rachel, his earthly sister, records his education and activities and finally chooses to die that he may live. Her response to the mud house—

its earthy smell, the roof's openness to the sky from which the star Canopus looks down upon her—recollects the earlier mud houses in Lessing's fiction, the native huts in *Grass*, Martha Quest's (and Doris Lessing's) first house, and the huts of the river people in *Briefing*. Seven families live in this single-story house, each with its own set of rooms and rooftop. Rachel, who becomes especially close to one family, Shireen and Nassim and Fatima, regrets her family's move to a modern flat in Tunis: "I felt perfectly at home in that mud rabbit warren. I loved living there" (250).

That Moroccan house is a version of the Coldridge house in *The Four-Gated City*, as the Sherban family is a version of the Coldridge family. Wherever the Sherban family is there are others with them, talking, learning, loving. Once again, Lessing imagines a family partly biologically and partly nonbiologically related. When Rachel, her brother Benjamin, Shireen, Nassim, Fatima, and many others are dead, the two orphaned children George had asked Rachel to look after carry on. The boy, called Kassim Sherban, is the Joseph Batts of *Shikasta*, the special survivor who participates in the rebuilding of the ancient cities that begins at the end of the Century of Destruction.

Kassim's letter effectively ends the novel. (A brief bibliography for Canopean students follows it.) In it, Kassim tells of a town with "a central square and a fountain. It is all done in stone" (358). Like Charles Watkins, he is vaguely reminded of something, but Kassim's memory of the archetypal city is triggered by a good copy of it, whereas Charles's memories of the archetypal city are fading in a debased environment. Kassim's voyage after Catastrophe is the familiar eternal return, one that moves backward as well as forward in time.

Lessing's efforts to modify the determinism that hangs so heavily over the Canopean cosmos are more convincing at the end of *Shikasta* than perhaps anywhere else in the Canopus novels. Kassim's discoveries have a certain spontaneity. The magic of the city in the shape of a six-pointed star entrances him and everyone else. But how did this city come about? In this compulsively over-ordered universe, there is, oddly enough, no apparent plan for it: "There were no plans. No architect. Yet it grew up symmetrical and on the shape of a six-pointed star" (358). Kassim hears tales from the Indians about Giants who were there long before known explorers arrived. He finds another city, a circle with scalloped edges, and then another composed of six linked hexagons. Continuing his journey with his jaguar and dog amid new kinds of people he calls George-people, Kassim finds four new cities: a triangle, a square, another circle, a hexagon. People begin to move out of the older cities into the new ones. When Kassim meets George, both set out to start a new city. How can we know where to put the center, Kassim asks George. Later, the twenty or so in the party suddenly all "knew quite clearly where the city should be. We knew it all at once. Then we found a spring, in the middle of the place. That was how this city was begun. It is going to be a star city, five-points" (363). The gardens and the fields soon follow. George leaves to complete one more task in Europe, after which he will die. Kassim's final line, "And here we all are together, here we are . . ." (364), echoes Martha's last line in The Four-Gated City, "Here, where else, you fool, you poor fool, where else has it been, ever . . ." (591). Both lines emphasize the here and now. Kassim's underlines the shared nature of the human enterprise.

The primal cities are only a memory trace for Kassim. For Ambien II, in The Sirian Experiments, they have a similar status, although she was alive during the eighteen thousand years of the Rohandan ideal period when they flourished. When Ambien I told her about them, Ambien II had insisted on seeing one. She was flown from Sirian Territory to an island in Canopean territory, where she saw below "a magnificent white city, circular, with many surrounding channels and causeways" (47). That memory never leaves Ambien's mind. She longs for these cities, misses them as she never misses Sirius, although she "had not been back to our Home Planet for millennia: this was because I was thoroughly happy on Rohanda . . . In short, Rohanda had become my home" (44).

The Sirian Experiments, a first-person narration, could have been called The Education of Ambien II. In it Ambien has done her "best to chronicle the slow, difficult growth" of her understanding of Canopus (270). Her bias toward Sirian technological overkill and Sirian genetic experimentation on animal and human subjects is quite eroded in the course of her employment in the Sirian colonial service.

In thinking "of the mathematical cities of the pre-Disaster phase," Ambien is astonished that on the Canopean Mother Planet, there is "nothing so advanced" (68). When Ambien questions Klorathy, her evasively tutelary Canopean agent, about this apparent oddity, his answer is the same answer he always gives: "'Cities, buildings—the situations of cities and buildings on any planet—are designed according to need'" (68). His answer makes Ambien feel cheated. The reader, allowed some superiority over Ambien, knows that the famous mathematical cities are not the highest form of architecture. There is a pattern yet more advanced, one wholly inner, one we— and Ambien—cannot fathom.

Ambien cannot forget the remarkable cities: "On a new planet I was always on the watch for them: they had perhaps become something of a fixation with me. My mental picture of the Canopean Empire included planets covered with these fabulous, these extraordinary cities" (100). But Ambien's adventures unfortunately also take her to cultures below the city-building level and to corrupt cities. Once, in Lelanos, Ambien does encounter a positive city. The bluish gray stone of its evil double, Grakconkranpatl, is "lightened with a glistening white quartz and thin bands of red" (187).[7] Ambien thinks she perceives a pattern in the city's design, "or even several interlocking patterns in the way the buildings were set out, but I never grasped it wholly" (187). She finds the view from above pleasing: "There was a variation, and informality; there were no frowningly dominant buildings; no temples; no threat of stone, and rock, and earth being used to imprison or weight the tender—and so brief—flesh of Rohanda" (187).

Ambien looks back from Lelanos, from "this lovely civilised city," to its "horrible opposite across the mountains" (191), where she nearly lost her life. Negatives have always had a way of helping to define positives. What Grakconkranpatl is not helps us to define what cities should be like. In Grakconkranpatl the stones are the opposite of sacred: "Their lowering colour, their massing and crowding arrangement, gave an impression of hostility and threat" (164). Crucial elements of the sacred city are missing: "There were no gardens or green. No central open space" (164). The buildings are windowless. Ambien has a difficult time trying to decipher the social structure these buildings reflect. She describes the roads as "insane," for they are absolutely straight, making "no concession to the terrain, to ups and downs, or even mountains and precipices" (165).

The primary evil city in the novel, however, is not Grakconkranpatl but Koshi, perhaps because it is a degenerated archetypal city.

It is Lessing's City of Dis. Twenty-one very tall, narrow, conical buildings rise up from a desert landscape, "crammed together, in a small space, looking as if their bases touched" (109). Yet the spaces between the cones are filled with ten- or eleven-story buildings that house the poor. Ambien describes the immediately apparent disparity between rich and poor in Koshi as "*punishable*" (108). This Babylon has a vivid taste and smell and noise for which "the silences of space had ill-prepared" Ambien (111). The tall cones are remainders and reminders of an earlier time. Once again, Ambien tries to search out their pattern: "if there was one . . . it could perhaps be said they were built in two very deep arcs that intersected" (112). "'How long has it been,'" Ambien later asks, "'since this city was allowed to spoil its original design?'" (123). She has "understood" by this time that the original design did contain the cones "in a certain alignment—probably interlocking arcs—and that the huddle of poor buildings around their bases, and the spreading new suburbs, were a dereliction of an original purpose" (123). Of course, Ambien recalls the mathematical cities, which "were never far from my mind" (123).

The adventures in Koshi are effective partly because the symbolic design of the city is so aptly and evocatively imagined. They are also effective because the dry, correct Ambien begins to fall into the power of Shammat under the influence of the city and the influence of Nasar, the only fallen Canopean agent she will ever encounter. In Nasar and in Elylé, a descendant of the obliterated matriarchy of Adalantaland, Ambien encounters her own temptations, and the seductiveness of evil at last begins to be credible. The relentless didacticism of the novel recedes.

Behind the sacred cities in *Shikasta* and *The Sirian Experiments* lie the mud villages, houses, and cities in *The Grass Is Singing*, the five Martha Quest novels, *Going Home*, *Briefing for a Descent into Hell*, and *The Memoirs of a Survivor*. It is possible to see these cities as an evolution from the mud villages; it is also possible to see them as a contradiction of these villages, for they certainly represent a new epistemology.

When roads are called "insane," or the Grakconkranpatl architecture "frowning," or the Lelannian architecture "the architecture of the smile" (197), we are in the presence of something more than personification or the pathetic fallacy. In Lessing's new system, the material world is a mirror of the psychic world.[8] The Coldridge house was a mirror, too, but it was a house first. In *Briefing* the balance shifts; the mind, not matter, becomes the source of reality. (Hindsight suggests that the Crystal Charles Watkins is waiting for is Canopean, for in Shikasta and The Sirian Experiments Canopeans fly about in crystal aircraft.)

Lessing's system of thought since Briefing resonates with parallels to medieval and Renaissance thought on the correspondences between architectural form and the harmony of the cosmos. If, in fact, we substitute the word "city" for the word "church" in passages by or about architectural theorists, these passages could be by or about Lessing. Consider the following sentence: "This implies that if a city has been built in accordance with essential mathematical harmonies, we react instinctively; an inner sense tells us, without rational analysis, that we perceive an image of the vital force behind all matter" (Wittkower, describing Alberti, 25). The word "city" has, of course, been substituted for the word "church." The city is, in Lessing's Canopean world, a sacred entity. It is, indeed, what the church was to the medieval world. City architecture, like church architecture, mirrors the eternal harmony. It reflects an effort to recreate the perfection of the sacred archetype.

Renaissance architects "firmly adhered to the Pythagorean conception, 'All is number,'" and its elaboration by Plato, the Neoplatonists, and "a long chain of theologians." These architects "were convinced of the mathematical and harmonic structure of the universe and all creation" and its ability to permeate our souls (Wittkower, 24). No wonder that musical consonances became "the audible tests of a universal harmony which had a binding force in all the arts" (Wittkower, 110). No wonder that geometry became the basis of the builder's art (Von Simson, 13). No wonder the cacophony of the stones drives Giants and Natives to madness, suicide, and flight. No wonder the cities of the First Time are mathematical. (To call them geometrical might have meant having to leave out the crescent and the oval shapes.)

In a fifteenth-century treatise, the architect Alberti recommends nine basic forms for churches, six of which derive from the circle and three from the square (Wittkower, 4). He adds that these basic forms can be enriched by chapels. The point is not that Lessing necessarily saw this treatise or the many others like it but that her thinking so deeply reflects and recollects this once pervasive habit of mind. What she has done is to apply centuries of hermetic and mainstream religious thought about the meaning and the shape of buildings singly and in agglomeration to the city. Religious writings often describe the church as the sanctuary. In Lessing's Canopean novels, all buildings should be sanctuaries that reflect human union with the divine.

Lessing seems especially partial to her circle and star cities. The city Ambien sees from the air, for example, is circular and gleaming white. The first mathematical city Kassim sees is a six-pointed star. The one he is building when *Shikasta* ends is a five-pointed star. The circle is the familiar, the expected, perfect figure. The meaning of the star is less obvious. The collocation of a six-pointed and a five-pointed star suggests Islam and Judaism. This collocation is not accidental in a novel whose Christ figure, George/Johor, explicitly represents Islamic, Jewish, and Christian organizations and roots. Furthermore, Canopus and Sirius are stars, the two brightest stars in the heavens. Star shapes are the right symbolic forms for Canopean cities, as the cross shape is the right symbolic form for the Christian church. The third layer of meaning in the star shape relates it to the city of Renaissance architects, for the star shape describes the radial form so favored by them. Campanella's city was radial and circular, as was Filarete's Sforzinda, though the first had seven and the second eight rings. But the radial city is not exclusively circular. The city of Vitruvius, the major source of Renaissance radial theories, was radial and octagonal (Manuel and Manuel, 163; Dougherty, 61). Hermes/Mercury is credited with founding the magical city of Adocentyn, which was radial and possibly circular. The prosaic hygienic basis for Vitruvian radial design quite vanishes when the sacral imagination of Renaissance theorists takes over.[9]

This sacral imagination is surely behind the curative powers of geometric forms first presented in *Briefing* and developed at some length in *The Sentimental Agents*. Charles Watkins delights in the "continuous geometrical patterns" before him, but his hospital treatment does not include the use of such shapes, as Incent's does. Incent is bound to recover, as Charles is bound not to.

One geometrical pattern is negative. The modern city, often described as a city without a center, has the gridiron for its mandala: "It has neither garden nor agora nor shrine" (Dougherty, 100). Although Romans contemporary with Vitruvius preferred the grid pattern to his radial plans, we choose to think of the grid as peculiarly ours. Lessing has Ambien accept this assumption. As Ambien looks over an entire continent from a Canopean Crystal, she sees "a mesh of absolutely regular rectangles," which are of course not merely visual signs but "a map, a chart, of a certain way of thinking ... a set of mind made visible ... the mind of the white conquerors" (277). "This stamp of rigidity" covers the continent. Ambien describes the grid with new insight as "a pattern of ownership, a multiplication of the basic unit of the possession of land," an incarnation of Shammat (278). The city Ambien finally enters is one of ours, "filled with poisonous smoke," whose skyscraper buildings "emerged from the fumes like islands from water" (278).

There is no sacred space in our cities, Ambien tells us. Her stance is expected. Unexpected is her assignment of rigidity to the grid pattern and organic pattern to the Canopean world and to her own perceptions. The theoretical spontaneity attributed to the Canopean outlook is rarely if ever convincing. Kassim's knowledge of where to site his new city is described as spontaneous and inner, but images of disobedience and compulsive tidiness overwhelm these two novels, even if we allow for Ambien's deliberately limited bureaucratic character.

Lessing's mud house and her sacred city are very different constructions. The mud house may be an idealized outsider view of native closeness to nature, another version of the primal paradise, but its rhythms are less intellectualized, its version of obedience is less compulsive. It represents another kind of First Time architecture. "These fabulous, these extraordinary cities" do, however, have a vivid imaginative life, one Ambien captures in her role as almost one of us. They represent Lessing's newer sacramental imagination at its momentary best. The evocation of the historical London of the 1950s and 1960s, in all its brilliant detail and protean force, represents a different kind of triumph. It denies perfection and celebrates change, validating the palimpsestic nature of history and human experience.

Afterword

... it was in her power to cut the cycle.

Doris Lessing, *A Proper Marriage*

In a 1973 review of *The Summer before the Dark*, David Lodge defines "the most striking feature of this distinguished writer's work: her remarkable development from being a conventionally realistic novelist to being an experimental, mythopoeic one" (81). He cites as his examples the unexpected trajectory from the early Martha Quest novels to "the apocalyptic conclusion of the series in *The Four-Gated City*"; *The Golden Notebook*, with its "skeptical internal scrutiny" of "the conventions of fictional realism"; and finally, *Briefing for a Descent into Hell*, "in which hallucinatory visions fusing the imagery of Blake, science fiction, R.D. Laing's schizoid patients and hermetic philosophy almost completely displace the rational daylight world of realism" (81).

The Canopus novels that were yet to come presumably reinforced Lodge's judgment of Lessing's "most striking feature." A number of comments are in order. Lessing's mythopoeic stature has yet to be adequately appreciated. But no such appreciation can or should try to devalue the force and vividness of what Lodge calls her conventional realism. The paradox of Lessing's example is that her straining against the boundaries of realism has proceeded without modernist strategies—that, as I see it, she has created her own usable past, one that leaps from nineteenth-century realism to the post–World War II (or postmodern) world, that excises the modernist example. Her excisions are different from T. S. Eliot's or other reconstructions of the literary canon, but they should be recognized as excisions.

Evaluating the radical nature of Lessing's example cannot be conventionally accomplished, for her experimentations are not formally radical; they cannot, for example, be called a mimesis of disorder or chaos. (Anna Wulf talks very lucidly about her division and breakdown; the hero of *Briefing* is more disordered, but not exceptionally so.) Her language is pointedly ordinary; Lessing wants to invest commonplace diction and syntax with unexpected reverberations. At her best, she does give simple language extraordinary dimensions: "Martha took off her nightdress and was alone with her body" (*A Proper Marriage*, 63). Her usually somber, sometimes lighter, doubletalk is another pervasive presence: Anna, ironically born a Freeman, needs to learn to become all the Free Women she is. Although often undercut, questioned, and qualified, Lessing's feminism is nonetheless an inescapable presence in her work.

Lessing's radical example remains, though it does not fit the usual frames of reference. Lodge's words continue to point in a direction that more and more readers of Lessing will be taking— and have been taking (e.g., Draine, Rose, Rubenstein, Schweickart, Whitlock)—toward Lessing's literary strategies. Lodge's comments are also an ironic reminder that our views of what he calls the conventional realistic novels have been changing. These novels no longer appear so conventional after all. They too have their provocative patterns and exclusions. *The Grass Is Singing* and the first four Martha Quest novels are, for example, suffused with imagery, irony, and pattern that earlier feminist criticism could not and should not have been expected to see. The earlier feminist search for "images of women" was part of the need to document the "authority" of women's experience. That search takes a different direction today. It is contained in more complex critical approaches that are at once more literary and more political and still feminist (see Moi).

If two such open-minded and omnivorous critics as Karl Miller and Burton Pike could, in their respective works on doubling and the image of the city, omit the example of Lessing, then we know that Lessing's work is still not part of the standard academic curriculum. That gargantuan gap cries out for closing. Lessing must, for example, be a central figure in any discussion of the double and the city in literature.

Doris Lessing's quest plot is still being written. Its long meditation on character presents us with figures who contradict the stable, monolithic view of personality in favor of one that is permeable, volatile, various, and interchanging. Her remembering mirrors —her Marthas, her Annas, her Jannas—are a haunting, unsettling presence. They do not go away. They assert, to use Elizabeth Abel's formulation, that "female identity is constituted, not threatened by a mirroring other" ("Reflections," 6). Lessing's example undermines Miller's judgment that "comparatively few women are awarded doubles, or write about them" (52).

Multiple characters—female/female and female/male, connected by naming patterns—make a formidable appearance in Lessing's work. (DuPlessis calls them "multi-personed or cluster protagonists" in *The Four-Gated City* and *Memoirs* ["Feminist Apologues," 2]; the phrase applies more widely.) Only less formidable is Lessing's early and continuing commitment to mixed narrative forms. (Bertelsen calls them "portmanteau" for Canopus [*Doris Lessing*, 22]. Abel uses the word "composite" for *The Golden Notebook*.) One mode characteristically undermines or is incomplete without the other. In *A Proper Marriage*, Martha tears up her "real" letters to Douglas and sends him cheery, conventional letters (177). In the later novels, Lessing found a way to accommodate and to represent such simple as well as more complex contradictory, multiple texts.

Lessing has been more interested in "fissured, disjointed, problematic, texts" (Hanson, 107) and truths than she is usually given credit for. To use a recent critic's words, "If the utopian ideal is not a certainty but a potentiality, the same is true of the meaning of the text" (Schweickart, 278). If Lessing's diction and syntax have been simple, her repetitions and her explorations of language—its silences and sounds—have not been simple. The transformation of the monster repetition into something sacramental and desirable represents a complex journey. The silences/sounds and kaffir/English/tribal of *The Grass Is Singing* initiate a parallel exploration of language. The varied writing forms of *The Golden Notebook* are primary discourse in that novel; they suit a novel about a writer with a writer's block. The walls, houses, and cities of *The Four-Gated City* are a different kind of primary pattern; they suit a novel about a protagonist in search of a viable private/collective life.

Like Martha, Doris Lessing is still testing out "various other shells for living in," one at a time or in cluster (*A Proper Marriage*, 65). Her testing out has taken her into galactic space and back again to Maudie Fowler's room or to Alice Mellings's house. From one point of view Lessing explodes the claustrophobia that haunts nineteenth-century fiction by women, a claustrophobia meticulously documented by feminist critics (e.g., Gilbert and Gubar, Showalter, Brownstein). The claustrophobia is there, in the rooms Martha, Anna, Kate Brown, and other women protagonists occupy in Lessing fictions.[1] (Its opposite is also there, for the room can be a place of love and visionary experience.) Martha felt this claustrophobia even in the midst of the veld. Something like Martha's experiential paradox may be said to characterize the Canopus series, which should have catapulted women out of their domestic space ("For women have sat indoors all these million years" [Woolf, 91]) into the greatest of all outdoors. In fact, these galactic novels are often as suffocating, as claustrophobic, as deterministic, as *The Grass Is Singing* or *A Ripple from the Storm*. One point about this paradox is that getting there never quite happens in Lessing's worlds. Displacement, not arrival, is at the center of her imagination, even in her galactic novels. In making displacement the organizing metaphor of her study of Doris Lessing (Africa, England, "New Worlds"), Lorna Sage describes an element so central in Lessing's work that virtually all critics have commented on it. Displacement defines the varied shapes of Lessing's otherness—her female, white, colonial, political selves.

Lessing's city image can be described as ambivalent (protean or metamorphic would be more accurate). It does, in part, reflect the double view of the city as temporal and transcendent, as corruption and archetype.[2] That double view belongs to a larger dialectical habit of mind. Sometimes that habit of mind uses binary modes; more often it accepts the collaboration/contradiction/intersection between binary and multiple modes (as Karl Miller does in his discussions of the double). The city is always the crucial center of human collective life. Historically described as female and entered by men, it is a construction normally out of bounds to the woman. Lessing has appropriated the fact and the dream of the city for women.

Martha's "real" letters, the ones she does not send, and her "apparent" letters, the ones she does send, recall Jane Somers's serious sociological book, *Real and Apparent Structures*. The title suggests (and simultaneously undermines) current critical jargon, the kind Lessing would never use. It also suggests the double and multiple structures Lessing has in fact been analyzing all her life.

Notes

Introduction: Doubling as Dialectic and Repetition

1. The first phrase is Roberta Rubenstein's (*Novelistic Vision*, 9). The second belongs to Betsy Draine, who boldly proposes to reverse the usual stress on Lessing's content and explore "form as an imperative in itself" (*Substance*, xii). We are all moving in similar directions. Bakhtin formulations like dialogic, polyphonic, and double-voiced could also be usefully applied to Lessing's novels.

In his introduction to a volume of George Eliot criticism, Creeger comments on "the [nineteenth] century's most characteristic pattern of thought—that of Hegelian dialectic, with its thesis and antithesis resolving themselves, but not coming to final rest, or synthesis" (3). Lessing's work shares in the revision of Hegelian and Marxist dialectic that is still in progress in our century.

2. French feminists have been more hospitable to psychoanalysis than American feminists. Luce Irigaray and Julia Kristeva are psychoanalysts; Irigaray valorizes woman's special relation to mystical thought and experience. See Toril Moi's excellent analytic history of feminist theory.

3. The words of an academic historian turned mystic, William Irwin Thompson, are a pure example of the conflation of Marxist and mystic dialectic that occurred in the 1960s: "Mysticism seems impractical in technological culture because it is the dialectical negation of the culture and the affirmation of the next culture" (140).

4. See the bibliography for my earlier articles on doubles, names, and numbers. Other critics (e.g., Stimpson, DuPlessis, Lurie) have begun to speculate on Lessing's naming patterns in gender-related ways. Peter Caracciolo's highly original studies of naming must also be cited.

5. Lessing's recent autobiographical essay "Autobiography: Impertinent Daughters" corroborates Seligman's earlier information that Alfred was known as Michael at home and that Emily Maude went by her middle name. As Lessing puts it, "It was 'Maude' and 'Michael' Tayler who arrived in Persia. My mother had always disliked Emily, I suppose because it was the name of her mother, but she liked Maude, because of Tennyson's Maud. She had been trying to shed Emily for years. She would not have Alfred for my father: a common name. And what did he think about it? I can hear him: 'O Lord, old thing, who cares? What does it matter? If it makes you happy, then . . .'" (59–60).

Lessing claims, as many women would, her lack of attachment to the various surnames she has had—Tayler, Wisdom, Lessing. She also claims a lack of attachment to the name "Doris," suggested, according to family story, by the doctor who delivered her. She concludes: "I sometimes wonder what my real name is: surely I have one?" (*Diaries*, viii).

6. See Katherine Fishburn's astute analysis of *Making* as an end point to the Canopus series (chap. 6).

Chapter 1. The Grass Is Singing (1950)

1. In her introduction to *Doris Lessing*, published after the completion of this manuscript, Eve Bertelsen corroborates the new interest in *Grass*: "It is now being conceded that the book anticipates most of Lessing's later concerns and provides a microcosm for most of her future styles" (17). She cites several southern African critics whose work is as yet unavailable in the United States (44 n. 8).

2. In an interview with Eve Bertelsen, Lessing says that the figure of Mary is based on a woman she knew. But the genesis of a fictional character is always more complicated, as Lessing of course knows. For example, in the same interview Lessing also says she wove a modified version of her own first sight of an adult male penis into the scene in which Mary happens upon Moses washing himself. She had herself happened upon a family servant naked and washing himself; the scene in the novel had to be less overtly sexual.

3. See chapter 7 on *A Ripple from the Storm* for additional discussion of the *Waste Land* imagery in Lessing. *Retreat to Innocence* uses an epigraph from Eliot; *Briefing* uses lines from "Sweeney"; and so on. Lessing's fictional uses of Eliot have an artistic and historical significance. Others may, as Rubenstein also suggests (*Novelistic Vision*), want to explore them further.

4. See Anthony Chennell's comment on Lessing's demythologizing of white settler ideology (42).

5. Bertelsen examines the lexical and syntactic repetitions in the last four pages of the novel (*Doris Lessing*, 23–24). These pages continue to excite debate (see, for example, Taylor).

6. See Betsy Draine's comparison of *The Grass Is Singing* with Anna Wulf's novel *The Frontiers of War* in *The Golden Notebook* (*Substance*, chap. 4).

Chapter 2. Retreat to Innocence (1956)

1. The rich, incestuous layers in Lessing's fiction have begun to be addressed. See Linda Weinhouse's dissertation and Sprague, "Politics of Sibling Incest."

Chapter 4. Doubletalk and Doubles Talk:
The Golden Notebook (1962)

1. Lessing's essay on The Golden Notebook was originally published as an introduction to an English paperback reprint. It did not appear in the United States until 1973, in Partisan Review 14: 14–30. It is also republished in A Small Personal Voice.

2. The first two books on Lessing were Dorothy Brewster's and Paul Schlueter's. Selma Burkom's early essay should also be noted. John L. Carey, Joseph Hynes, Martha Lifson, Marjorie Lightfoot, Anne M. Mulkeen, and Annis Pratt all published close appreciations of structure in The Golden Notebook within a few years of Lessing's essay. Hynes and Lifson have a particularly rich analysis of the interrelationships between structure and theme in the novel. Schweickart points out in a recent essay: "Left to their own devices, Lessing's critics would have found their way to the reading she has sketched" (in her 1971 essay/introduction). In a recent essay Schweickart describes The Golden Notebook as "a collection of canceled novels" (274) based on a pattern of hinged and dialectical articulation. Rubenstein's earlier analysis of the novel draws attention to its simultaneously existing psychological and structural unity: "Ultimately, then, The Golden Notebook is one story with one major character, split, divided, and refracted through a variety of invented personas, situations, and experiences" (Novelistic Vision, 108).

3. From the Jungian point of view, Anna can be described as needing to recognize her animus self. Parts of the novel are clearly Jungian—the notion of "negative selves," for example, which Anna says belongs to Mrs. Marks/Mother Sugar. The male selves in the novel can be described as negative and/or animus selves. The Jungian element is in the novel, but so are other ways of seeing dominant and submerged selves or conflict and contradiction.

4. My quip may be useful. Lessing may indeed overturn the nineteenth-century pattern so persuasively argued by Gilbert and Gubar.

5. I owe to Roslyn Stein (personal communication) the perception that Anna is a palindromic name.

6. Keppler believes that the terms "double" and "doppelgänger" are so loosely used that "they have no real meaning." He prefers the term "second self" (2). We are probably stuck with both terms. I find "double" preferable for Lessing; it gives the other self greater independence from the primary self.

7. According to the Freudian view, a woman can acquire the phallus she lacks through the son she bears.

8. In Jungian terms, Michael can be described as the hidden or anima side of Alfred (who, as noted, was Michael at home). For Anna to have a lover named Michael makes for witty oedipal fulfillment. Compare this hidden incestuous motif with Maryrose's open one. The names "Anna/Michael" almost exactly duplicate "Alfred/Michael." The implications of these repetitions for an under-

standing of the interrelationship beween Lessing's life and her fictions are undeniably rich. So far critical interest in how Lessing uses and distorts her life in her work has been minimal. As that interest grows, her naming patterns will come to be seen as more and more revealing.

9. I assume Lessing deliberately altered the title from *Stalin on the National Question*; in the context of the novel, "Colonial" is much more apt than "National." Lessing has altered or mistaken other titles. Mrs. Van, for example, is said to have read *The Story of a South African Farm* instead of *The Story of an African Farm*, and Olaf Stapledon's novel is listed as *First and Last Men* instead of *Last and First Men*.

10. Giles sees a snake still alive, "choked with a toad in its mouth. The snake was unable to swallow; the toad was unable to die" ([New York: Harcourt, Brace & World, 1941], 99).

11. Anna and Saul have enacted what Freud describes as "all the unfulfilled but possible futures to which we still like to cling in phantasy, all the strivings of the ego which adverse external circumstances have crushed, and all our suppressed acts of volition which nourish in us the illusion of Free Will" (630).

12. Betsy Draine has a positive view of the boulder-pushing image. See "Nostalgia and Irony," 31–48.

13. Lifson is the only other critic I know to have explored Anna's name. Her view is different from mine: "It has been her immersion in chaos and cruelty, in the 'Wulf' part of her name, that enables her to move towards the joy of freedom ('Freeman'), to peace, order, endurance, and even creativity" (105). Wulf doesn't have to be male, but in colloquial parlance it is, and in conjunction with Freeman it is more so.

14. As noted earlier, Lessing derives her middle name, May, from her grandmother, who was a Caroline May. By giving her middle name to her fictional mother, Lessing surely displaces and dominates her. Anna's mother is also a May, May Fortescue (*Golden Notebook*, 467).

15. Hynes is also interested in the question of thirds (108).

16. But more incestuous than adulterous if biographical speculations are also considered. See n. 8 to this chapter.

17. In the Yellow Notebook, the Molly figure, Julia, has no child. She and Anna/Ella share child care. When Ella is out, Julia babysits Michael/Janet. There can be no more perfect babysitter than one's other self.

18. It is also possible that Lessing displaces and disguises the three children she actually bore, two boys and a girl, into the three children in the novel—Tommy, Michael, and Janet—and that Tommy is the son she took with her to England. Tommy has more reality than either of the other two. From one perspective, therefore, Anna, Molly, and Ella may be the three faces of Lessing as mother. Such splitting serves complex artistic as well as private needs equally well.

19. As Lessing puts it, Free Women "is an absolutely whole conventional novel, and the rest of the book is the material that went into making it" ("A Talk with Florence Howe," in *A Small Personal Voice*, 81).

20. In *The Four-Gated City*, Lessing extends her use of doubling to environments. See chapter 5.

21. The "truth" of the Blue Notebook is by no means absolute. Anna has two birth dates, for example (as does Tommy). In her 19 January 1950 entry Anna says she is thirty-three (234), which would make her birth year 1923 or 1924. On 17 October 1954 Anna says she was born on 10 November 1922 (467).

22. Thomas Stern's manuscripts in *Landlocked* are very much like the mixed forms in *The Golden Notebook*. Thomas's go further; they are written over, dense with marginalia, torn, rained on, spotted, ant-eaten. Compare the practice of French novelists like Michel Butor and the English novelist Christine Brooke-Rose. See also Anne Hedin's parallel interest in direct visual presentation of Lessing's narrative patterns in *The Golden Notebook*.

23. Only two of Sybil Dorsett's sixteen selves were male. Sybil "had developed more alternating selves than had any other multiple personality"; furthermore, she "was the only known woman personality whose entourage of alternating selves included males" (Schreiber, 214). See also Stoller and Mollinger.

Chapter 5. Multiple Mirrors: *The Four-Gated City* (1969)

1. Compare Roberta Rubenstein's provocative description of the "three-tiered universe" of *The Four-Gated City*, which, like my hypothesis, stresses the environments in the novel. For Rubenstein, "the room, the house and the city correspond to intrapsychic, interpersonal, and public dimensions of being" (*Novelistic Vision*, 234).

2. See, for example, Frederick R. Karl, *Reader's Guide*, p. 304, which describes the novels as expressions of the "linear" 1950s, as a "working out of entire chapters" of Simone de Beauvoir's *The Second Sex* (1949): "Childhood," "The Young Girl," "Sexual Awakening," and so on. Compare Barnouw, DuPlessis, and Whitlock on the *Children of Violence* novels as Bildungsromane.

3. DuPlessis accepts and develops this A/M naming hypothesis. She suggests, for example, that "the alliterative repetition foreshadows the transpersonal protagonist" (*Writing beyond the Ending*, 189).

4. Roberta Rubenstein also perceives the "correspondence between dwellings and interior states" in Lessing's work; see "A Room of the Self." In "A Womb with a View" Carey Kaplan examines the house metaphor as "typologically female" and uterine. Compare Bachelard on the house as intimate space and Pratt's discussion of the contraries in *The Four-Gated City* (*Archetypal Patterns*, 164).

5. Frederick R. Karl takes the four gates in the title to refer to four houses in the novel—a restaurant, Mark's house, Jack's house, Paul's house. More important than this inexact equivalence is Karl's sense of Lessing's dwellings as psychic reflectors. See "Doris Lessing in the Sixties." If Lessing's four gates are discovered to have a precise referent, it is likely to be a religious or mythic source.

6. Dr. Stern of *A Proper Marriage* is described as "my pet lamb" (11). Mrs. Marks

(Marx), Anna's analyst, is familiarly known as Mother Sugar. (Compare Dr. Lamb in *The Four-Gated City*.)

7. Nicole Ward Jouve is one of several critics who thinks Martha was originally destined to be an artist.

8. Lessing likes this image of doubleness and take-over. Perhaps its most extended form appears as the blueprint image in *Briefing for a Descent into Hell*, which seems to coalesce with the possessed personality image. See n. 10 to this chapter.

9. See n. 19 to Chapter 4.

10. According to Henri F. Ellenberger, "The phenomenon of possession, so frequent for many centuries, could well be considered as one variety of multiple personality" (127). Martha is herself "possessed" by the Devil in her major "descent" into the self. Anna and Saul, in *The Golden Notebook*, are also possessed during their comparable "descent." The image of possession, the being-taken-over image, is noticeable in Lessing's post-1960 work.

11. Compare Martha's predictive dream of her future in the Coldridge house early in the novel: "she saw a large layered house ... and it was full of children, not children, half-grown people, and their faces as they turned them towards her were tortured and hurt, and she saw herself, a middle-aged woman ... An anxious face, a face set to endure, to hold on ... and she heard herself crying: she had dropped back fast through layers of herself to find Jack holding her" (62).

12. I suppose R. D. Laing could be summoned as an influence, but the Coldridge house is not a house of schizophrenics; Paul's house is closer to the kind of Laingian house described in Clancy Segal's *Zone of the Interior* (New York: Popular Library, 1976).

13. Dagmar Barnouw (197) has also noticed this repetition with a difference of the triad's names: she also considers the Martha/Mark/Lynda triad as collective protagonist. DuPlessis has developed the concept of the multiple/collective protagonist; she calls the triad a "communal protagonist." See especially *Writing beyond the Ending*, 186–96.

14. Several years ago the *New York Times* reported government sponsorship of research into the control of telepathy.

Chapter 6. Mothers and Daughters/Aging and Dying

1. Mona Knapp, letters to the author, 13 January 1986 and 6 February 1986; the quotation is from an article in *Frankfurter Allgemeine Zeitung*, no. 254, 2 November 1981, p. 21. See also, Mona Knapp, "Lessing on the Continent," 9. Lessing's fictional Anton stayed in Rhodesia amid the white settler community; the historical Lessing returned to East Germany and became, as Murray Steele reports, "East German consul at Dar-es-Salaam in the 1960s" (54).

2. Lessing does mention elsewhere her delayed realization that her mother "could, I think, be something like Jane Somers if she lived now" ("Autobiography: Impertinent Daughters," 58).

3. See Fishburn for an excellent overview of Lessing's use of narrator guides in the Canopus novels.

4. Miller's rich discussion of Joyce's "prodigious doubling," with its "elements both of division and dispersal," has no counterpart discussion of Lessing's (or Virginia Woolf's) "prodigious doubling" (37). Although his *Doubles* has sections on Jane Austen, Charlotte Brontë, Edith Wharton, and Sylvia Plath, Miller notes: "The literature of duality is at once submissive and rebellious. But a male rebelliousness looms large. Comparatively few women are awarded doubles, or write about them" (52). Although *Doubles* was published in 1985, it neglects the feminist analysis of the doubles phenomenon, especially in works by Adrienne Rich (her essay on *Jane Eyre* was originally published in 1973 and was republished in 1979 in *On Lies, Secrets, and Silence*) and Sandra Gilbert and Susan Gubar (their book, *The Madwoman in the Attic*, was published in 1979). This absence is a shock in so omnivorous a work. Lessing is referred to only once as the author of a favorable review of Flora Rheta Schreiber's *Sybil*, a study of multiple personality (339).

Chapter 7. Radical Politics: *A Ripple from the Storm* (1958)

1. Lessing both "merged" and "fragmented" historical events, to use the words of Murray Steele that interestingly duplicate, from my point of view, Lessing's merging and fragmentation of personality.

2. See chapter 5 on *The Four-Gated City*; see also Barnouw (507), DuPlessis (*Writing beyond the Ending*), and Whitlock.

3. Maisie's child will be Rita Gale, who may be a fictional displacement of Lessing's second child, Jean Wisdom. John and Jean Wisdom were born between 1939 and 1943. Peter Lessing was born in 1948. Rita Gale, who succeeds Lynda and Martha as Mark Coldridge's partner in *The Four-Gated City*, is Maisie Gale (and Martha) reimagined in a fulfilling marriage. A circle is completed when Rita, a descendant of Maisie/Martha, marries Mark.

4. Most readers have responded to Lessing's use of the African landscape. Few have noted, as Bertelsen does, that weather in the *Children of Violence* novels is also "used as both index and icon" (*Doris Lessing*, 24). *Ripple* is a superb and unnoticed example of the imagistic correlation of weather with personal/political contradictions and destinies. Its return to the wasteland imagery of *Grass* and *Retreat* has also gone unnoticed.

5. Roberta Rubenstein has another suggestion, which sounds plausible but lacks textual support. She believes that "the action of the novel develops out of the isolated ripples of socialist revolution generated years earlier in Europe and

Russia" (*Novelistic Vision*, 57). She also accurately notes the "rather mixed metaphor" in the title of the novel.

Chapter 8. From Mud Houses to Sacred Cities: Martha Quest to Ambien II

1. Lessing expands here her earlier comment that "the whole concept of a city, four-gated or otherwise, is so archetypal, so is the mythology of all nations, when you start looking" (Bikman, 26).

2. Solomon's Temple was considered archetypal, and its proportions were deciphered and emulated during the High Middle Ages and the Renaissance.

3. Lee Edwards appropriately uses the term "Hobbesian" for these children (567).

4. To Ellen Cronan Rose's comprehensive architectural and philosophical documentation in her "*Città Felice*" article the emotional force of the millennial drive should be added. These two strands are major keys to Lessing's Canopus ethos. (The millennial strand is equally central to her earlier Marxist outlook.) See also Snitow and Harris. Revolutionary medieval messianism was recently the subject of a best-selling novel: Umberto Eco's *The Name of the Rose* (1980; New York: Warner Books, 1985).

5. Lessing's emphasis on eugenic mating in the Canopus series has been a source of unease to many of her readers. The Marxist geneticist J. B. S. Haldane was well known when Lessing was active in left-wing politics. Lessing's reference to him in the preface to *The Sirian Experiments* (vii) is unrelated to his eugenic studies, but her knowledge of them can be assumed.

6. See Betsy Draine's thorough analysis of *Shikasta* as a revision of Jewish and Christian testaments and traditions (*Substance*, chap. 3).

7. The Grakconkranpatl society combines elements of Aztec and Incan cultures; Lelannian society suggests an older, now-contested, view of Mayan culture as pacific.

8. In an interview with Minda Bikman, Lessing describes her "serious query about the effect the proportions of buildings have on the people who live in them" (26). Compare Bachelard's speculations about the relationships between interior and exterior space. See also Snitow.

9. The star Sirius has a special mystery. It is binary. The visible Sirius A has a companion star called Sirius B that is invisible to the naked eye (Gingerich, 94).

Afterword

1. Karl places Lessing in a line of male writers whose space is claustrophobic—Kafka, Beckett, Pinter (*Reader's Guide*).

2. These lines from Pike are worth quoting: "From the beginning the image of the city served as the nexus of many things, all characterized by strongly ambivalent feelings: presumption (Babel), corruption (Babylon), perversion (Sodom and Gomorrah), power (Rome), destruction (Troy, Carthage), death, the plague (the City of Dis), and revelation (the heavenly Jerusalem). In Christian thought, the city came to represent both Heaven and Hell" (6–7).

Works Cited

Novels by Doris Lessing

Asterisks indicate editions cited.

The Grass Is Singing. London: Michael Joseph, 1950; New York: Thomas Y. Crowell, 1950. *Reprint. New York: Popular Library, 1976.

Martha Quest. Vol. 1 of *Children of Violence.* London: Michael Joseph, 1951; New York: Simon & Schuster, 1964. *Reprint. New York: New American Library, 1970.

A Proper Marriage. Vol. 2 of *Children of Violence.* London: Michael Joseph, 1954; New York: Simon & Schuster, 1964. *Reprint. New York: New American Library, 1970.

Retreat to Innocence. London: Michael Joseph, 1956. *Reprint. New York: Prometheus, 1959.

A Ripple from the Storm. Vol. 3 of *Children of Violence.* London: Michael Joseph, 1958; New York: Simon & Schuster, 1966. *Reprint. New York: New American Library, 1970.

The Golden Notebook. London: Michael Joseph, 1962; New York: Simon & Schuster, 1966. *Reprint. New York: Bantam Books, 1973.

Landlocked. Vol. 4 of *Children of Violence.* London: MacGibbon & Kee, 1965; New York: Simon & Schuster, 1966. *Reprint. New York: New American Library, 1970.

The Four-Gated City. Vol. 5 of *Children of Violence.* London: MacGibbon & Kee, 1969; New York: Alfred A. Knopf, 1969. *Reprint. New York: Bantam Books, 1970.

Briefing for a Descent into Hell. London: Jonathan Cape, 1971; New York: Alfred A. Knopf, 1971. *Reprint. New York: Bantam Books, 1972.

The Summer before the Dark. London: Jonathan Cape, 1973; New York: Alfred A. Knopf, 1973. *Reprint. New York: Bantam Books, 1974.

The Memoirs of a Survivor. London: Octagon Press, 1974; New York: Alfred A. Knopf, 1975. *Reprint. New York: Bantam Books, 1976.

Re: Colonised Planet 5, Shikasta. Vol. 1 of *Canopus in Argos: Archives.* London: Jonathan Cape, 1980; *New York: Alfred A. Knopf, 1980. Reprint. New York: Random House, Vintage Books, 1981.

The Marriages between Zones Three, Four, and Five. Vol. 2 of *Canopus in Argos: Archives.* London: Jonathan Cape, 1980; *New York: Alfred A. Knopf, 1980. Reprint. New York: Random House, Vintage Books, 1981.

The Sirian Experiments. Vol. 3 of *Canopus in Argos: Archives.* London: Jonathan Cape,

1981; *New York: Alfred A. Knopf, 1981. Reprint. New York: Random House, Vintage books, 1982.

The Making of the Representative for Planet 8. Vol. 4 of *Canopus in Argos: Archives.* London: Jonathan Cape, 1982; *New York: Alfred A. Knopf, 1982. Reprint. New York: Random House, Vintage Books, 1983.

Documents Relating to the Sentimental Agents in the Volyen Empire. Vol. 5 of *Canopus in Argos: Archives.* London: Jonathan Cape, 1983; *New York: Alfred A. Knopf, 1983. Reprint. New York: Random House, Vintage Books, 1984.

The Diaries of Jane Somers. *New York: Random House, Vintage Books, 1984. Originally published in 2 vols. by Jane Somers [pseud.] as *The Diary of a Good Neighbour* and *If the Old Could* . . . London: Michael Joseph, 1983–84; New York: Alfred A. Knopf, 1983–84.

The Good Terrorist. London: Jonathan Cape, 1985; *New York: Alfred A. Knopf, 1985. Reprint. New York: Random House, Vintage Books, 1986.

Other Works by Doris Lessing

Going Home: Autobiographical Essay. *London: Michael Joseph, 1957. Rev. ed. New York: Ballantine Books, 1968.

A Man and Two Women. London: MacGibbon & Kee, 1957; New York: Simon & Schuster, 1963. *Reprint. New York: Touchstone, 1984.

Particularly Cats. London: Michael Joseph, 1967; New York: Simon & Schuster, 1967. *Reprint. New York: Simon & Schuster, 1978.

A Small Personal Voice: Essays. Edited by Paul Schlueter. New York: Alfred A. Knopf, 1974. *Reprint. New York: Random House, Vintage Books, 1975.

"Autobiography: Impertinent Daughters." *Granta* 14 (1984): 51–68.

"Autobiography (Part Two): My Mother's Life." *Granta* 17 (1985): 227–38.

"Doris Lessing Talks about Jane Somers." *Doris Lessing Newsletter* 10, no. 1 (1986): 3–5, 14.

Secondary Works

Abel, Elizabeth. "Reflections on the Female Double." Paper presented at the annual meeting of the Modern Language Association, 1980.

———. "*The Golden Notebook:* 'Female Writing' and 'The Great Tradition.'" Paper presented at the annual meeting of the MLA, 1981. In Sprague and Tiger, 101–7.

Bachelard, Gaston. *The Poetics of Space.* Translated by Maria Jolas. 1958. Boston: Beacon Press, 1964.

Bakhtin, Mikhail. *Problems of Dostoevsky's Poetics.* Minneapolis: University of Minnesota Press, 1984.

Bardolph, Jacqueline. "Woman and the World of Things: A Reading of *The Grass Is Singing*." 1978. Reprinted in Bertelsen, *Doris Lessing*, 121–26.

Barker, Paul. "Doris Lessing: The Uses of Repetition." *New Society*, 24 June 1965, 27–28.

Barnouw, Dagmar. "'Disorderly Company': From *The Golden Notebook* to *The Four-Gated City*." *Contemporary Literature* 14 (1973): 491–515. Reprinted in Sprague and Tiger, 115–25.

Bertelsen, Eve. "Interview with Doris Lessing, January 9, 1984." In Bertelsen, *Doris Lessing*, 93–118.

———, ed. *Doris Lessing*. Johannesburg: McGraw-Hill, 1985.

Bikman, Minda. "A Talk with Doris Lessing." *New York Times Book Review*, 30 March 1980, 1, 24–27.

Brewster, Dorothy. *Doris Lessing*. New York: Twayne Publishers, 1965.

Brownstein, Rachel. *Becoming a Heroine*. New York: Viking Press, 1982.

Burkom, Selma. "Only Connect: Form and Content in the Works of Doris Lessing." *Critique* 11 (1968): 511–68.

Caracciolo, Peter. "Doris Lessing's 'Lights of Canopus': Oriental Sources of Space History." *Foundation*, no. 31 (1984): 18–30.

———. "What's in a Canopean Name?" *Doris Lessing Newsletter* 8, no. 1 (1984): 15.

Carey, John L. "Art and Reality in *The Golden Notebook*." *Contemporary Literature* 14 (1973): 437–56.

Chennells, Anthony. "Doris Lessing and the Rhodesian Settler Novel." 1985. In Bertelsen, *Doris Lessing*, 31–44.

Cohn, Norman. *The Pursuit of the Millennium*. New York: Harper & Row, 1957.

Cousins, Ewert. *Bonaventura and the Coincidence of Opposites*. Chicago: Franciscan Herald Press, 1978.

Creeger, George, ed. *George Eliot*. Englewood Cliffs, N.J.: Prentice-Hall, 1970.

Dassin, Joan. "Good-bad Writing." *New Boston Review*, Fall 1975, 4.

Deleuze, Gilles. *Logique du sens*. Paris: Editions de Minuit, 1969.

Dinnage, Rosemary. "In the Disintegrating City." *New York Review of Books*, 17 July 1975, 38–39.

Dougherty, James. *The Five-Square City: The City in the Religious Imagination*. Notre Dame, Ind.: University of Notre Dame Press, 1980.

Draine, Betsy. "Nostalgia and Irony: The Postmodern Order of *The Golden Notebook*." *Modern Fiction Studies* 26 (1980): 31–48.

———. *Substance under Pressure: Artistic Coherence and Evolving Form*. Madison: University of Wisconsin Press, 1983.

DuPlessis, Rachel Blau. "The Feminist Apologues of Lessing, Piercy, and Russ." *Frontiers* 4, no. 1 (1979): 1–8.

———. *Writing beyond the Ending: Narrative Strategies of Twentieth Century Women Writers*. Bloomington: Indiana University Press, 1985.

Edwards, Lee. "Flights of Angels: Varieties of a Fictional Paradigm." *Feminist Studies* 5, no. 3 (1979): 547–70.

Eliade, Mircea. *Cosmos and History: The Myth of the Eternal Return.* 1949. New York: Harper & Row, 1954.

———. *Myths, Dreams, and Mysteries.* New York: Harper & Row, 1960.

Ellenberger, Henri. *The Discovery of the Unconscious.* New York: Basic Books, 1970.

Enright, D. J. "Shivery Games." *New York Review of Books,* 31 July 1969, 22–24.

Fishburn, Katherine. *The Unexpected Universe of Doris Lessing.* Westport, Conn.: Greenwood Press, 1985.

Freud, Sigmund. "The Uncanny" (1919). In *Standard Edition of the Complete Psychological Works,* edited and translated by James Strachey and Anna Freud, 17:619–39. London: Hogarth Press, 1971.

Gilbert, Sandra, and Susan Gubar. *The Madwoman in the Attic.* New Haven: Yale University Press, 1979.

Gingerich, Owen. "Sirius Enigmas." In *Astronomy of the Ancients,* edited by Kenneth Brecher and Michael Fiertag, 91–116. Cambridge: MIT Press, 1979.

Hanson, Clare. "The Woman Writer as Exile: Gender and Possession in the African Stories of Doris Lessing." Paper presented at the annual meeting of the MLA, 1984. In Sprague and Tiger, 107–14.

Harris, Marvin. "Messiahs." In Harris, *Cows, Pigs, Wars and Witches,* 133–52. 1974. New York: Random House, Vintage Books, 1978.

Hedin, Anne. "The Mandala: Blueprint for Change in Lessing's Later Fiction." Paper presented at the annual meeting of the MLA, 1980. In Bertelsen, *Doris Lessing,* 163–68.

Heilbrun, Carolyn. *Toward a Recognition of Androgyny.* New York: Harper & Row, 1973.

Howe, Irving. "Neither Compromise nor Happiness." *New Republic* 147 (15 December 1962): 17–20. Reprinted in Sprague and Tiger, 177–81.

Hynes, Joseph. "The Construction of *The Golden Notebook.*" *Iowa Review* 4 (1973): 100–113.

Irwin, John T. *Doubling and Incest/Repetition and Revenge.* Baltimore: Johns Hopkins University Press, 1975.

Jouve, Nicole Ward. "Of Mud and Other Matter—The Children of Violence." In *Notebooks/Memoirs/Archives: Reading and Re-reading Doris Lessing,* edited by Jenny Taylor, 75–134. London: Routledge & Kegan Paul, 1982.

Jung, Carl G. *The Collected Works of Carl G. Jung,* Vol. 4, *Freud and Psychoanalysis.* Vol. 7, *The Relations between the Ego and the Unconscious.* Vol. 12, *Psychology and Alchemy.* New York: Pantheon, 1959.

———. *Man and His Symbols.* 1964. New York: Doubleday, 1969.

Kaplan, Carey. "A Womb with a View: The House on Radlett Street in *The Four-Gated City.*" *Doris Lessing Newsletter* 7, no. 1 (1983): 3–4.

———. "Britain's Imperialist Past in Doris Lessing's Futurist Fiction." Paper presented at the annual meeting of the MLA, 1984.

Karl, Frederick R. "Doris Lessing in the Sixties: The New Anatomy of Melancholy." *Contemporary Literature* 13 (1972): 15–33.

————. *A Reader's Guide to the Contemporary English Novel.* New York: Farrar, Strauss & Giroux, 1972.

Kawin, Bruce F. *Telling It Again and Again: Repetition in Literature and Film.* Ithaca, N.Y.: Cornell University Press, 1972.

Keppler, Carl E. *The Literature of the Second Self.* Tucson: Arizona University Press, 1972.

Kierkegaard, Søren. *Repetition.* Translated by Walter Lawrie. Princeton: Princeton University Press, 1942.

Knapp, Mona. *Doris Lessing.* New York: Frederick Ungar, 1984.

————. "Lessing on the Continent: How Germany Finally Lost Its Heart." *Doris Lessing Newsletter* 10, no. 1 (1986): 8–9, 13.

Lehmann-Haupt, Christopher. "Books of the Times." Review of *The Making of the Representative for Planet 8. New York Times,* 29 January 1982, C25.

Leonard, John. "The Spacing Out of Doris Lessing." *New York Times Book Review,* 7 February 1982, 1, 35. Reprinted in Sprague and Tiger, 204–9.

Lifson, Martha. "Structural Patterns in *The Golden Notebook.*" *Michigan Papers in Women's Studies* 2, no. 14 (1978): 95–108.

Lightfoot, Marjorie. "Breakthrough in *The Golden Notebook.*" *Studies in the Novel* 7 (1975): 277–85.

Lodge, David. "Keeping Up Appearances." *New Statesman,* 4 May 1973. Reprinted in Bertelsen, *Doris Lessing,* 81–83.

Lurie, Alison. "Bad Housekeeping." *New York Review of Books,* 19 December 1985, 8–10.

Manuel, Frank E., and Fritzie P. Manuel. *Utopian Thought in the Western World.* Cambridge, Mass.: Harvard University Press, 1979.

Miller, J. Hillis. *Fiction and Repetition: Seven English Novels.* Cambridge, Mass.: Harvard University Press, 1982.

Miller, Karl. *Doubles: Studies in Literary History.* London: Oxford University Press, 1985.

Mitchell, Juliet. *Psychoanalysis and Feminism.* New York: Random House, Vintage Books, 1975.

Moi, Toril. *Sexual/Textual Politics: Feminist Literary Theory.* London: Methuen & Co., 1985.

Mollinger, Robert. "Self-Defense: Comments on Multiple Personality." Paper presented at the annual meeting of the MLA, 1979.

Morphet, Fiona. "The Narrowing Horizon: Two Chapter Openings in *The Grass Is Singing.*" *Doris Lessing Newsletter* 9, no. 2 (1985): 14–15.

Mulkeen, Anne M. "Twentieth Century Realism: The 'Grid' Structure of *The Golden Notebook.*" *Studies in the Novel* 4 (1972): 262–74.

Newquist, Roy. "Interview with Doris Lessing." 1963. Reprinted in *A Small Personal Voice,* 45–60.

Norman, Liane. "Risk and Redundancy." PMLA 90 (March 1978): 285–91.

Oates, Joyce Carol. "Last Children of Violence." Saturday Review 52 (17 May 1969): 48.

Parrinder, Patrick. "Descents into Hell: The Later Novels of Doris Lessing." Critical Quarterly 22 (1980): 5–25.

Pike, Burton. The Image of the City in Modern Literature. Princeton: Princeton University Press, 1981.

Pratt, Annis. Archetypal Patterns in Women's Fiction. Bloomington: Indiana University Press, 1981.

———. "The Contrary Structure of Doris Lessing's The Golden Notebook." World Literature Written in English 12 (1973): 150–60.

Rich, Adrienne. Of Woman Born. 1976. New York: Bantam Books, 1977.

———. On Lies, Secrets, and Silence. New York: W. W. Norton & Co., 1979.

Rogers, Robert. The Double in Literature. Detroit: Wayne State University Press, 1970.

Rose, Ellen Cronan. The Tree Outside the Window. Hanover, N.H.: University Press of New England, 1976.

———. "Doris Lessing's Città Felice." Massachusetts Review 24, no. 2 (1983): 369–86.

Rosenfield, Claire. "The Shadow Within: The Conscious and Unconscious Use of the Double." Daedalus 92 (1963): 326–44.

Rubenstein, Roberta. The Novelistic Vision of Doris Lessing: Breaking the Forms of Consciousness. Urbana, Ill.: University of Illinois Press, 1979.

———. "A Room of the Self: Psychic Geography in Doris Lessing's Fiction." Perspectives on Contemporary Literature 5 (1979): 69–78.

Sage, Lorna. Doris Lessing. London: Methuen & Co., 1983.

Sale, Roger. "A Small Personal Voice." New York Times Book Review, 22 September 1974, 22.

Schlueter, Paul. The Novels of Doris Lessing. Carbondale: Southern Illinois University Press, 1973.

Schreiber, Flora. Sybil. Chicago: Henry Regnery Co., 1973.

Schweickart, Patrocinio P. "Reading a Wordless Statement: The Structure of The Golden Notebook." Modern Fiction Studies 31, no. 2 (Summer 1985): 263–79.

Showalter, Elaine. A Literature of Their Own: British Women Novelists from Brontë to Lessing. Princeton: Princeton University Press, 1977.

Seligman, Dee. "The Four-Faced Novelist." Modern Fiction Studies 26 (1980): 3–6.

Sennett, Richard. The Uses of Disorder. New York: Random House, Vintage Books, 1970.

Singleton, Mary Ann. The City and the Veld: The Fiction of Doris Lessing. Lewisburg, Pa.: Bucknell University Press, 1977.

Snitow, Ann. "Houses Like Machines, Cities Like Geometry, Worlds Like Grids of Friendly Feeling: Doris Lessing—Master Builder." Doris Lessing Newsletter 7, no. 2 (1983): 13–14.

Sprague, Claire. "Dialectic and Counter-Dialectic in the Martha Quest Novels."

Journal of Commonwealth Literature 14 (1979): 39–52. Based on a paper given at the Berkshire Conference of Women Historians, 1978.

———. "'Without Contraries Is No Progression': Lessing's *The Four-Gated City*." *Modern Fiction Studies* 26 (1980): 99–116.

———. "From Anna/Saul to Martha/Mark: Mixed Doubles in Doris Lessing." Paper presented at the annual meeting of the MLA, 1981.

———. "Doubletalk and Doubles Talk in *The Golden Notebook*." *Papers on Language and Literature* 18 (1982): 181–97.

———. "May and Martha, Susan and Kate: Aging Women in Doris Lessing's Fiction." Paper presented at the annual meeting of the MLA, 1982.

———. "The Politics of Sibling Incest in Doris Lessing's 'Each Other.'" *San Jose Studies* 11 (1985): 42–49.

———. and Virginia Tiger, eds. *Critical Essays on Doris Lessing*. Boston: G. K. Hall & Co., 1986.

Steele, Murray. "Doris Lessing's Rhodesia." 1985. In Bertelsen, *Doris Lessing*, 44–54.

Stimpson, Catharine R. "Doris Lessing and the Parables of Growth." In *The Voyage In: Fictions of Female Development*, edited by Elizabeth Abel, Marianne Hirsch, and Elizabeth Langland, 186–295. Hanover, N.H.: University Press of New England, 1983.

Stoller, Robert. *Splitting: A Case of Female Masculinity*. New York: Dell Publishing Co., Delta Books, 1973.

Taylor, Jenny. "Introduction: Situating Reading." In *Notebooks/Memoirs/Archives: Reading and Re-reading Doris Lessing*, edited by Jenny Taylor, 1–42. London: Routledge & Kegan Paul, 1985.

Thompson, William Irwin. *Passages about Earth*. New York: Harper & Row, 1974.

Tymms, Ralph. *The Double in Literary Psychology*. Cambridge: Bowes & Bowes, 1949.

Von Simson, Otto. *The Gothic Cathedral*. New York: Pantheon Books, 1956.

Wannenburgh, Alf, and Ian Murphy. *Rhodesian Legacy*. Cape Town: C. Struik, 1978.

Weinhouse, Linda. "Doris Lessing and Incest." Ph.D. dissertation, Hebrew University, 1983.

———. "Incest and Repression in *The Grass Is Singing*." *Revista canaria de estudios ingleses* 8 (1984): 99–117.

Whitlock, Gillian. "Fashion and Form: *Children of Violence* as Bildungsroman." 1985. In Bertelsen, *Doris Lessing*, 132–39.

Wittkower, Rudolph. *Architectural Principles in the Age of Humanism*. 1949. London: Tiranti, 1952.

Woolf, Virginia. *A Room of One's Own*. 1929. New York: Harcourt Brace & World, 1957.

Yates, Frances. *Giordano Bruno and the Hermetic Tradition*. Chicago: University of Chicago Press, 1964.

Index

Lightning Source UK Ltd.
Milton Keynes U
UKOW05f0421080813

215015UK00001B/102/P